Hurricane Maria in Puerto Rico

Hurricane Maria in Puerto Rico

Disaster, Vulnerability, and Resiliency

Edited by
Marie T. Mora, Havidán Rodríguez, and
Alberto Dávila

LEXINGTON BOOKS
Lanham • Boulder • New York • London

Published by Lexington Books
An imprint of The Rowman & Littlefield Publishing Group, Inc.
4501 Forbes Boulevard, Suite 200, Lanham, Maryland 20706

www.rowman.com

6 Tinworth Street, London SE11 5AL, United Kingdom

1. Photo of impassable road with fallen tree and other debris following Hurricane Maria in Puerto Rico. Courtesy of Marla Perez Lugo
2. Photo of beach house irreparably damaged by Hurricane Maria in Puerto Rico. Courtesy of Fernando Rivera
3. Photo of the Aguirre thermoelectric power plant before Hurricane Maria. Courtesy of Marie T. Mora, Alberto Dávila, and Havidán Rodríguez
4. Photo of Catedral Basílica Metropolitana de San Juan Bautista (Metropolitan Cathedral Basilica of Saint John the Baptist) with setting sunlight. Courtesy of Marie T. Mora
5. Satellite image of Hurricane Maria overlaid with outline of Puerto Rico. Courtesy of National Oceanic Atmospheric Administration (NOAA) National Environmental Satellite, Data, and Information Service
6. Photo of coquí found during disaster recovery efforts in Puerto Rico. Courtesy of Havidán Rodríguez
7. Photo of home destroyed by Hurricane Maria in Puerto Rico. Courtesy of Fernando Rivera
8. Photo of aerial view of the northern coast of Puerto Rico with dramatic storm clouds. Courtesy of Marie T. Mora
9. Photo of flooded road following Hurricane Maria in Puerto Rico. Courtesy of Marla Perez Lugo
10. Photo of aerial view of San Juan showing damage from Hurricane Maria. Courtesy of Sgt. Jose Diaz-Ramos, National Guard. The appearance of U.S. Department of Defense (DoD) visual information does not imply or constitute DoD endorsement.

11. Voter Registration and Turnout among Island-Born and Mainland-Born Puerto Ricans in the 2018 U.S. Congressional Elections Mark Hugo Lopez, Pew Research Center; Antonio Flores, Pew Research Center; and Jens Manuel Krogstad, Pew Research Center.

British Library Cataloguing in Publication Information Available

Library of Congress Cataloging-in-Publication Data

Names: Rodríguez, Havidán, editor. | Mora, María Teresa, editor.
Title: Hurricane Maria in Puerto Rico : disaster, vulnerability & resiliency / edited by Havidán Rodriguez, Maria T. Mora, and Alberto Dávila.
Description: Lanham : Lexington Books, 2021. | Includes bibliographical references and index. | Summary: "Bringing together scholars in various fields (including economics, sociology, demography, psychology, disaster research, political science, education, the arts, and others), this volume represents one of the first interdisciplinary sets of studies analyzing the effects of Hurricane Maria, including the slow response and recovery, on island and stateside Puerto Ricans"— Provided by publisher.
Identifiers: LCCN 2021026626 (print) | LCCN 2021026627 (ebook) | ISBN 9781793603074 (cloth) | ISBN 9781793603081 (ebook)
Subjects: LCSH: Hurricane Maria, 2017. | Hurricanes—Puerto Rico. | Hurricane damage—Social aspects—Puerto Rico. | Hurricane damage—Puerto Rico—Psychological aspects.
Classification: LCC HV636 2017 .P9 H87 2021 (print) | LCC HV636 2017 .P9 (ebook) | DDC 363.34/922097295—dc23
LC record available at https://lccn.loc.gov/2021026626
LC ebook record available at https://lccn.loc.gov/2021026627

We dedicate this book to the memory of Dr. Joy Lynn Suárez-Kindy (1974–2020), an admirable Puerto Rican colleague, collaborator, educator, and contributing coauthor to this book. We also dedicate this book to the victims of Hurricane Maria in Puerto Rico who have suffered an enormous and unprecedented loss as a consequence of this devastating hurricane, which has been exacerbated by an ongoing economic crisis, a flurry of recent earthquakes, and a global pandemic. Yet, the people of Puerto Rico remain a strong, vibrant, and resilient community.

Contents

List of Illustrations

List of Tables

Foreword

Antecedents and Consequences of Inequity: The Praxis of Nation-Community Rebuilding

Ruth Enid Zambrana

Hurricane Maria in Puerto Rico: Disaster, Vulnerability, and Resiliency is an interdisciplinary and scholarly tour de force on the historic and contemporary social, economic, and political reality of the U.S. colonial territory of Puerto Rico. The goals of the book are to examine the effects of Hurricane Maria (September 20, 2017) on the island and on stateside Puerto Ricans. In my view, the book addresses three key questions: What were the principal social, economic, and political antecedents that contributed to the unfathomable impact of Hurricane Maria on the Puerto Rican people? What were the actual economic, health, and mental health consequences of Hurricane Maria on the lives of youth, families, and communities? Who engaged in recovery efforts and what was the level of response at the federal, state, and local levels and the diasporic Puerto Rican peoples?

The editors of this volume are distinguished knowledgeable scholars in their fields of economics and sociology, and in the sociopolitical status of Puerto Rico. The chapter authors, who are predominantly social scientists, encapsulate a depth of understanding of the intersections of power relations, disasters, and pre- and post-economic conditions that is aberrant in traditional disciplinary descriptive and explanatory scholarship. The editors and coauthors are deeply embedded in knowledge production of disaster research drawing on prior scholarship and knowledge, representing accomplished professionals and scholars who live, work, and practice in the Puerto Rican systems. These insightful narratives are refreshing and informative in contrast to the opinions and shallow analyses often proffered by opportunistic pop-up experts from the United States on colonial matters of race inequity and maltreatment. The depth of knowledge offered in the pages of this book is fortified by the critical intersectional analytic lens applied to the economic and social antecedents and consequences of a hurricane to a colonial territory. Many of the chapters interrogate the ways in which power relations, as exemplified in hierarchical structures within the federal system, operate, such as delays in the delivery of supplies or resources to inaccessible places and other communities in need. Other chapters focus attention on the long-standing weak infrastructure that promoted a lack of responsiveness to the outstanding need for medical personnel and transport vehicles to the interior areas of the island that were most deeply affected by the hurricane. Intersectional analyses seek to dismantle and make visible inequitable processes that disadvantage classes of people. An intersectional analytic lens seeks to engage in praxis, that is, to produce knowledge that can be transformative so as to inform institutional practice and promote more just and fair systems. The analyses presented in this anthology engage a process of praxis to create new knowledge and institutional analyses so that these processes inform each other.

The first question, in my view, is *What were the principal social, economic, and political antecedents that contributed to the unfathomable impact of Maria on the Puerto Rican people?* The authors adeptly address the calamitous effects of the underlying economic, social, and political antecedents of Hurricane Maria. Puerto Rico began a serious economic decline during the recession that started in 2006 with the departure and decrease of industries provoked by the expiration of the Section 936 corporate tax exemption program. The recession resulted in the loss of industry, jobs, and earnings that was associated with a loss of bank deposits, financial capital, and tax revenue collected by the government. These losses were further exacerbated by government corruption, long-term neglect of the electrical grid, and significant out-migration of the population. A robust analysis of the economic profile of labor market changes, wage structure, and employment trends by age cohort is presented in several chapters. These antecedents to poverty and low socioeconomic status depict the structural processes in place, including U.S. interventions that contribute to the inability of a nation and its people to achieve economic mobility and stability. The initial chapters set the stage for understanding how economic (downward trend of healthcare employment due to the economic crisis) and political forces (debt crises) eroded infrastructures in the community, particularly the healthcare system, that exacerbated the crisis caused by Hurricane Maria.

The second question is *What were the actual economic, health, and mental health consequences of Hurricane Maria on the lives of youth, families, and communities?* The second set of chapters provides a powerful assessment of the role of social determinants, inequitable structures, and their confluent impact on population health that exacerbates preexisting and current disaster-produced conditions rather than ameliorate health and mental conditions. The authors cogently weave together prior economic woes and infrastructure weaknesses to assess the impact of Hurricane Maria on health and mental health outcomes. Strikingly, all of these conditions heightened the consequences of the disaster on youth, families, and communities and demonstrate parallel, explanatory insights into the intersections of economic, health, and mental health outcomes of the population across sectors. The authors address with clarity the events that stalled the ability to understand the impacts and extent of the damage leveled on the island by Hurricane Maria on health and human services and the subsequent increases in mortality (e.g., youth suicide and morbidity). The disastrous aftermath devitalized all critical infrastructures that could inform the efforts, as data collection systems, health systems, and electrical and water systems were initially inoperable throughout the island and even a few months later were still inoperable throughout a large portion of the island. These inoperable systems prevented not only an accurate account of fatalities and mortalities but also created a staggering loss of jobs, lack of access to healthcare services, food stamps, and public assistance. Earlier events, including the impact of the recession that started in 2006, contributed to high population loss due to the out-migration of many Puerto Ricans from the island to the mainland. These population losses adversely impacted recovery efforts as there were shortages of workers at all levels. The simultaneous degrading of all infrastructure systems that were already weak left the island with little to no operable infrastructure, deeply impacted all health and human services, and left the population to recover alone in many instances. The weakened systems, jointly with poor leadership at the U.S. federal level, eviscerated the initial recovery efforts.

In answering the third question—*Who engaged in recovery efforts and what was the level of response at the federal, state, and local levels and the diasporic Puerto Rican peoples?*—several chapters present data and proclaim a resounding recognition of how the people of Puerto Rico, on the island and stateside, expressed their talents, skills, and will to resist oppression and neglect and lift their communities. The resistant mechanisms predominantly discussed include the production of visual arts projects and artistic performances led by community members and artists, provoking key insights into the role of the humanities (novels, theater, visual arts including community projects, etc.) to describe and to see the emotional toll of disaster. The authors of chapter 10 describe "an inventory of aesthetic reactions of Puerto Rican arts to the traumatic experiences of Hurricane Maria." These efforts are beautifully described, revealing and affirming the role of art in depicting the impacts of disastrous events and social structure on communities. The arts are a primary vehicle to express the voice, narratives of lived experiences, and responses of the people to social and environmental events. Chapter 10 describes a series of visual arts projects that illustrate critical themes of the relationships among disaster, colonization, climate change, and artistic expression, revealing the power of the affective aesthetic lens of Puerto Rican visual arts in describing the impact of Hurricane Maria.

The role of diasporic Puerto Ricans as leaders and members of the U.S. resource-rich infrastructures played a key role in coalescing forces for the good of the people through universities and state entities. The last chapters cogently address the power of the people through voting patterns, comparing island and stateside Puerto Rican challenges in disaster management, and as chapter 12 describes, using a case study methodology, how leadership can engage and create responsive and transformational power structures to design responses to strengthen, rather than debilitate, an already vulnerable population. Universities are important institutions in the United States and represent a "kingdom" of resources, brain power, and human capital in their students, faculty, and administrators. In this case study, collaboration and teamwork are an extraordinary exemplar of capitalist generosity, experiential learning, and how structural power in higher education is amenable to opportunistic equitable transformation. Collaborative efforts can serve as a future template for decolonizing efforts and promoting equity and social justice.

The major contributions of this book are its dialogic engagement with the roots of U.S. power and the historic stripping away of resources and its persistent disinvestment in the development of human and economic capital on the island. This book adds to the eminent corpus of scholarship on Puerto Rico through its distinct embedding of the discourse in a deep political understanding of power arrangements under capitalist governance. In many of the chapters, the discourses do not elude the role of bureaucratic systems of health, utilities, and transportation, among other systems that were weak prior to Hurricane Maria. Pointedly the authors describe the disservice to the residents of Puerto Rico that resulted from the opportunistic endeavors of U.S. relief efforts that sought to compromise human suffering and insure economic gain for those in power, both from the island as well as the U.S. government.

Another contribution is its critical analytic eye on the broader spectrum of antecedents inclusive of key historical events and the destructive force of Hurricane Irma (2017). Equally notable are the evidence-based and data-driven analyses and trends presented to demonstrate prior social and economic conditions, and assess the impacts of the disaster and governmental (non) action. The most stellar contribution of the book in my view is the focused, critical, conscious theorizing of the authors of the powerful role of the intersections of structural arrangements in economics, employment sector, industry, and colonial status and its impact on population well-being across sectors. The fact that poverty exacerbates the impact of the disasters and that poverty is nurtured by failing and inequitable capitalist enterprises is a global trend and a historic practice of U.S. capitalism. Much to their credit, the chapters are focused on different systemic impacts, yet each is informed by the prior and current economic, social, and political conditions of Puerto Rico. This approach disallows for individual victim blaming and cultural deficit approaches, but rather shines a clear light on colonial practices and the resultant institutional systemic failures.

The book represents a well-rounded intersectional critical analysis of antecedents, determinants, and consequences of neglectful colonial rule. Scholarly academics, practitioners, and scholar-activists provide well-written and superbly contextualized descriptions of the consequences of historic colonial status and prior and current events that shaped the impact of Hurricane Maria and will continue to reverberate on the economic, political, and social structures of Puerto Rico for decades to come.

What sets this book apart from others is its capturing of an event and addressing issues of subordination and domination as a contextualized foundational theme. In effect, the sociopolitical relationship and power structures are cogently embedded as antecedent social conditions. In this respect, the victims are not to be blamed, but rather failing structures contributed to adverse conditions prior to disaster and heightened the adverse conditions post-disaster. Although not dwelled upon, a few facts remain uppermost in our minds. First, the U.S. government and its primary disaster organization failed the Puerto Rican people miserably and with little remorse. Second, the Puerto Rican people both island and stateside, the Puerto Rican diaspora, showed tremendous self-reliance and worked together to support their communities on the island and in New York, Florida, and other parts of the United States. Stateside Puerto Ricans also launched, under the leadership of state governments, university systems, and other public entities/organizations, efforts to collaborate to restore people's hope and access to resources to improve their well-being.

This is a must read for political scientists, sociologists, economists, colonial and postcolonial theorists, and Latin American and Caribbean scholars. This is not a book about theory—rather, it is a book about the lived experiences of peoples under the guise of a "colonial democracy" and about whom scholars theorize but know little of what it means to the people. This book is a layered narrative of stories within stories that defy what was public information and confirms what the supportive first responders saw, what the artists perceived, what the people experienced as observed by professionals, and as expressed to providers.

What the future holds for Puerto Rico is uncertain. What can be stated with certainty is that this book proffers a template for future accurate, truthful, and authentic descriptions of not only colonial and postcolonial experiences but also of racism, inequity, and maltreatment among Puerto Rican communities in the United States. It is my hope that future generations of Puerto Rican and other racial/ethnic scholars will initiate analyses with an intellectual starting point of assessing historic, economic, and social dimensions of power relations linked to race, class, ethnicity, and gender and other dimensions of inequality to assure the "origin story" guides the analyses.

Preface

Just two days after Hurricane Maria struck Puerto Rico with sustained 155 mile-per-hour windspeeds in September 2017, we received our page proofs from Lexington Books for our monograph *Population, Migration, and Socioeconomic Outcomes among Island and Mainland Puerto Ricans: La Crisis Boricua*. At that time, we had spent over four years intensively studying one of the deepest economic crises in the island's recent history, surging since 2006 (which we referred to as "La Crisis Boricua") that led to unprecedented government debt and the subsequent Puerto Rico Oversight, Management, and Economic Stability Act (PROMESA) of 2016; a loss of industry and jobs; record net island-to-mainland migration; a rapidly aging and shrinking population; and a weakened (and as with the electrical grid, dilapidated) infrastructure. Despite the lack of immediate official information, we had no doubt Hurricane Maria would wreak devastating havoc on the millions of American citizens living in Puerto Rico and exacerbate (at least temporarily) the massive net out-migration to the mainland.

We were able to include an addendum in that book to highlight how our findings on pre-Maria conditions and outcomes on the island can be used to inform and anticipate post-Maria conditions, but we immediately realized the need to further explore how Hurricane Maria intensified the island's deteriorating socioeconomic conditions, the rapidly aging and shrinking of its population, and net out-migration. In the months that followed, after discussing how we could meet this need with Joseph Parry, the acquisitions editor at Lexington Books, we invited colleagues from a variety of disciplines (including economics, sociology, demography, health, psychology, disaster research, political science, education, the arts, etc.) who enthusiastically agreed to collaborate.

This book represents one of the first interdisciplinary sets of studies dedicated to analyzing the effects of Hurricane Maria on Puerto Rico and Puerto Ricans, but it will certainly not be the last. As we mention in chapter 1, the grave and unprecedented challenges encountered by the nine million self-identified Puerto Ricans who live in Puerto Rico and the U.S. mainland (3.2 and 5.8 million, respectively), we expect that scholars, artists, educators, and others will continue to write about Hurricane Maria for years if not decades to come. Much of the writing and analysis for this book occurred throughout 2018 and 2019, meaning that neither the earthquakes that began rocking the southern coast of the island in December 2019 (still ongoing as of June 2021) nor the COVID-19 global pandemic in 2020 and 2021 is integrally discussed in the chapters. The primary focus of this volume started as—and remained on—Hurricane Maria. As Edwin Meléndez, director of the Center for Puerto Rican Studies at Hunter College, succinctly stated on October 28, 2017, at the *Puerto Rico, Puerto Ricans Symposium*, "Maria changed everything." Nevertheless, we expect the information presented here will help inform future research on how the serial earthquakes and COVID-19 compounded the longer-term effects of Hurricane Maria and La Crisis Boricua for Puerto Ricans living on the island and U.S. mainland.

As with our previous book, this volume, including our own chapter contributions (chapters 1 and 13), greatly benefitted from feedback and input from the external reviewers as well as from colleagues and students since the beginning of the project. Given the particular importance and value of soliciting insights and feedback from Puerto Ricans, we intentionally discussed and presented our work while it was still in progress with colleagues at institutions on the island—including the Puerto Rico Institute of Statistics; University of Puerto Rico Cayey; InterAmerican University Metropolitan campus; and Centro Comprensivo de Cancer, University of Puerto Rico-Río Piedras—as well as the Center for Puerto Rican Studies at Hunter College, City University of New York. We, along with other chapter contributors, also had the opportunity to discuss our work in panel discussions organized by the American Society of Hispanic Economists at the 2018 Western Economic Association International conference in Vancouver, British Columbia, and the 2019 Southern Economic Associational annual conference in Fort Lauderdale, Florida. (See the Acknowledgments section for additional details.)

One of the major challenges we encountered while working on this volume was that the news continued evolving, including the amount of time that elapsed to restore electricity to the island post-Maria (which in some cases, as noted throughout the book, took nearly a year), the estimated number of fatalities related to Hurricane Maria (with the official estimate standing at 2,975 as this volume went to press), and controversies over the disbursement of aid and supplies as well as financial assistance for rebuilding, among others. Even without the earthquakes and COVID-19, the slow recovery and rebuilding efforts following Hurricane Maria along with the continued controversies surrounding PROMESA and migration patterns will likely serve as fodder for future research for years to come.

We leave this section reminding readers that Hurricane Maria exacerbated but did not create Puerto Rico's current crisis. As we pointed out in our aforementioned book, the seeds of La Crisis Boricua had been brewing for decades, often rooted in the complicated relationship Puerto Rico has had with the U.S. mainland. The path of Puerto Rico's longer-term recovery will depend on effectively and strategically addressing the island's chronic socioeconomic conditions. We remain concerned and committed to contributing to these policy discussions.

Acknowledgments

In the eight years of intensively studying Puerto Rico's severe economic crisis and the socioeconomic and migration outcomes of Puerto Ricans on the island and U.S. mainland, we have been fortunate to receive invaluable insights, feedback, and input from numerous friends and colleagues who helped shape and guide our work, including directly impacting the work that resulted in this edited volume. With regards to the latter, we are particularly grateful to Mario Marazzi Santiago, Mark Hugo Lopez, Francisco Rivera-Batiz, José Caraballo-Cueto, Edwin Meléndez, María Enchautegui, Antonio Fernos, Orville Disdier, Xavier F. Totti, William Spriggs, Hector Cordero Guzmán, Andra Gillespie, Juan DelaCruz, Charles Venator-Santiago, Zadia Feliciano, Jose Fernandez, Fernando I. Rivera, José Javier Pérez, Frank Conway, Alexis Santos, and William Vélez.

We also acknowledge the participants who provided feedback during our presentations at various conferences, seminars/workshops, and panel discussions as this volume was underway, which included the following:

- AFL-CIO, Washington, DC, March 2018;
- *Puerto Rico: The Road to Recovery and Reconstruction* conference, sponsored by the Albert Shanker Institute, American Federation of Teachers, and the Hispanic Federation, Washington, DC, March 2018;
- Center for Puerto Rican Studies (Centro), Hunter College, City University of New York (CUNY), April 2018;
- University of Puerto Rico Cayey, May 2018;
- American Society of Hispanic Economists panel on Puerto Rico's Humanitarian and Economic Crises, *Western Economic Association International* annual conference, Vancouver, BC, June 2018;

- *Economic Issues Affecting Hispanic and African American Communities* conference, sponsored by the American Society of Hispanic Economists and the Department of Economics at Texas A&M University, College Station, TX, October 2018;
- Puerto Rico Institute of Statistics, San Juan, PR, February 2019;
- Centro Comprensivo de Cancer, University of Puerto Rico-Rio Piedras, February 2019;
- InterAmerican University Metropolitan Campus, February 2019;
- Lehman College, CUNY, Bronx, NY, February 2019;
- Presidential Session on Puerto Rico's Challenges and Solidarity, *Latin American Studies Association* conference, Boston, MA, May 2019;
- Department of Economics, University of Missouri—St. Louis, October 2019;
- *RISE: Transforming University Engagement in Pre- and Post-Disaster Environments*, sponsored by the National Council for Science and the Environment and the University at Albany, SUNY, Albany, NY, November 2019;
- James Weldon Johnson Institute for the Study of Race and Difference, Emory University, November 2019;
- American Society of Hispanic Economists panel on Hurricane Maria in Puerto Rico, *Southern Economic Association* annual conference, Fort Lauderdale, FL, November 2019; and
- AEA Summer Program (virtual), Michigan State University, July 2020.

In addition to the chapter authors for their enthusiastic willingness to contribute to this book, we sincerely appreciate Ruth Enid Zambrana for writing such an insightful and thoughtful Foreword, as well as the American Society of Hispanic Economists for their willingness to host various conference sessions and panel discussions about Puerto Rico and Puerto Ricans. Finally, we gratefully acknowledge Tony Lynch for his excellent research assistance; Kimberly A. Comproski, Kristen M. Marlow, Sherri Jenkins, Marina Rodriguez, and Mary Jane Thaxton for their much-appreciated administrative support; and last (but certainly not least), Joseph Parry, as this edited volume would not have come into being without his enthusiastic encouragement and support throughout the entire process.

Chapter 1

Hurricane Maria in Puerto Rico

Context and Ramifications

Marie T. Mora, Havidán Rodríguez, and Alberto Dávila

With its 155 mile-per-hour sustained windspeeds, the near-Category 5 Hurricane Maria brought catastrophic devastation and destruction as it diagonally crossed the Commonwealth of Puerto Rico from the southeast to the northwest on September 20, 2017. The official death toll estimate of 2,975 lost lives (representing nearly one-tenth of a percentage point (0.09%) of Puerto Rico's entire population, and over 1,000 more fatalities than the 1,833 lives lost due to Hurricane Katrina in the U.S. Gulf Coast in August 2005) means this record storm became one of the most devastating hurricanes not only for Puerto Rico but for the United States. Many of these deaths, as well as the prolonged human suffering, were attributed to what was described as inadequate disaster response and slow restoration of basic services (including running water, electricity, and the provision and distribution of food and medicine), and not to the direct impact of the hurricane itself. For example, even one month after Hurricane Maria made landfall, more than 8 out of 10 (83%) island residents and businesses remained without electricity, and one-third (33%) still lacked running water (Center for Puerto Rican Studies 2018a, 2018b).

At the same time, as we have discussed elsewhere (e.g., Mora, Dávila, and Rodríguez (MDR) 2018, 2019), Hurricane Maria made landfall when Puerto Rico had been confronting a severe economic crisis surging for over a decade (see also Meléndez and Venator-Santiago 2018). This crisis (which we have referred to as "La Crisis Boricua") began in 2006 and was characterized by a significant loss of industry and jobs, a deteriorating infrastructure (including for the provision of public utilities, education, and healthcare services), record net out-migration, a shrinking and rapidly aging population, rising healthcare undercoverage, a bankrupt government, and federal legislation restricting fiscal policy decisions made by elected officials on the island. Thus, Hurricane Maria exacerbated the effects of La Crisis Boricua on the socioeconomic, health, and demographic outcomes affecting Puerto Ricans on the island and U.S. mainland.[1]

Bringing together scholars and artists from a wide variety of disciplines (including economics, sociology, demography, health, psychology, disaster research, political science, education, the arts, etc.), this book represents one of the first interdisciplinary sets of studies dedicated to analyzing the effects of Hurricane Maria on island and stateside Puerto Ricans, but it will certainly not be the last. Given the grave and unprecedented challenges encountered by the nine million Puerto Ricans who live in Puerto Rico and the U.S. mainland (3.2 and 5.8 million, respectively), we expect that scholars, artists, educators, and others will continue to write about this catastrophic event. We expect some of this future work will couple the discussion of Hurricane Maria (including the much-criticized response by the federal government) with the COVID-19 global pandemic and the series of earthquakes that started affecting the island in December 2019 and continued for at least 1.5 years.

Specific topics in this volume cover Hurricane Maria's impact on labor market outcomes, including wages and employment by industry; health implications, including mental health; changes in artistic expression; civic engagement; and disaster response and recovery. A common thread through many of the chapters was the destruction of Puerto Rico's electrical grid and the prolonged restoration of electricity and other essential services that resulted in the loss of thousands of lives. We conclude this volume summarizing what we have learned, but also raise questions that remain to be answered, and we hope will encourage additional research.

Providing the context for the upcoming chapters, the remainder of this chapter presents an overview of Puerto Rico's socioeconomic, demographic, and political reality when Hurricane Maria made landfall. We also discuss the massive net out-migration from Puerto Rico to the U.S. mainland before and shortly after Hurricane Maria, which represents the largest exodus in terms of the numbers of migrants and the second largest in terms of the migration scale, relative to the island's population (the largest being in the 1950s during the period known as the "Great Migration"). As part of this discussion, we highlight Florida's recent prominence in becoming home to the largest number of Puerto Ricans outside of Puerto Rico, thus removing the state of New York from that position. We also discuss how the socioeconomic and demographic characteristics of recent Puerto Rican migrants from the island were similar between those who migrated before versus after Hurricane Maria, which allows us to use the characteristics of pre-Maria migrants to predict the transition and needs of post-Maria Puerto Rican migrants. Finally, we provide insights into the socioeconomic, demographic, and health challenges, which Hurricane Maria exacerbated in Puerto Rico.

OVERVIEW AND CONTEXT OF HURRICANE MARIA'S DEVASTATION

Hurricane Maria was the strongest storm on record to hit Puerto Rico in nine decades since Hurricane San Felipe II made landfall on September 13, 1928; the latter had official estimates of sustained 160 miles per hour windspeeds, and unofficial estimates of 180–200 miles per hour (Puerto Rico Hurricane Center (PRHC) 2019). Like Hurricane Maria, Hurricane San Felipe II led to catastrophic destruction across the island, damaging essentially every building and decimating the agricultural sector (PRHC 2019). At the same time, Hurricane San Felipe II's estimated death toll of 312 lost lives was a fraction of the 2,975 deaths attributed to Hurricane Maria. In fact, since the arrival of the Spanish in the late 1400s, only Hurricane San Ciriaco, which struck Puerto Rico on August 8, 1899, had a higher estimated death toll (at 3,369) than Hurricane Maria (PRHC 2019). As such, as this volume went to press, Hurricane Maria held the official record for the largest loss of lives in Puerto Rico since the collective granting of U.S. citizenship to Puerto Ricans in 1917. Moreover, as noted in upcoming chapters, other unofficial estimates place Hurricane Maria's death toll even higher (e.g., Kishore et al. 2018).

The power of Hurricane Maria's windspeeds, storm surge, and heavy rainfall across the island resulted in widespread catastrophic destruction. As seen in figure 1.1, Hurricane Maria made landfall in Puerto Rico's southeast corner near Yabucoa and diagonally crossed the island, exiting on the northwest coast, just west of Arecibo. As discussed in the 2019 National Hurricane Center (NHC) Tropical Storm Report, Maria's eyewall replacement shortly before landfall resulted in approximately tripling its eye diameter, which increased Puerto Rico's areal exposure to Hurricane Maria's strongest winds as it moved across the island (Pasch, Penny and Berg 2019) and resulted in "tornado-like damage across a swath of the island" (Meyer 2017). Hurricane Maria was technically a Category 4 storm upon making landfall in Puerto Rico, but the NHC Tropical Storm Report noted that "in Puerto Rico, winds of Category 5 intensity were almost certainly felt at some elevated locations on the island" (Pasch, Penny and Berg 2019, p. 5).

Beyond the wind, Hurricane Maria caused flooding from the storm surge as well as the heavy rainfall. As seen in figure 1.1, the combined effect of the storm surge and tide produced inundation levels of 6–9 feet above ground level just to the north of where Hurricane Maria made landfall; 4–7 feet above ground level south of the landfall; 3–5 feet in other areas along the southern

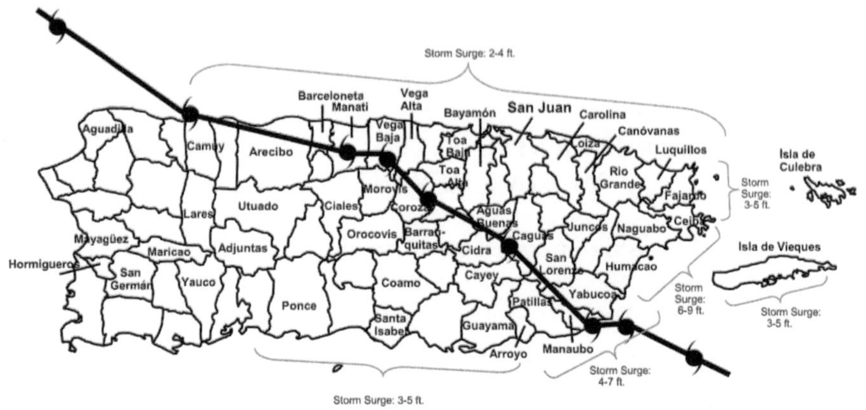

Figure 1.1 Hurricane Maria's Path across Puerto Rico: September 20, 2017. *Note*: The boundaries show Puerto Rico's 78 municipios (municipalities). Given space constraints, not all of the municipios are labeled. The levels of storm surge reflect the estimated storm surge inundation for coastal areas; coastal areas not marked (southwest, northwest, and west coasts plus Culebra) had 1–3 ft of estimated storm surge inundation. *Source*: Authors' depictions based on information in the Center for Puerto Rican Studies (2018b) and the National Hurricane Center (Pasch, Penny and Berg 2018).

coast plus the island of Vieques; 2–4 feet on most of the northern coast; and 1–3 feet on the western, far southwestern, and far northwestern coasts plus the island of Culebra (Pasch, Penny, and Berg 2019). Ten percent of the island received more than 500 millimeters (approximately 19.7 inches) of rain (Ramos-Scharrón and Arima 2019), peaking at 37.9 inches in Caguas (Pasch, Penny and Berg 2019), which caused widespread flooding, flash flooding, and landslides, further leading to the destruction of critical components of infrastructure, including electrical, transportation, and communication systems.

In the immediate aftermath of Hurricane Maria, the entire island was without electricity. As noted earlier, 83 percent of residents and businesses remained without electricity a full month after Hurricane Maria, and 33 percent still lacked running water (Center for Puerto Rican Studies 2018a, 2018b). Even three months after Hurricane Maria's landfall, electricity had not been restored to nearly half of the island's then 3.3 million American citizens (Robles and Bidwood 2017), and in some cases, it took nearly a year. Moreover, approximately 97 percent of the roads and highways were impassable immediately after Maria, some remaining so for months (Government of Puerto Rico 2018).

Hurricane Maria resulted in the costliest disaster in Puerto Rico to date, at an estimated $94.4 billion in damages as reported by the 2019 NHC Tropical Storm Report, which shattered Puerto Rico's previous costliest hurricane on record—Hurricane Georges, with approximately $5 billion (in 2017 dollars) in damages (Pasch, Penny and Berg 2019). As reported by the U.S. Government Accountability Office (2020), the Government of Puerto Rico estimated that $132 billion in funding would be needed over a 10-year period to repair and reconstruct the infrastructure damaged by Hurricanes Maria and Irma (the Category 5 storm whose eyewall passed just north of Puerto Rico two weeks before Hurricane Maria).

It is not surprising that a hurricane of this magnitude would be devastating to the location in which it made landfall. However, as we have noted elsewhere, the demographic, social, economic, and political context in which Hurricane Maria transpired, and the ensuing number of lost lives and prolonged human suffering in the wake of the inept response and recovery on multiple levels (including at the commonwealth and federal levels), transformed this "natural hazard" (e.g., hurricane) into a socially constructed disaster. A number of factors contributed to this chronic situation, including the preexisting severe economic crisis and the dilapidated infrastructure. At least initially, Hurricane Maria all but decimated the already weakened and deteriorating economy that had struggled through more than a decade of a severe economic crisis (e.g., MDR 2018; Meléndez and Venator-Santiago 2018; Aja et al. 2018). The next three chapters by María E. Enchautegui, Zadia M. Feliciano, and José Caraballo-Cueto provide new insights into how Puerto Rico's labor market began the recovery process as rebuilding efforts got underway.

The electrical grid on the island—described by Glanz and Robles (2018) in a *New York Times* article as "decrepit, corroded and poorly maintained" after decades of underfunded maintenance, including during La Crisis Boricua—had been further weakened by the effects of Hurricane Irma. In fact, two years after Hurricane Maria, the American Society of Civil Engineers (ASCE) assigned a failing grade to Puerto Rico's energy infrastructure in its infrastructure report card, indicating "the infrastructure in the system is in unacceptable condition with widespread advanced signs of deterioration" and "many of the components of the system exhibit signs of imminent failure" (ASCE 2019). (More details will be discussed on the electrical grid in chapter 5 by Marla D. Pérez-Lugo, Cecilio Ortiz-García, and Didier Valdés.) Furthermore, the destruction of Puerto Rico's transportation infrastructure and an almost complete loss of telecommunications resulted in challenges and delays in providing many communities with emergency aid, supplies (e.g., drinking water, food, medicine), and services (e.g., medical care) desperately needed by the population (Rodríguez and Mora 2020; Meléndez and Venator-Santiago 2018).

Moreover, Hurricane Maria further eroded the healthcare system (which was already in a precarious situation), and it would not be able to respond to the critical and emerging healthcare needs post-Hurricane Maria, especially given the inadequate delivery of medical supplies and slow restoration of electricity to millions of residents (e.g., Orengo-Aguayo et al. 2019). As such, health implications and outcomes, including mental health, were of serious concern. Upcoming chapters by Jose M. Fernandez; Fernando I. Rivera and colleagues; Amy Nitza and Shao Lin; and María Rolón-Martínez, Joy Lynn Suárez-Kindy, and Rosaura Orengo-Aguayo discuss such outcomes in more detail, including the increased number of suicides.

Given these impacts, it is not surprising that Hurricane Maria accelerated the massive net exodus from Puerto Rico to the U.S. mainland that had been ongoing for more than a decade (e.g., MDR 2017a, 2017b, 2018, 2019; Meléndez and Venator-Santiago 2018; Hinojosa, Román, and Meléndez 2018; Cohn, Patten, and Lopez 2014; Figueroa-Rodríguez 2013). As we discuss later in this chapter, the massive net out-migration presented an additional set of demographic, socioeconomic, and healthcare challenges on the island and mainland, including a rapidly aging population, as well as a significant decline in the island's population.

LA CRISIS BORICUA AND PROMESA

La Crisis Boricua, or Puerto Rico's severe economic crisis, began surging in 2006 as numerous interrelated factors came into play, essentially creating a domino effect. By the time Hurricane Maria made landfall, since 2006 Puerto Rico only had one year of positive economic growth (half a decade earlier, in 2012), which reflected the crippling scaling back of industries spurred by the expiration of IRS Code Section 936, starting on January 1, 2006. This code had provided U.S. corporations with tax incentives to operate on the island, but it was repealed in 1995 with a 10-year phase-out period. In our previous work, we estimated the island lost 37,000 manufacturing jobs between 2006 and 2014 (albeit not all could be directly attributed to the expiration of Code 936) in addition to previous estimates of 30,000 jobs lost in the phase-out period (MDR 2017a, 2017b). Zadia Feliciano and Andrew Green—in a 2017 National Bureau of Economic Research working paper—found that the phase-out and elimination of the Section 936 tax exemption program was related to an 18.7–28.0 percent reduction in the number of manufacturing establishments and a 16.7 percent decline in manufacturing wages relative to the U.S. mainland between 1995 and 2012.

As such, with the loss of industry, jobs, and earnings came a loss of bank deposits, financial capital, and tax revenue collected by the government. As we discuss elsewhere (e.g., MDR 2017a, 2017b, 2018), as part of the means to address its budgetary issues, the commonwealth government eliminated numerous public sector jobs, which led to a further loss of jobs, earnings, bank deposits, and tax revenue. The loss of private and public sector jobs, among other factors, spurred the largest net out-migration in terms of the number of migrants, and the second largest (since the Great Migration of the 1950s) in terms of the number of migrants relative to the population size (e.g., MDR 2017a, 2018).

The government also imposed a sales tax (*Impuesto a las Ventas y Uso*), starting in 2006 at 7.0 percent, which was previously nonexistent, and raised it in 2015 to 11.5 percent (a rate currently higher than any state sales tax in the continental United States). These issues were further compounded by the island's loss in credit ratings on municipal bonds in 2014, and the government's unprecedented $74 billion public debt, plus an additional $49 billion in unfunded pension obligations (e.g., MDR 2017a, 2017b). This fiscal deterioration resulted in a series of defaults on debt payments starting in August 2015, just weeks after then-governor Garcia Padilla described the debt ($72 billion at the time) as a "death spiral" and "not payable."

Given Puerto Rico's dependency status with the United States,[2] the island was unable to enact its own bankruptcy law while also being ineligible to file for federal bankruptcy protection (all due to its status as a U.S. territory). Because the federal bankruptcy code authorizes Congress, not territories, to enact bankruptcy legislation, Congress created the nonelected Oversight Board (not accountable to the island's residents) to restructure the island's debt through the passage of the Puerto Rico Oversight, Management, and Economic Stability Act (PROMESA), which was signed into law by President Barrack Obama in June 2016. PROMESA and the Oversight Board reinvigorated debates on Puerto Rico's pseudo-colonial status and lack of representation in Congress.[3]

As we and others have highlighted (e.g., MDR 2017a, 2018; Meléndez 2018a, 2018b; Aja et al. 2019; Cabán 2019; Rodríguez and Mora 2020), concerns over PROMESA include:

- The absence of provisions to address economic development and chronic socioeconomic issues;
- Removing Puerto Rico's autonomy and decision-making power, including over the Board's appointments, scope, decisions, and outcomes;
- The lack of accountability to the Puerto Rican government and the island's inhabitants; and
- The potential focus on bond holders, adversely impacting rebuilding and public services provisions.

PUERTO RICAN ISLAND-MAINLAND MIGRATION BEFORE AND AFTER HURRICANE MARIA

With all these significant challenges, it is not surprising that Puerto Ricans had been leaving the island in record numbers before Hurricane Maria. Updating our previous estimates of this net out-migration (e.g., MDR 2017a,

Table 1.1 Puerto Rico's Estimated Population, Natural Increase, and Net Migration between July 1, 2006 and July 1, 2019

Characteristic	*Estimates (All Pertain to July 1)*
Panel A: Pre-Maria Estimates—2006–2017	
Population in Puerto Rico: 2006	3,805,214
Population in Puerto Rico: 2017	3,325,286
Total Change in PR population: 2006–2017	−479,928
Natural Increase in PR (*live births – deaths*): 2006–2017	129,164
Estimated net migration: July 1, 2006–July 1, 2017	−609,092 *(16.0% 2006 pop.)*
Panel B: Post-Maria Estimates—2017–2018	
Population in Puerto Rico: 2018	3,193,354
Total Change in PR population: 2017–2018	−131,932
Natural Increase in PR (*live births – deaths*): 2017–2018	−8,553
Estimated net migration: July 1, 2017–July 1, 2018	−123,379 *(3.7% of 2017 pop.)*
Panel C: Post-Maria Estimates—2018–2019	
Population in Puerto Rico: 2019	3,193,694
Total Change in PR population: 2018–2019	340
Natural Increase in PR (*live births – deaths*): 2018–2019	−7,393
Estimated net migration: July 1, 2018–July 1, 2019	7,733
Estimated net migration: July 1, 2006–July 1, 2018	724,738 *(19.0% of 2006 pop.)*

Note: The 2017 population estimates differ from those reported in Mora, Dávila, and Rodríguez (e.g., 2018) due to updated population estimates from the U.S. Census Bureau (2019).
Source: Authors' estimates using data from the U.S. Census Bureau data (2019 and earlier) and Mora, Dávila, and Rodríguez (2018).

2018), table 1.1 provides the estimated population size on the island, natural increase (the difference between live births and deaths), and estimated net migration pre-Maria (panel A), immediately after Hurricane Maria up through July 1, 2018 (panel B) and then through July 1, 2019 (panel C), based on our estimates using data from the U.S. Census Bureau (2019).[4] In 2006, Puerto Rico's population stood at 3.81 million. By July 1, 2017 (a few months before Hurricane Maria), the island's population had declined by nearly half a million people (479,928) to 3.33 million. When accounting for the natural increase of 129,164, the estimated net out-migration from Puerto Rico was 609,092, representing nearly one-sixth (16.0%) of the island's entire 2006 population. This number of net migrants exceeded the estimated number of net migrants from Puerto Rico during the Great Migration period of the 1950s (470,000), but on a relative basis compared to the population size, it fell short of the one-fifth representation migrants comprised at that time (MDR 2017a).

Not surprisingly, Hurricane Maria initially expedited Puerto Rico's population loss. As seen in panel B of table 1.1, between July 1, 2017, and July

1, 2018, Puerto Rico's population continued to fall by 131,932 individuals. With the negative natural increase (meaning there were more deaths than births that year) of 8,553, Puerto Rico lost an estimated 123,379 residents due to net out-migration in the one year, which represented 3.7 percent of the island's entire population. That is, within a 12-month period, Puerto Rico lost approximately 1 out of every 26 residents due to out-migration in the time surrounding Hurricane Maria.

Of interest, however, as the island began to recover, Puerto Rico's population loss came to a halt by July 1, 2019. For the first time in 15 years, Puerto Rico had a slight estimated population increase of 340 residents (table 1.1, panel C). Natural increase remained negative (−7,393) but net in-migration of 7,733 offset the loss. Whether the in-migration that year was driven by temporary out-migrants due to Hurricane Maria or if it reflects a changing dynamic in the island-mainland migration flows remains to be seen (especially given the subsequent COVID-19 pandemic). Still, cumulatively between 2006 and 2018, an estimated nearly three-quarters of a million (724,738) residents left the island on net, representing almost one in five residents (19.0%)—a similar share to the one observed in the Great Migration period.

While these estimates reflect net out-migration, it is important to note that despite massive out-migration from Puerto Rico during La Crisis Boricua, Puerto Rico also received a significant number of in-migrants from the mainland (e.g., MDR 2017a, 2018; Cohn, Patten, and Lopez 2014); otherwise the island's population loss would have been greater. Figure 1.2 presents the number of Puerto Rican migrants who left the island for the mainland (the top line), as well as the number who left the mainland for the island (the bottom line) in each year between 2006 and 2018.[5]

The effect of Hurricane Maria on out-migration is one of the striking features of figure 1.2, given the sharp upturn in the number of Puerto Rican out-migrants from the island between 2017 and 2018. The number of Puerto Rican in-migrants to the island, however, while lower than in 2016, did not appear to be aberrant compared to other recent years. But the historically large net out-migration resulting from La Crisis Boricua is also visible in figure 1.2. Despite the emergence of La Crisis Boricua in 2006, this figure shows that the out-migration from the island tapered off and in-migration increased as the U.S. mainland encountered the Great Recession (which ran from December 2007 through June 2009), dampening incentives to migrate (MDR 2017a). As the mainland labor market slowly recovered—but Puerto Rican labor market did not—out-migration to the mainland surged, but eventually slowed and stabilized after 2014, until Hurricane Maria. In-migration to Puerto Rico sharply declined after 2010 (coinciding with the mainland's economic recovery) but became relatively stable the following year.

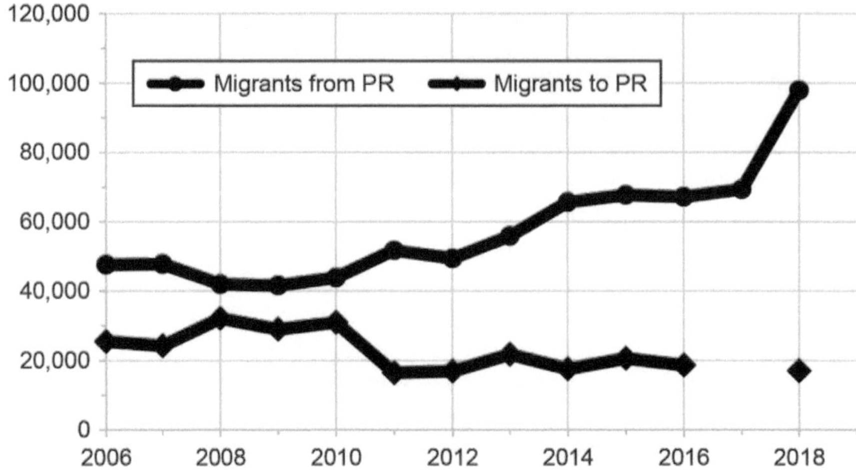

Figure 1.2 Annual Migration Flows of Puerto Ricans between the Island and Mainland: 2006–2018. *Note*: These estimates only include individuals who self-identify as Puerto Rican. The 2017 data for Puerto Rico are not shown because data collection for that year was incomplete due to the suspension of data collection efforts on the island by federal statistical agencies after Hurricane Maria. The 2018 estimates include some pre-Hurricane Maria migrants. *Source*: Authors' estimates using 2006–2018 ACS/PRCS data in the IPUMS.

FLORIDA AS THE MAJOR DESTINATION AREA OF PUERTO RICAN MIGRANTS PRE- AND POST-MARIA

In terms of where Puerto Rican migrants from the island were moving, Florida became the top destination area during La Crisis Boricua as well as post-Hurricane Maria. In previous work (MDR 2017a, 2018, 2019), we discussed how Florida received one-third of all migrants from the island between 2006 and 2016—a larger share than any other state (see also Cohn, Patten and Lopez, 2014). Florida was also the largest receiving area of Puerto Rican interstate migrants during that time. These changes, along with relatively high fertility rates of mainland Puerto Ricans, resulted in Florida becoming home to more Puerto Ricans than the state of New York shortly before Hurricane Maria. Post-Hurricane Maria, solidifying Florida's prominence in the Puerto Rican community, initial estimates based on different sources and data collection methodologies consistently showed that Florida received an even larger share of the immediate migrants from Puerto Rico, ranging between 42 and 52 percent (see MDR 2019).[6] As such, by 2018, an estimated 1.17 million Puerto Ricans resided in Florida (more than one out of five of all Puerto Rican mainland residents), compared to 1.08 million in the state of New York.

Figure 1.3 presents the major pre- and post-Hurricane Maria receiving areas (for 2006–2016 and 2018), listed in order of the number of recent

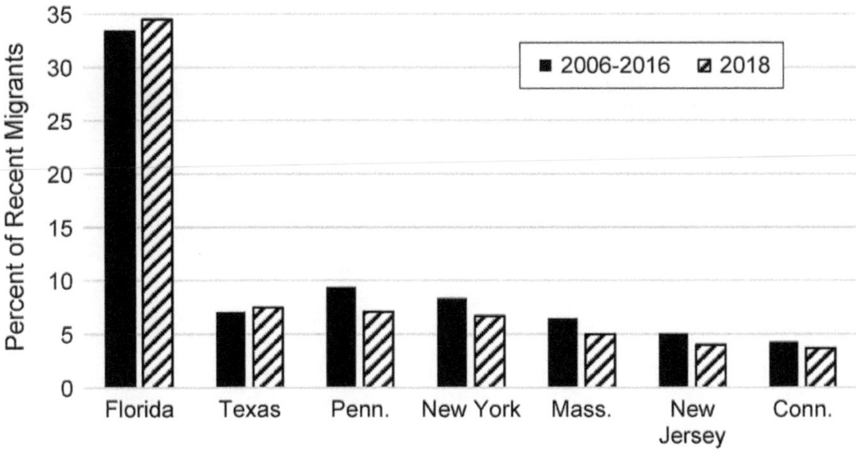

Figure 1.3 Major Receiving States of Puerto Rican Migrants Pre- and Post-Hurricane Maria. *Note*: These estimates only include individuals who self-identify as Puerto Rican. *Source*: Authors' estimates using ACS data in the IPUMS.

Puerto Rican migrants living in each state in 2018. It is clear from this figure that Florida ranked as the state with the largest number of recent Puerto Rican migrants from the island both pre- and post-Hurricane Maria, receiving one-third of all the migrants (33.4% vs 34.5%, respectively), with no statistically significant difference separating migrants between the two periods.

Although receiving only a fraction of the number of post-Hurricane Maria migrants as Florida, Texas—a nontraditional receiving area—moved into second place in 2018, being the recipient of 7.5 percent of incoming Puerto Ricans from the island. The state had ranked as the fourth largest receiving area between 2006 and 2016, with 7.1 percent of Puerto Rican migrants. Other prominent states receiving pre- and post-Hurricane Maria Puerto Rican migrants include traditional settlement areas of Puerto Ricans, namely Pennsylvania, New York, Massachusetts, New Jersey, and Connecticut, which housed 7.1, 6.7, 5.0, 4.0, and 3.7 percent, respectively, of post-Maria migrants. Despite marginal differences in the rankings pre- and post-Hurricane Maria, this figure indicates that the pre-Maria migration patterns continued after Hurricane Maria made landfall.

With respect to the specific metropolitan areas into where Puerto Rican migrants from the island have settled, Florida's dominance is further evident as it contains three of the top five receiving areas of Puerto Ricans pre- and post-Hurricane Maria (see table 1.2): Orlando-Kissimmee-Sanford, Miami-Fort Lauderdale-West Palm Beach, and Tampa-St. Petersburg-Clearwater. (For the pre-Maria period here, we focus on the 2014–2016 years.) The Orlando area, which topped the list in both periods, received more migrants than the next three metropolitan areas combined.[7] Between 2017 and 2018,

Table 1.2 Top 10 Mainland Receiving Metropolitan Areas of Puerto Rican Migrants from Puerto Rico in 2014–2016 and 2018

Rank	*2014–2016*	*2018*
1	Orlando-Kissimmee-Sanford, FL: 16.5%	Orlando-Kissimmee-Sanford, FL: 17.2%
2	Miami-Fort Lauderdale-West Palm Beach, FL: 5.5%	New York-Newark-Jersey City, NY, NJ, and PA: 7.3%
3	Tampa-St. Petersburg-Clearwater, FL: 5.4%; and New York-Newark-Jersey City, NY, NJ, and PA: 5.4%	Miami-Fort Lauderdale-West Palm Beach, FL: 5.3%
4	—	Tampa-St. Petersburg-Clearwater, FL: 4.2%
5	Dallas-Fort Worth-Arlington, TX: 3.9%	Philadelphia-Camden-Wilmington, PA, NJ, DE, and MD: 2.9%; and Springfield, MA: 2.9%
6	Philadelphia-Camden-Wilmington, PA, NJ, DE, and MD: 3.8%	—
7	Providence-Warwick, RI and MA: 2.6%	Hartford, CT: 2.8%; and Lakeland-Winter Haven, FL: 2.8%
8	Cleveland-Elyria, OH: 2.6%	—
9	Springfield, MA: 2.0%	Columbia, SC: 2.7%
10	Allentown-Bethlehem-Easton, PA and NJ: 1.9%	Dallas-Fort Worth-Arlington, TX: 2.0%

Note: The percentages shown indicate the percent of all recent Puerto Rican migrants who lived in the respective metropolitan area. These estimates only include individuals who self-identify as Puerto Rican. The metropolitan receiving area is where individuals resided at the time of the ACS survey; as such, these areas do not necessarily reflect the initial point-of-entry for individuals who moved multiple times in the past 12 months after entering the mainland. The 2018 data include some pre-Maria migrants.
Source: Authors' estimates using ACS data in the IPUMS.

approximately one of six (17.2%) of all incoming migrants from the island moved to the Orlando-Kissimmee-Sanford metropolitan area.

Traditional receiving areas, including the New York-Newark-Jersey City, Philadelphia-Camden-Wilmington, and Springfield, MA, metropolitan areas were in the top 10 in both periods, with New York rising from a tied third to second place, receiving 7.3 percent of incoming migrants post-Hurricane Maria. Still, nontraditional areas for Puerto Rican migrants are also represented, notably Dallas-Fort Worth-Arlington pre- and post-Maria—highlighting the increased importance of Texas to the Puerto Rican diaspora—as well as Columbia, SC, following Hurricane Maria.

SOCIOECONOMIC CHARACTERISTICS OF PUERTO RICAN MIGRANTS IN MAINLAND DESTINATION AREAS

The scale of the exodus from Puerto Rico that started even before Hurricane Maria has socioeconomic, demographic, and political implications for the island, but migration flows also impact the mainland receiving areas. We previously identified that before Hurricane Maria, the socioeconomic and demographic characteristics of Puerto Ricans varied with respect to the destination area. For example, the education levels and socioeconomic indicators tend to be higher among recent Puerto Rican migrants in Texas and to a lesser extent in Florida, compared to those moving into traditional settlement areas (MDR 2017a, 2018). Because the pre- and post-Hurricane Maria settlement areas appear similar for recent Puerto Rican migrants, presumably their socioeconomic and demographic characteristics are as well. We now have access to data to test this premise that were unavailable when we conducted our previous work.

POVERTY RATES AMONG RECENT PUERTO RICAN MIGRANTS PRE- AND POST-HURRICANE MARIA

We present in figure 1.4 the poverty rates of all recent Puerto Rican migrants living stateside as well as those living in the five largest receiving states between 2014–2016 and 2018—shortly before and after Hurricane Maria. We focus on the 2014–2016 years to narrow the pre-Hurricane Maria timeframe (hence,

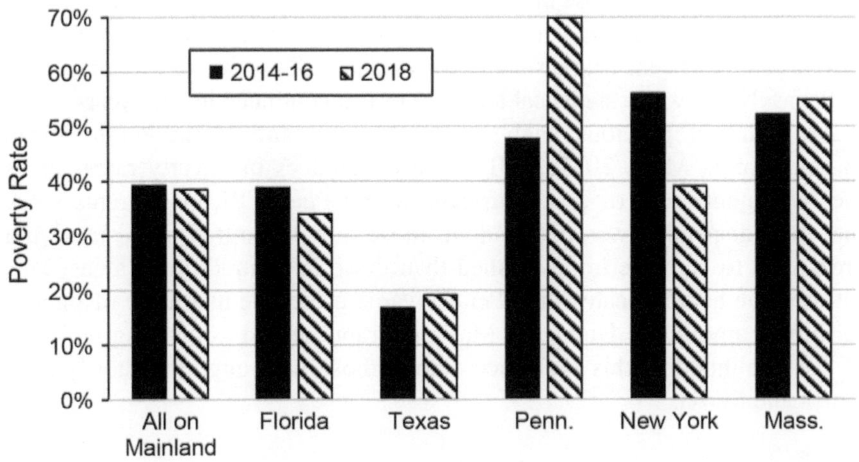

Figure 1.4 Poverty Rates of Recent Puerto Rican Migrants on the Mainland, by Selected State of Residence, 2014–2016 and 2018. *Note*: These estimates only include nongroup quarter residents who self-identify as Puerto Rican. Statistical tests (including Pearson χ^2- and design-based F-tests) indicate that the difference in poverty rates between pre- and post-Hurricane Maria Puerto Rican migrants in Pennsylvania is statistically significant at the 5 percent level; the remaining differences between the 2014–2016 and 2018 migrants, including for mainland overall, were not statistically significant at the 10 percent level. Details can be provided by the authors. *Source*: Authors' estimates using ACS data in the IPUMS.

mainland economic conditions) to the time shortly before the storm. We exclude 2017 from this analysis because data collected that year include nearly nine months of data on pre-Hurricane Maria migrants, a demographic that cannot be distinguished from post-Hurricane Maria migrants in this public-use dataset.

Overall, poverty rates differed little between Puerto Ricans who moved to the mainland shortly before and after Hurricane Maria; approximately 4 in 10 were below the poverty line in both periods (39.1% in 2014–2016 vs 38.4% in 2018). Poverty rates also differed little between pre- and post-Hurricane Maria migrants within the major receiving states except Pennsylvania. For example, the incidence of poverty was higher among pre- and post-Hurricane Maria recent migrants in Florida (38.8% vs 34.0%) and in New York (55.6% vs 39.1%), and lower among pre- versus post-Hurricane Maria recent migrants in Texas (16.7% vs 19.1%) and Massachusetts (52.5% vs 54.9%), but none of these differences were statistically significant at conventional levels.

In Pennsylvania, figure 1.4 indicates that recent Puerto Rican migrants who left the island shortly after Hurricane Maria had considerably higher poverty rates than those who migrated shortly beforehand; more than two-thirds (69.9%) of the post-Hurricane Maria migrants were below the poverty line in 2018 compared to less than half (47.7%) in 2014–2016. Note that post-Maria migrants in Pennsylvania also had the highest poverty rate in the states; the next highest in 2018 occurred among those in Massachusetts. As future data become available, researchers should analyze whether the significantly higher incidence of poverty among post-Hurricane Maria versus pre-Hurricane Maria Puerto Rican migrants in Pennsylvania was a statistical anomaly or if it continued in later years.

As with our previous analyses of pre-Hurricane Maria Puerto Rican migrants (e.g., MDR 2017a, 2018), the differences in poverty rates across the settlement areas of post-Hurricane Maria Puerto Rican migrants show that their dispersion was not random; those moving to traditional receiving areas tend to be more impoverished than those in nontraditional areas. This information also indicates that, Pennsylvania aside, the incidence of impoverishment among pre-Hurricane Maria migrants served as a strong indicator of the likelihood of this incidence among those who migrated shortly after Hurricane Maria.

LABOR FORCE STATUS AND EDUCATIONAL ATTAINMENT

Further analyses indicate that poverty rates were not the only socioeconomic indicator that remained similar between pre- and post-Hurricane Maria Puerto Rican migrants on the U.S. mainland. To illustrate, using the labor force status among Puerto Rican adult migrants between the ages of 25 and 64, as seen in panel A of figure 1.5, 59.1 percent were employed and another 11.1 percent

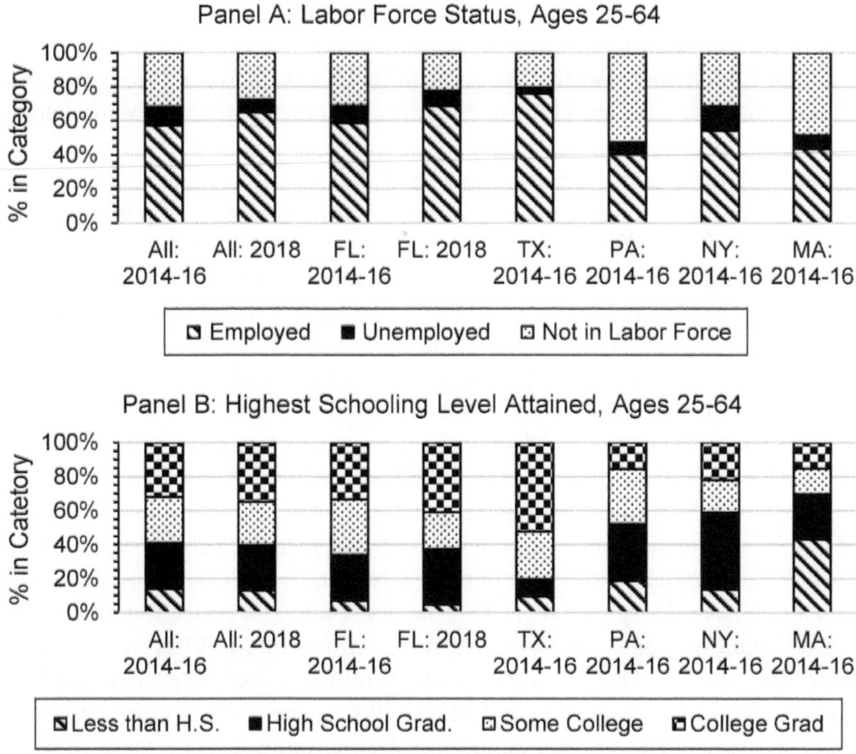

Figure 1.5 Labor Force Status and Educational Attainment of Recent Puerto Rican Migrant Adults, Ages 25–64, in 2014–2016 and 2018, and by Selected State of Residence. *Note*: These estimates only include adults ages 25–64 who self-identify as Puerto Rican. The unemployed indicates the percentage reporting being unemployed, not the unemployment rate. Statistical tests (including Pearson χ^2- and design-based F-tests) indicate that the difference in the distributions of labor force status and educational attainment between pre- and post-Hurricane Maria Puerto Rican migrants overall and in Florida was not statistically significant at the 10 percent level. Details can be provided by the authors. *Source*: Authors' estimates using ACS data in the IPUMS.

were unemployed in 2014–2016. While on the surface these labor market outcomes improved to employment and unemployment rates of 65.0 and 7.6 percent, respectively, among those who moved stateside following Hurricane Maria, the distribution of their market activities did not statistically differ from those of their pre-Hurricane Maria counterparts at conventional levels.

The education distributions were also statistically similar between Puerto Rican adults ages 25–64 who moved to the mainland before and after Hurricane Maria (see panel B of figure 1.5). On average, 14.0 percent versus 12.9 percent of pre- versus post-Hurricane Maria Puerto Rican migrants living stateside had less than a high school education; approximately one-quarter were high school graduates (26.9% vs 26.8%); approximately one-quarter had some college, but not a four-year college degree (27.2% vs 25.6%); and approximately one-third were college graduates (31.9% vs 34.7%).

Figure 1.5 further shows that the distributions of labor force activities and educational attainment differed little between pre- and post-Hurricane Maria Puerto Rican adult migrants in Florida, the largest receiving area of Puerto Ricans who moved from the island to the mainland. As with poverty rates, the consistency in these distributions indicates that the socioeconomic conditions of pre-Hurricane Maria Puerto Rican migrants served as a strong indicator of such conditions for those who migrated from the island in the aftermath of Hurricane Maria.

For comparison purposes, we report in figure 1.5 the distributions of the labor force status and educational attainment for pre-Hurricane Maria Puerto Rican adult migrants in the other major receiving states; we do not report the corresponding distributions for 2018 owing to the relatively small sample sizes of Puerto Rican adult migrants in these states that year. Still, based on the other patterns, we anticipate that the socioeconomic outcomes of Puerto Rican adults who moved from the island post-Hurricane Maria to Texas were relatively high, while those moving to traditional receiving areas, such as New York, Pennsylvania, and Massachusetts, were relatively low. As we have previously discussed (e.g., MDR 2018), the economic and educational needs of Puerto Rican migrants following Hurricane Maria likely differ according to where they locate. Those moving to the traditional receiving areas, including New York, Pennsylvania, and Massachusetts, may need more assistance with accessing education and employment opportunities while those moving to newer destination areas, such as Texas, may need more assistance with respect to better matching their education levels to employment and finding housing and transportation close to their places of work.

THE SHRINKING AND RAPIDLY AGING POPULATION LEFT BEHIND IN PUERTO RICO

The Puerto Rican migratory exodus from the island to the mainland, which was aggravated by Hurricane Maria, has far-reaching effects not only for those who relocate as well as for their mainland communities, but also for Puerto Ricans who remain on the island. As discussed earlier in this chapter, the island's population was shrinking for more than a decade when Hurricane Maria made landfall, driven largely by net out-migration during La Crisis Boricua. Because younger people (often in their prime childbearing years) tend to be the ones who migrate, combined with the low fertility rates and relatively long lifespans on the island, the massive net out-migration from Puerto Rico increased the average age of the island's population, leaving a situation described by Raúl Figueroa-Rodríguez (2013) as the "elders' colony". Even without Hurricane Maria, the demographic challenges on the island included an increased need for healthcare services and a shrinking labor force to generate income and tax revenue, supporting retirees and other elderly populations.

According to our estimates, the average age of Puerto Ricans on the island significantly increased by 4.5 years, from 36.0 years in 2006 to 40.5 years in 2016. It increased again by another 1.5 years following Hurricane Maria, to 42.0 years in 2018. As noted earlier in this chapter, in recent years live births in Puerto Rico have fallen short of deaths, further contributing to the increasingly elderly population on the island.

To better visualize this expedited aging, figure 1.6 shows the age-population pyramids of Puerto Ricans on the island in 2006 (the year La Crisis Boricua got underway) in panel A, 2016 (after a record exodus of Puerto Ricans during the first decade of La Crisis Boricua) in panel B, and 2018 (shortly after Hurricane Maria made landfall, which expedited the mass exodus from the island, as discussed earlier in this chapter) in panel C. A standard demographic tool, comparing age-population pyramids over time, shows how the age and gender composition of a population have changed. The population pyramid for a youthful population has a typical pyramidal shape, with a wide base representing the younger ages of the population, and a narrow top representing the relatively small older population segments. As populations age, these pyramids change in shape and start bulging like a beehive as more individuals are represented in middle ages as opposed to youthful ages. These pyramids become top-heavy when larger shares of the population are represented in the older age ranges.

Figure 1.6 shows that, between 2006 and 2018, Puerto Rico's age structure went through a significant aging transition, continuing the transition that started decades beforehand (MDR 2017a; Figueroa-Rodríguez 2013). In addition to changes in the age composition of island residents, this figure also shows a gender shift toward females. The net out-migration of younger populations is particularly salient in figure 1.6, given the "hollowing out" of the age-population pyramids for people in their late 20s and 30s, including in 2018, which has immediate and long-term implications for the island's fertility rates (already among the lowest in the world) and a continued demographic shift. As we noted before Hurricane Maria (MDR 2017a), "such rapid changes have important ramifications for the island's already low labor force participation rates and deteriorating and overstretched healthcare sector, particularly for women." It remains to be seen if the cessation in Puerto Rico's population loss between 2018 and 2019, discussed earlier in this chapter, represented a one-time event or the beginning of a new demographic shift spurred by net in-migration.

DISCUSSION AND CONCLUDING REMARKS

It is important to emphasize that Puerto Rico was encountering an economic crisis (described by some as a humanitarian crisis) that had been

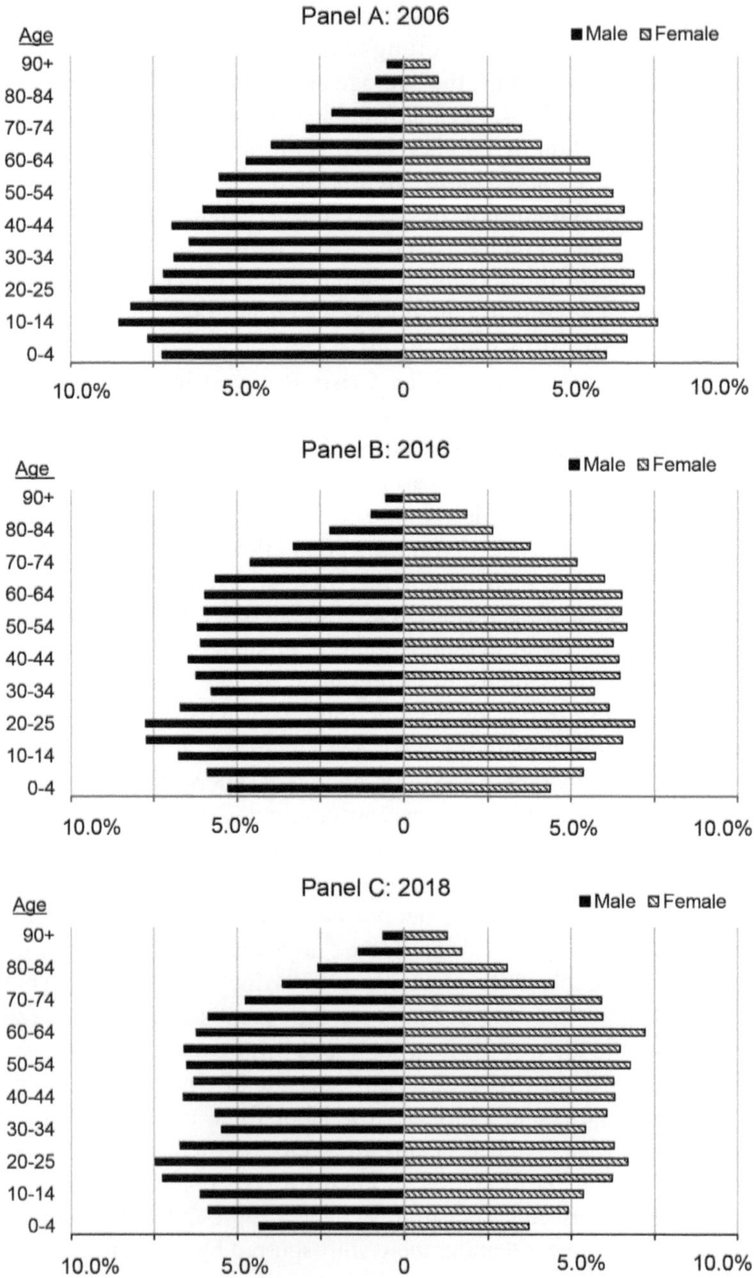

Figure 1.6 Age-Population Pyramids in Puerto Rico: 2006, 2016, and 2018. *Note*: These estimates only include individuals who self-identify as Puerto Ricans. *Source*: Authors' estimates using PRCS data in the IPUMS.

surging for more than a decade when Hurricane Maria made landfall. With its massive net out-migration, dilapidated infrastructure, demographic shift, the loss of public and private sector jobs, and a bankrupt government lacking fiscal autonomy, the island was ill-equipped to respond to the needs of Puerto Ricans during the aftermath of Hurricane Maria (e.g., MDR 2018, Meléndez and Venator-Santiago 2018; Aja et al. 2018; Rodríguez and Mora 2020).

Moreover, the federal government's immediate and subsequent response following Maria, including the delay in the disbursement of approved federal aid in September 2019 and the slow housing inspection process and grant awards by the Federal Emergency Management Agency,[8] raised questions about the nature of Puerto Rico's true relationship with the United States. It should be noted that as a territory, Puerto Rico's residents lack voting representation in Congress, but the nearly six million Puerto Ricans living stateside have this representation, more than ever before. It will be important to learn how the voting tendencies and other forms of civic engagement of mainland Puerto Ricans will influence the socioeconomic outcomes of post-Hurricane Maria Puerto Ricans on the island and mainland in the years to come.

NOTES

1. Throughout this volume, references to Puerto Ricans on the U.S. mainland and living stateside include those living in the 50 states plus Washington, DC. Moreover, for convenience the chapters refer to the Commonwealth of Puerto Rico as an island, but readers should be aware the commonwealth is technically comprised of several islands.

2. We provide an overview of this "dependency status" in our book (MDR 2017a). Congress has the constitutional authority to revise or revoke the powers of self-government currently exercised in Puerto Rico under Article IV, Section 3, Clause 2 of the U.S. Constitution: "Congress shall have the Power to dispose of and make all needful Rules and Regulations respecting the territory or other Property belonging to the United States." For a recent discussion of the history of territorial incorporation bills for Puerto Rico, see Charles Venator-Santiago (2018).

3. As noted by MDR (2017a), in 2017 Nobel laureate Joseph Stiglitz and Martin Guzman stated Puerto Rico was "*de facto* an American colony," and that the enactment of PROMESA reflected "the standard colonialist view that a colony cannot be trusted to make independent decisions." See also the April 2017 *Harvard Law Review*. For a detailed discussion of the politics and economics behind PROMESA, see Edwin Meléndez (2018a, 2018b); Pablo Guzmann, Martin Guzman, and Joseph Stiglitz (2018); and Alan Aja and colleagues (2018).

4. The population estimates in table 1.1 do not distinguish between people who self-identify as Puerto Rican versus those who do not. While this topic goes beyond

the scope of this chapter, in previous work (MDR 2018), we reported that individuals who did not self-identify as Puerto Rican were overrepresented among net out-migrants from Puerto Rico, at least prior to Hurricane Maria.

5. Unless otherwise specified, the remainder of our analyses in this chapter employs 2006–2018 public-use microdata from the American Community Survey (ACS) and the Puerto Rican Community Survey (PRCS) conducted by the U.S. Census Bureau and made available in the Integrated Public Use Microdata Series (IPUMS) by Steven Ruggles et al. (2019). All analyses employ the IPUMS-provided sampling weights; details are available from the authors. We identify recent migrants based on their place of residence 12 months before the ACS/PRCS survey. As such, the 2017 data include post-Maria migrants for households surveyed after September 20, 2017, while the 2018 data include pre-Maria migrants for individuals who moved between January 1 and September 19, 2017, and were surveyed before September 20, 2018.

6. These sources include the 2018 work by Jennifer Hinojosa, Nashia Román, and Edwin Meléndez at the Center for Puerto Rican Studies, based on school enrollment data, prior migration data, and other sources; an analysis by Teralytics, based on a sample of nearly half a million smartphones between October 2017 and February 2018 (Echenique and Melgar 2018); and analyses by CNN investigative reporters (Sutter and Hernandez 2018), based on requests to the U.S. Postal Service to change mailing addresses from Puerto Rico to a mainland destination between October 1, 2017, and December 31, 2017, as well as on the applications for disaster assistance from the Federal Emergency Management Agency from mainland zip codes between September 20, 2017, and November 11, 2017.

7. So prominent has the Orlando area become as a destination area for Puerto Rican migrants that GFR Media (the parent company of Puerto Rico's largest circulating newspaper, *El Nuevo Día*) relocated one of its editors, José Javier Pérez, from San Juan, Puerto Rico, to Orlando, Florida, in 2017 to cover news about Puerto Ricans in the area (Villafane 2017).

8. The Department of Housing and Urban Development refused to start disbursing $9.7 billion in aid in September 2019 allocated by Congress, citing concerns about "corruption" and "financial mismanagement" on the island (e.g., Sommerfeldt 2020). Moreover, hundreds of thousands of households were still waiting to have their homes inspected by FEMA an entire year after Hurricane Maria, and the FEMA awards Puerto Rican households had received fell considerably short of the requested amounts (Rodríguez and Mora 2020).

Chapter 2

Employment and Wages in Puerto Rico after Hurricane Maria

María E. Enchautegui

ABSTRACT

This chapter examines whether employment and wages grew after Hurricane Maria and compares such changes across industry sectors. Unemployment claim data show the slow recovery after Maria. No job gains were detected in any of the industry sectors 19 months following Maria's landfall, and the position of Puerto Rico relative to Florida deteriorated. However, wages grew, especially in the construction sector, which could stem from a combination of a declining labor supply, increased demand, out-migration, and legislation. Longer-term impacts on wages and employment in Puerto Rico have yet to be examined.

When Hurricane Maria hit Puerto Rico with high-end Category 4 windspeeds on September 20, 2017, its center crossed the island diagonally from the southeast through northwest (shown in figure 1.1 in the previous chapter), leaving immense catastrophic damage. The electric grid, a topic that will be further addressed by Marla D. Pérez-Lugo, Cecilio Ortiz-García, and Didier Valdés in chapter 5, was virtually destroyed, leaving households without electricity for an average of 106 days (Román et al. 2019). Also destroyed were 95 percent of cellular communication sites and 80 percent of aerial optical fiber installations (U.S. Homeland Security 2018).

In 2018, the then-governor of Puerto Rico estimated that it would take as much as $132 billion to reconstruct Puerto Rico (Government of Puerto Rico 2018), although the 2019 National Hurricane Center Tropical Storm Report noted damage estimates of $94.4 billion. The Federal Emergency Management Agency (FEMA 2018) reported that by September 2018, 462,000 households received a total of $1.4 billion in individual assistance for essential home repairs, rental assistance, and other disaster-related costs. The Federal Oversight and Management Board (one of the provisions of PROMESA discussed in the previous chapter by Marie T. Mora, Havidán Rodríguez, and Alberto Dávila) anticipated $83 billion in federal and private recovery funds in the 10 years following the hurricane (Commonwealth of Puerto Rico 2019).

The recovery funds represent a sizeable injection of money to an economy that had been undergoing a severe economic crisis since 2006 and have the potential of rekindling economic growth and creating jobs. However, concerns were raised whether there would be enough skilled labor to go around. In particular, with the declining population discussed in the previous chapter by Mora and colleagues, along with incoming recovery funds, one would expect to see wages grow as the island rebuilt, particularly in the construction industry. In light of these issues, I seek to answer the following overarching questions. Did employment and wages grow in Puerto Rico following Hurricane Maria? If so, what sectors were the most affected?

Identifying the effects of Hurricane Maria on the labor market is challenging. The poor performance of the Puerto Rican economy leading up to Maria makes it difficult to determine if employment losses are a continuation of a trend or the result from the adverse impact of the hurricane (Zadia M. Feliciano in the following chapter also makes this point). Moreover, part of the observed employment decline stems from the contraction in the labor supply caused by the island's shrinking population. Limitations and data availability lags present another difficulty. It may be too soon to see positive effects on employment if they end up emerging slowly. My approach is to first point to additional effects on employment in the post-Maria period overall and by industry after accounting for time trends. Second, I conduct a more sophisticated analysis that uses employment in Florida as a comparison. Finally, I provide a descriptive wage analysis, tracing wage growth before and after Hurricane Maria.

I selected Florida as a comparison because, as discussed in the previous chapter, it is the state receiving the largest number of Puerto Ricans from the island, suggesting Florida is a relevant labor market for Puerto Ricans. More importantly, Florida was not directly impacted by Hurricane Maria.[1] My analysis shows employment losses in Puerto Rico overall and in almost all the industries analyzed 19 months after Hurricane Maria. The employment position of Puerto Rico relative to Florida also deteriorated after Maria. At the same time, there were gains in wages on the island, especially in construction, which likely started to take place in the second part of 2018. At least in the first year and a half after the hurricane, the recovery funds had not been enough to revert the pattern of employment decline driven by a sluggish economy and population decline in Puerto Rico.

OVERVIEW OF THE EFFECTS OF NATURAL DISASTERS ON LABOR MARKETS

Natural disasters can affect labor markets. At the heart of these effects is how the economy responds to the injection of recovery funds that often enter after natural disasters, the out-migration that can take place, and the resilience of the population in reinvesting in their communities.

After Hurricane Katrina made landfall in Louisiana on August 29, 2005, employment in the New Orleans metropolitan area declined by 34 percent in September 2005 (*Monthly Labor Review* 2006). The Federal Reserve Bank of Dallas (2017) estimated a loss of 6,400 jobs from Hurricane Harvey in 2017, and Hurricane Andrew wiped out 6,600 jobs in the Miami metropolitan area in 1992 (Jacobs and Davidson 2017).

Another potential labor market impact is the reduction in labor supply as people leave the affected areas and migrate internally or internationally (Belasen and Polachek 2013; Bengtsson, Xin and Holme 2017; McIntosh 2008; Mbaye and Zimmermann 2016). Partly if not largely driven by Hurricane Katrina, the population of Louisiana declined from 458,000 in 2000 to 230,000 by July 2006 (Plyer 2013). Floods, wet mass movements, drought, wildfire, and extreme high temperatures have also boosted migration from developing countries to the six main Organization for Economic Co-operation and Development receiving countries of Australia, Canada, France, Germany, the UK, and the United States (Mbaye 2017).

Brusentsev and Vroman (2017) found that Hurricanes Sandy in New York and New Jersey, and Ike and Andrew in Florida did not appear to have significant employment effects during the three months after they made landfall. But Hurricane Katrina had statistically significant negative employment effects in Louisiana and Alabama although not in Mississippi.

Most research shows that the negative impacts of natural hazards on employment are short lived (Belasen and Polacheck 2009, Groen, Kutzbach and Polivka 2016, Strobl 2011, Karoly and Zissmopoulos 2010, Ewing and Kruse 2005). At the same time, the medium- and long-term effects of disasters on employment are theoretically ambiguous (Belasen and Polachek 2009). While destruction of infrastructure and other forms of physical capital may impede labor market activity in the short run, federal disaster assistance, cleanup and recovery activity funded locally, and the production of replacement capital can be accelerating factors toward economic recovery (Strobl 2011).

The unemployment rate for Louisiana rose sharply after Hurricane Katrina to 12.1 percent but it began falling in December 2005, and in June 2006 it was near its pre-hurricane level (*Monthly Labor Review* 2006). Similarly, the five hurricanes that passed by or near Wilmington, NC, between 1996 and 1999 had only temporary effects on unemployment (Ewing and Kruse 2005).

Whether the recovery has long-run effects has also been addressed but results are inconclusive (Shabnam 2014). Ewing and Kruse (2005) found long-term reductions in unemployment from one of the five hurricanes affecting Wilmington, NC, leading them to conclude that reconstruction and improvements may result in long-run positive economic impacts. In contrast, Strobl (2011), using 1970–1995 county data for 409 counties located in the North Atlantic Basin, concluded that the net effects of hurricanes on employment over the long run are negligible.

The behavior of wages follows the changes in labor supply and demand brought about by hurricanes and other natural hazards. In the immediate aftermath, losses in labor demand may translate into lower earnings. But thereafter wages may increase for two reasons: (1) the destruction of physical capital may lead to a substitution toward labor, increasing labor demand and raising wages, and (2) labor supply may be reduced due to out-migration. Belasen and Polachek (2009) found that counties directly hit by hurricanes experienced earnings growth of up to 4.35 percent during a period of close to two years. And after that period, earnings settled at a level about 0.4 percent higher than before the storm while neighboring counties experienced reductions in earnings. Groen, Kutzbach, and Polivka (2016), exploring the economic impacts of Hurricanes Katrina and Rita, also found wage declines at first that ultimately turned into wage gains.

Industry-Specific Labor Market Effects

Not all industries are affected equally by natural disasters. Hurricanes Katrina and Harvey had large employment effects on the leisure and hospitality industry (*Monthly Labor Review* 2006, Bureau of Labor and Statistics 2018, Federal Reserve Bank of Dallas 2017). In developing countries, the agricultural sector is highly affected by natural disasters, leaving thousands without their livelihoods and without work. The agricultural sector—including crops, livestock, fisheries, and forestry—absorbs approximately 22 percent of the economic impact caused by medium- and large-scale natural hazards and disasters in developing countries (Food and Agricultural Organization of the United Nations 2005). Guimarães, Hefner, and Woodward (1993) focused on the effects of Hurricane Hugo that struck South Carolina in 1989, and found that Hugo had no effect on income and employment overall although it had sectoral effects as evidenced on the income of construction, agriculture, retail trade, and transportation and utilities. In Groen, Kutzbach, and Polivka's (2016) study of Hurricanes Katrina and Rita, earnings gains were the highest for construction workers, even in the short run, presumably tied to the increased demand for construction services related to post-storm cleanup and rebuilding.

When writing this chapter, it was not possible to examine the long-term impacts of Hurricane Maria. In the short run—two years after the event—and considering the sizeable amount of recovery funds committed after the hurricane's landfall, as well as aid to the depressed economy before Hurricane Maria, positive employment effects are possible, particularly in construction. Consider also that that the large population decline as a result of Hurricane Maria may further stimulate wage growth via a decline of labor supply in the island.

ANALYSIS OF EMPLOYMENT AND WAGES

To examine the effects of Hurricane Maria on employment, I use unemployment insurance weekly claims data from September 2016 through September 2018 from the U.S. Department of Labor, as well as monthly employment data from January 2009 to July 2019, the most recent month for which these data were available at the time of this analysis. The employment data come from published reports from an establishment survey, a sample based on the Quarterly Census of Employment and Wages conducted by the U.S. Bureau of Labor Statistics and the Department of Labor and Human Resources of Puerto Rico.

For the employment analysis, I first provide pre- and post-Hurricane Maria comparisons for employment in Puerto Rico[2] and then analyze employment in the pre- and post-Hurricane Maria period using Florida as a comparison. The wage analysis is descriptive, comparing wage growth across industries based on the two-digit North American Industry Classification System (NAICS) between 2015–2016 and 2017–2018. Note that the 2018 wage data point covers the entire year of 2018. The wage data for 2019 were not available when this analysis was conducted.

Unemployment Insurance Claims

Unemployment insurance claims data indicate a slow recovery following Hurricane Maria. Figure 2.1 shows the initial unemployment claims from September 2016 through September 2018. The week of September 9, 2017, just prior to the hurricane, there were 1,709 new unemployment insurance claims, and the average for the six weeks before the storm was 1,055. In

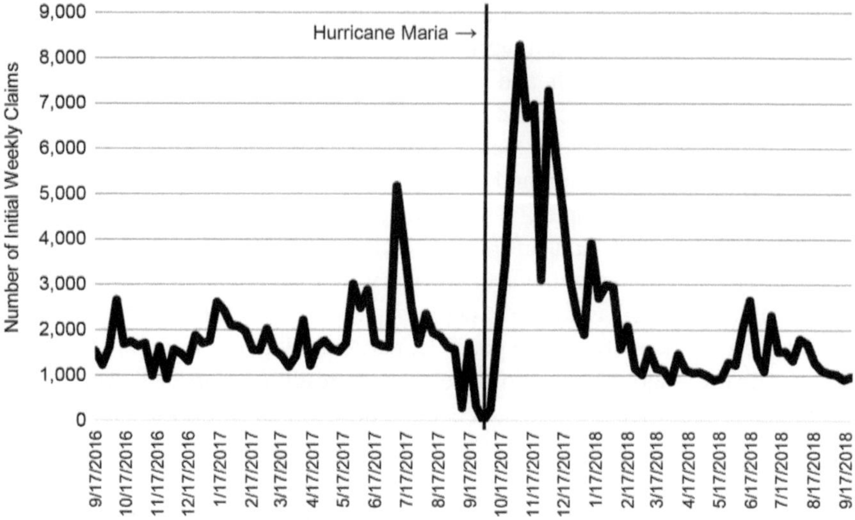

Figure 2.1 Initial Unemployment Insurance Claims in Puerto Rico before and after Hurricane Maria: September 2016–September 2018. *Source*: U.S. Department of Labor, Employment and Training Administration, Unemployment Insurance Weekly Claims Data.

the week ending October 28, 2017, new claims reached their highest point after Hurricane Maria: 8,281. It was not until five months later, the week of March 3, 2018, when unemployment claims started to decline consecutively and move back to resembling the pre-hurricane levels. However, as noted by Brusentsev and Vroman (2017), it is not possible to distinguish which of these claimants were under the regular Unemployment Insurance Program or under the Disaster Assistance Program.

As a point of comparison, a similar analysis (not shown in figure 2.1) was conducted for the two prior hurricanes: Category 2 Georges in 1998 and Category 3 Hugo in 1989, both of which passed over Puerto Rico the same week as Hurricane Maria. In both instances unemployment insurance claims had gone back to their pre-hurricane level by the end of November in the same year as the storm. The slow recovery and rebuilding following Hurricane Maria, including the continued lack of electricity, as well as the slow response of the distribution of recovery funds, likely contributed to the slow recovery of the post-Hurricane Maria labor market.

A More Detailed Analysis of Changes in Employment

I also estimated the average monthly change in employment for all industries and for selected industries owing to Hurricane Maria using data from January 2009 to June 2019.[3] These results are presented in table 2.1. The trend in overall employment was negative, amounting to a loss of about 700 jobs monthly. Among the selected industries, the government showed the largest decline followed by manufacturing. The industries of leisure and hospitality as well as professional and business services showed the strongest growth across time.

The post-Hurricane Maria effects, when statistically significant, are always negative, suggesting additional employment losses occurred after Hurricane Maria. Overall, in the post-Maria period of 19 months after the hurricane, 14,000 jobs were lost on net. Among the selected industries, leisure and hospitality show the largest declines after Hurricane Maria, followed by trade. This empirical observation is not surprising as the closing of major hotels following Hurricane Maria is well known. By June 2018, 3,500 rooms out of 15,000 were unavailable from closings due to Hurricane Maria (Rivera Sánchez 2018). Of interest, the construction industry had not lost nor gained jobs 19 months after Maria.

Employment Comparisons with Florida

The next analysis for employment takes Florida as the comparison, estimating whether the employment position of Puerto Rico relative to Florida deteriorated or improved after Hurricane Maria.[4] Table 2.2 presents the results of interest. It should be noted that Puerto Rico lagged in employment compared to Florida before and after Hurricane Maria. But this analysis shows the effects of interest are negative, meaning the employment gap between Puerto Rico and Florida deepened after Hurricane Maria. To illustrate, the employment disadvantage of Puerto Rico relative to Florida widened by 262,000 jobs following Hurricane Maria. Among the selected industries shown in table 2.2, the employment gap after the hurricane grew the most in the leisure and hospitality industry, followed by professional services. The least affected industry was information, where the employment gap grew the least, only by 3,000 jobs.

Wages in the Post-Maria Period

I also examined percentage changes in nominal average weekly wages by major industrial group for 2015–2016 and 2017–2018 using annual data. Figure 2.2 contains the results from this analysis. For Puerto Rico overall, wages remained flat for the 2015–2016 period but grew by 4.6 percent between 2017 and 2018. This wage growth occurred in almost all industries in the aftermath of Hurricane Maria, generally between 2 and 5 percent. The largest increase shown in figure 2.2 occurred in the construction industry, where weekly wages increased from $457.11 in 2017 to $617.89 in 2018, or by 35 percent. While wage increases in construction were expected, this large growth can also reflect the effect of Executive Order OE-2018-033 signed by Governor Ricardo Rosselló on July 30, 2018, setting to $15 the minimum

Table 2.1 Analysis of Monthly Employment (in Thousands) in Puerto Rico between January 2009 and July 2019: Regression Results for the Time Variable and Post-Maria Period, for Total Employment and by Selected Industries

	Time		*Post-Maria Period*	
Industry	*Coefficient*	*Standard Error*	*Coefficient*	*Standard Error*
Total Employment	−0.695	(0.088)***	−14.68	(8.14)*
Construction	−0.147	(0.025)***	1.96	(1.55)
Financial Services	−0.035	(0.007)***	0.07	(0.450)
Leisure and Hospitality	0.149	(0.013)***	−11.11	(1.01)***
Manufacturing	−0.156	(0.037)***	−2.39	(1.01)**
Professional and Business Services	0.146	(0.015)***	1.8	(1.48)
Government	−0.701	(0.043)***	1.5	(3.69)
Trade	−0.004	(0.018)	−8.66	(1.73)***
Transportation, Warehousing, and Utilities	0.013	(0.003)***	0.481	(0.269)*
Education	0.037	(0.013)***	−2.97	(1.21)***
Information	−0.008	(0.003)***	−0.506	(0.255)**
Health	0.089	(0.010)***	−6.52	(0.908)***
Other Services	0.006	(0.006)	−1.19	(0.442)***

***, **, * Statistically significant at the 1%, 5%, or 10% level.
Note: Other results not shown include coefficients for the binary variables for summer and winter months and a constant term. Estimates are corrected for first order serial correlation. See note 3 for details.
Source: Author's estimates based on monthly employment data in Puerto Rico from January 2009 through July 2019.

wage of construction workers in projects financed with public funds. However, the extent to which that order was implemented has been called into question (Diario de Puerto Rico 2019, Hernández Pérez 2019). The hourly wage reported for construction workers in the Occupational Employment Survey of May 2018 and before the Executive Order was $9.09, only $0.07 more than in May 2017. Therefore, it is likely the wage increase in construction observed in figure 2.2 took place after May 2018 and was likely the result from a combination of increased demand for construction labor and a declining labor supply.

These wage increases cannot be dismissed, even if temporary. Puerto Rico's wages prior to Hurricane Maria were surprisingly stagnant. Between 2010 and 2015 there was virtually no growth in nominal wages. The year-to-year wage growth from 2010 to 2015 was, respectively, 0.15, 1, −0.09, 0.59, and 1.33 percent. The 4.6 percent increase in wages for the 2017–2018 period was unique in the decade. María Enchautegui and Richard Freeman (2006) previously discussed some of the factors that have hindered wage growth in Puerto Rico. The authors suggested the threat of migration places a floor on wages: when unemployment is high and wages are about to decline, out-migration occurs and wages go back to their long-term level. The relatively high wage growth observed post-Hurricane Maria provides support for this

Table 2.2 Analysis of Monthly Employment (in Thousands) for Puerto Rico versus Florida between January 2009 and July 2019: Regression Results for Puerto Rico Relative to Florida after Hurricane Maria, for Total Employment and by Selected Industries

	Coefficient	*Standard Error*
All Industries	−262	(64.32)***
Construction	−29.34	(5.63)***
Financial Services	−8.64	(2.99)***
Leisure and Hospitality	−49.11	(12.84)***
Manufacturing	−8.98	(2.19)***
Professional and Business Services	−45.53	(9.98)***
Government	−26.66	(15.84)*
Trade	−26.30	(13.78)*
Transportation, Warehousing, and Utilities	−9.98	(3.10)***
Education	−8.13	(2.83)***
Other Services	−10.20	(1.96)
Information	−3.06	(1.08)***
Health	−22.54	(4.91)***

***, **, * Statistically significant at the 1%, 5%, or 10% level.

Note: Other results not shown include estimated coefficients for the time variable, a binary variable for Puerto Rico, the interaction between Puerto Rico and time, and a binary variable for the post-Maria period. See note 4 for details.

Source: Author's estimates based on monthly employment data in Puerto Rico and Florida from January 2009 through July 2019.

type of positive effect of out-migration resulting from the hurricane on wages in Puerto Rico.

DISCUSSION AND CONCLUDING REMARKS

Hurricane Maria destroyed lives, devastated homes and businesses, damaged important road arteries and telecommunications infrastructure, and crippled the whole electric grid in Puerto Rico. As discussed in the previous chapter, the declining economy, a shrinking population, a huge unpayable debt, and a federal oversight board were the backdrop of Hurricane Maria. The recovery funds coming into Puerto Rico represent a sizeable injection of money that could result in economic activity and job creation.

In spite of the expected stimulus that could have been produced by the recovery activity, in this chapter I found no statistically significant job gains 19 months following Hurricane Maria. On the contrary, employment fell overall and in the industries selected for analysis, continuing employment declines that started years before Hurricane Maria made landfall. It is possible the recovery activity materialized in a way that economic gains will be forthcoming in the near future. Or possibly the large population losses due to the spike in net out-migration after the hurricane were too large to reverse the declining employment trend. The analysis here indicates the employment gap between Puerto Rico and Florida grew after Hurricane Maria.

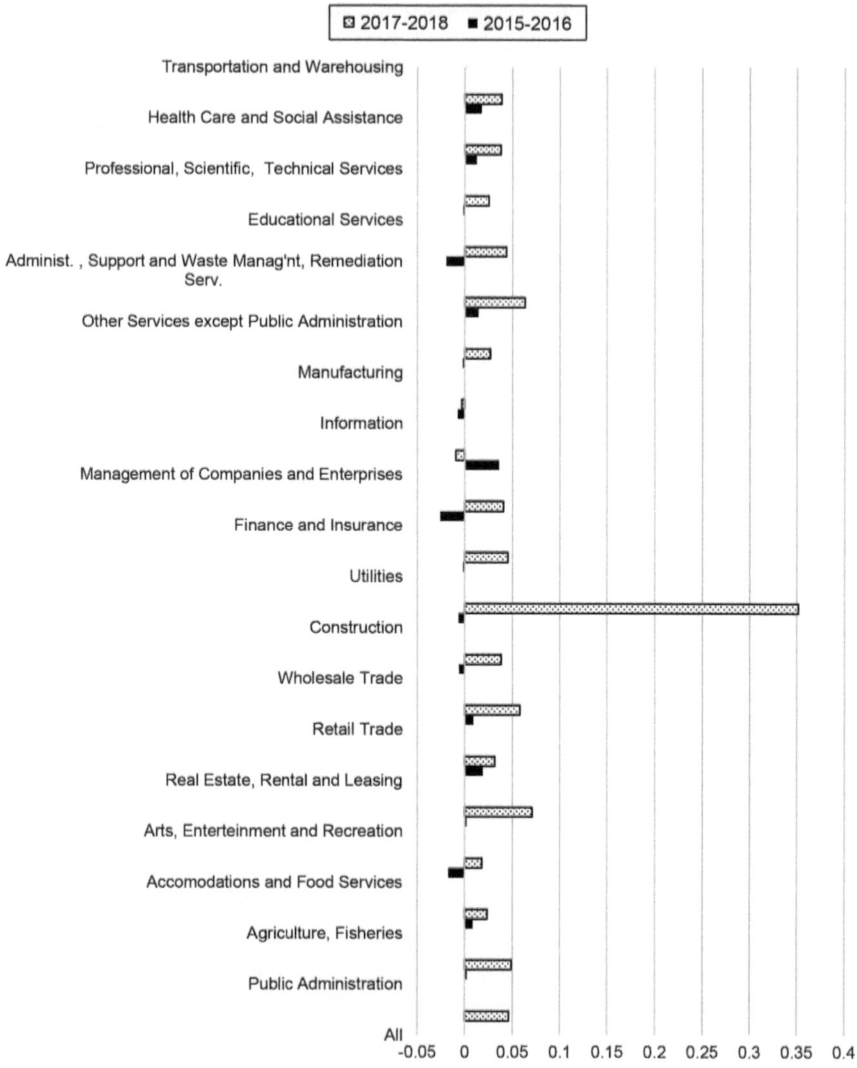

Figure 2.2 Percentage Change in Weekly Wages in Puerto Rico for All Workers and by Selected Industries: 2015–2016 and 2017–2018. *Source*: Author's estimates of wage growth across industries based on the two-digit NAICS between 2015–2016 and 2017–2018.

At the same time, consistent with other studies on the effects of natural disasters on labor markets, I found that wages grew in the year following Hurricane Maria. The wage gains could reflect an increased demand for labor in the midst of a strong decline in labor supply from out-migration. Also, as expected, the construction sector experienced a significant increase in wages after Hurricane Maria, likely related to demand and supply forces and bolstered by the Executive Order increasing the hourly wage of construction workers in government-funded projects to $15 per hour.

In all, the results presented here speak to the short- to medium-term effects of Hurricane Maria on employment and wages in Puerto Rico. As the economy continues to recover and the additional recovery funds reach the island, one must monitor longer-term impacts on the labor market as well as potential impacts on the path toward economic growth.

NOTES

1. Hurricane Irma hit Florida about two weeks prior to Hurricane Maria's landfall in Puerto Rico. Irma landed in the Florida Keys as Category 3 storm, and its intensity was reduced when entered through Naples and Fort Myers. In the metropolitan area of Naples, the reported area with the largest Irma effects, there appears to be no discernible effect on unemployment rate. According to the Local Area Unemployment Statistics from the Bureau of Labor Statistics for the Naples, Immokalee, Marco Island metropolitan areas in Florida, the unemployment rate fell from 4.8 percent in August 2017 to 4.2 percent in September and October, and 4.0 percent in November 2017. The unemployment rate of Florida continued its downward tendency after September 2017.

2. The establishment employment data are collected as of the full pay period that includes the 12th day of the month; hence the September 2017 employment figures do not include Hurricane Maria which made landfall on September 20 (Bureau of Labor Statistics 2017).

3. For these estimates, I used regression analysis for monthly employment that included a time trend variable, binary variables indicating summer and winter months, and a binary variable for the post-Hurricane Maria period equal to one for employment in October 2017 or later (and equal to zero otherwise) as regressors. The estimated coefficients reported in table 2.1 are those for the time trend and the post-Maria period variables. Contact the author for details.

4. Extending the analysis described in note 3, the analysis comparing Puerto Rico with Florida uses the "difference in difference" technique by further interacting a binary variable equal to one for Puerto Rico (and equal to zero for Florida) with the other variables in the regression model. Specifically, I estimate the following regression model:

$$Employment_t = \beta_0 + \beta_1 Time_t + \beta_2 Summer_t + \beta_3 Winter_t + \beta_4 PostMaria_t + \beta_5 PR + \beta_6 PR{*}Time_t + \beta_7 PR{*}PostMaria_t + \mu_t,$$

where $Employment_t$ represents the employment level in month t in Puerto Rico or Florida, the β's represent coefficients to be estimated, and μ_t is the error term. The coefficient of interest is β_7, the coefficient of the interaction term between the Puerto Rico and post-Hurricane Maria binary variables, which represents the change in the difference in employment between Puerto Rico and Florida before and after Hurricane Maria. Considering that Puerto Rico lags in employment to Florida, a negative coefficient means that the employment difference between Puerto Rico and Florida grew after Hurricane Maria. All models are corrected for first-order autocorrelation using the Prais-Winsten method.

Chapter 3

Hurricane Maria's Impact on Puerto Rico's Labor Market

Job Losses, Wage Changes, and Recovery of Municipalities Close to the Epicenter

Zadia M. Feliciano

ABSTRACT

This chapter presents details on changes in employment and wages, including at the municipality level, following Hurricane Maria. In addition to providing an overall account of job losses within the first year after Maria's landing, it analyzes changes in the structure of employment, showing the industries that experienced losses versus gains after the hurricane. Furthermore, detailed information on the impact of Hurricane Maria on Puerto Rico's municipalities is provided by analyzing how post-Maria labor market outcomes related to the distance from the epicenter.

Previous studies have demonstrated that hurricanes have strong negative effects on employment and earnings in affected areas but that these areas experience a speedy recovery.[1] I analyze the impact of Hurricane Maria on the Puerto Rican labor market, focusing on changes in employment and wages at the island and municipality levels. First, this chapter provides an overall account of job losses within the first year after Hurricane Maria's landing. Second, changes in the structure of employment are presented, showing the industries that experienced greater losses versus those that grew after the hurricane. Third, this chapter includes detailed information on the impact of Hurricane Maria on Puerto Rico's municipalities (*municipios* as they are known on the island) by analyzing how labor market outcomes related to the distance from Hurricane Maria's epicenter. This analysis presents evidence on how long it took for hard-hit municipalities to initiate their recovery and how many months these areas experienced a recovery relative to less affected municipalities.

As noted in chapter 1 by Marie T. Mora, Havidán Rodríguez, and Alberto Dávila, before Hurricane Maria struck Puerto Rico, Puerto Rico's government was undergoing proceedings similar to Chapter 9 of the U.S. Bankruptcy Court due to the island's severe economic and fiscal crisis. As such, in the analysis that follows, I attempt to disentangle the effects of the hurricane on the Puerto Rican labor market from those caused by the island's ongoing fiscal crisis.

HURRICANE MARIA'S IMPACT ON PUERTO RICO'S LABOR MARKET OUTCOMES

As discussed throughout this volume, Hurricane Maria was one of the most devastating environmental disasters to hit Puerto Rico in recent history, and its impact was exacerbated by Puerto Rico's aging infrastructure. To study the impact of Hurricane Maria on Puerto Rico's labor market outcomes, I use data on annual employment and wages by industry from the Quarterly Census of Employment and Wages, which are collected quarterly by the U.S. Bureau of Labor Statistics for every state in the U.S. mainland, Puerto Rico, and the U.S. Virgin Islands. (Note the previous chapter uses the same data.) Employment is defined as the number of filled jobs by either full-time or part-time workers. I also create panel data by municipality on employment and annual wages for the years 2016–2019 (monthly and quarterly depending on availability) from the Puerto Rico Department of Labor and U.S. Bureau of the Census.

Moreover, Hurricane Maria affected the entire island but some municipalities were impacted more than others. For example, the 10 most impacted municipalities by total number of damaged housing units were in San Juan (Puerto Rico's capital), Bayamón, Caguas, Ponce, Toa Baja, Carolina, Arecibo, Humacao, Canóvanas, and Guaynabo (Center for Puerto Rican Studies, 2018a). To investigate potential differences in the impact, I use geo-coded data from the Center for Puerto Rican Studies (2018a) to estimate the distance (in miles) of each of Puerto Rico's 78 municipalities from the epicenter of Hurricane Maria. (See figure 1.1 for a map of Puerto Rico showing the boundaries of these municipalities with Hurricane Maria's trajectory across the island.) I then analyze how the distance of a municipality from the hurricane's epicenter related to the percentage growth in employment in that municipality in a given month compared to the prior year. Similarly, I explore how distance from Hurricane Maria's epicenter related to the growth in wages in each municipality in a given quarter compared to a year earlier.

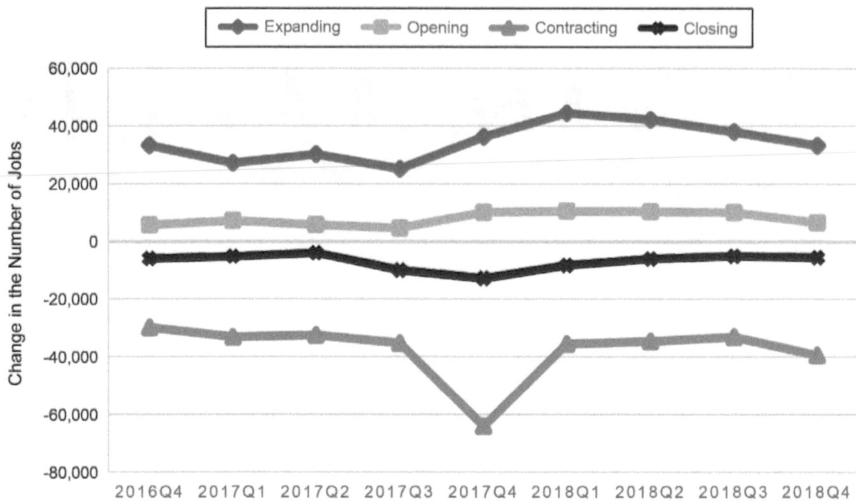

Figure 3.1 Number of Private Sector Jobs Gained and Lost in Puerto Rico: 2016–2018. *Source*: Author's tabulations using data from the Puerto Rico Quarterly Census of Employment and Wages, U.S. Census Bureau.

Quarterly wages for this analysis are used since monthly wages are not available by municipality.

Finally, I present evidence on changes in employment by industry and municipality. In particular, I estimate whether employment recovered in hotels and restaurants, manufacturing, construction, and retail trade differently in municipalities near the epicenter of the hurricane from those that were further away.

IMPACT OF HURRICANE MARIA ON AGGREGATE EMPLOYMENT AND WAGES

Figure 3.1 shows job gains and job losses in Puerto Rico from the fourth quarter of 2016 to the fourth quarter of 2018. Job gains are disaggregated by those originating from existing businesses and new businesses as are job losses. Puerto Rico experienced job losses during the third quarter of 2017 at the time of Hurricane Maria's landfall that, for the most part, originated from establishment closings. These job losses increased from 3,939 in the previous quarter to 10,114, while contracting establishments' job losses rose from 32,564 to 35,564. The largest decline in employment occurred in the fourth quarter of 2017 due to the contraction of existing establishments. That quarter's loss of 64,093 jobs almost doubled the number of jobs lost in existing establishments in the previous quarter, while employment owing to plant closings declined

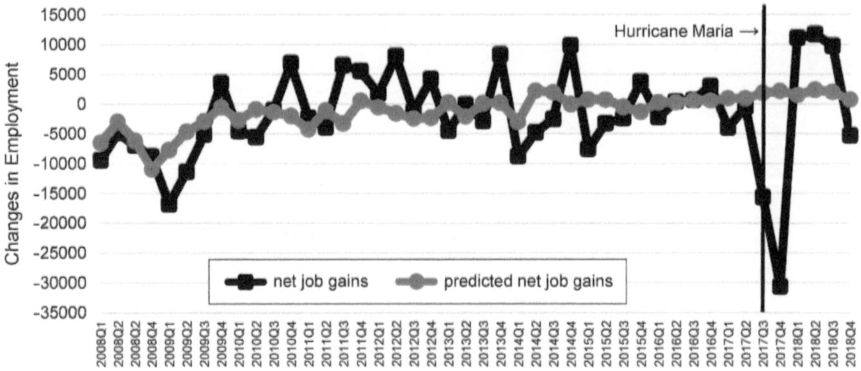

Figure 3.2 Actual and Predicted Net Job Gains in Puerto Rico: QI 2008–QIV 2018. *Note*: See note 4 for details. *Source*: Author's estimates using data from the Puerto Rico Quarterly Census of Employment and Wages.

by 12,899. However, the first quarter of 2018 saw an increase in 8,271 jobs (mostly from existing establishments). Moreover, job losses stemming from existing and closing establishments returned to pre-Hurricane Maria levels that quarter. But the growth in job gains slowed in the second to fourth quarters of 2018, supporting the view that labor market weaknesses persisted more than a year after Hurricane Maria. They also indicate that the increases in employment in 2018 as rebuilding got underway were not large enough to offset the initial losses that occurred in the last two quarters of 2017.

Figure 3.2 shows actual and predicted net job gains and losses from the first quarter of 2008 to the second quarter of 2018. I predict net job gains and losses by conducting statistical analysis where job growth in Puerto Rico depends on the U.S. GDP growth rate and annual fluctuations.[2] Consider that the Puerto Rican economy is greatly affected by movements in the U.S. economy (e.g., Rivera-Batiz 1996) and for this reason U.S. GDP growth rates can be used to predict Puerto Rico's job gains and losses. The main purpose of this analysis is to estimate net job gains under the hypothetical counterfactual that Hurricane Maria did not make landfall. The analysis takes into account trends in net job changes on the island over an extended period of time prior to the landing of Hurricane Maria, from the first quarter of 2008 to the second quarter of 2017, including adjustments to the slowdown in the labor market during the years prior to Maria. The effect of Hurricane Maria is clear, as figure 3.2 shows a large drop in net jobs in the fourth quarter of 2017 beyond what is predicted by my counterfactual model. The peak of job losses owing to the hurricane coincided with the tourist holiday season in Puerto Rico.

For further insight, table 3.1 presents estimates of job losses stemming from Hurricane Maria, focusing on the time between the second quarter of

Table 3.1 Actual and Predicted Employment Changes in Puerto Rico before and after Hurricane Maria: QII 2017–QIV 2018

Time	*Change in Net Employment*	*Predicted Change in Net Employment*	*Difference: Actual – Predicted Employment*	*Actual Net Change in Employment as Percent of Total Private Sector Employment*
QII 2017	−531	924	−1,455	0.0
*QIII 2017**	*−15,626*	*1,805*	*−17,431*	*−2.3*
QIV 2017	−30,635	2,145	−32,780	−4.7
QI 2018	11,106	1,478	9,628	1.6
QII 2018	11,736	2,360	9,376	1.8
QIII 2018	9,763	2,003	7,760	1.4
QIV 2018	−5,291	717	−6,008	−0.7

* Quarter when Hurricane Maria Landed in Puerto Rico.
Note: The final column measures gross job gains and gross job losses as a percentage of the average of the previous and current quarter employment levels.
Source: Puerto Rico Quarterly Census of Employment and Wages and Author's estimates.

2017 through the end of 2018. The second column shows actual net employment and the third column shows the predicted net employment. The difference between actual and predicted net employment, shown in the fourth column, is the estimated employment effect of Hurricane Maria. My estimates of net job losses from Hurricane Maria are 17,431 in the third quarter of 2017 and 32,780 jobs in the following quarter, for a total of 50,211 jobs lost on net. These net employment losses represented 2.3 percent of private sector employment in the third quarter of 2017 and 4.7 percent of private employment in the following quarter. Moreover, while net employment grew in the first three quarters of 2018 by a combined total of 26,764 jobs, the increase only restored about half of the jobs initially lost in the aftermath of Hurricane Maria. Employment fell by another 6,008 jobs in the fourth quarter of 2018, again indicating the weakness of Puerto Rico's post-Hurricane Maria labor market.

IMPACT OF HURRICANE MARIA ON INDUSTRY EMPLOYMENT AND WAGES

Table 3.2 shows employment and wages by industry before and after Hurricane Maria. I compare data on quarterly employment and wages in the second quarter of 2018, nine months after the hurricane, to that of the second quarter of 2017, approximately three months before the hurricane. Overall employment declined in the island by 2.4 percent but wages increased by 5.3 percent. The two industries hardest hit by the hurricane in percentage terms were agriculture, with an 18.3 percent decline in employment (which is not surprising

Table 3.2 Employment and Wages by Industry in Puerto Rico before and after Hurricane Maria: QII 2017 and QII 2018

Industry	*Empl. QII 2017*	*Empl. QII 2018*	*Percent Change Empl.: QII 2017–QII 2018*	*Wages QII 2017*	*Wages QII 2018*	*Percent Change Wages: QII 2017–QII 2018*
All Industries	877,238	855,817	−2.4	6,700	7,054	5.3
Agriculture, Forestry, Fishing, and Hunting	11,981	9,791	−18.3	2,440	2,475	1.4
Mining, Quarrying, and Oil Extraction	497	498	0.2	4,719	5,347	13.3
Utilities	8,673	8,253	−4.8	9,268	10,753	16.0
Construction	20,589	26,013	26.3	5,612	8,680	54.7
Manufacturing	71,594	71,412	−0.3	9,437	9,845	4.3
Wholesale Trade	29,394	28,966	−1.5	10,069	10,421	3.5
Retail Trade	127,110	121,146	−4.7	4,624	4,955	7.2
Transportation and Warehousing	19,369	19,604	1.2	8,744	9,083	3.9
Information Services	18,018	16,592	−7.9	9,297	9,094	−2.2
Finance and Insurance	29,222	28,372	−2.9	10,710	10,661	−0.5
Real Estate and Rental and Leasing	13,811	13,468	−2.5	6,477	6,636	2.5
Professional, Scientific, and Tech Services	30,522	31,275	2.5	10,125	10,533	4.0
Management of Companies and Enterprises	13,592	15,155	11.5	12,582	12,097	−3.9
Adm and Waste Mng and Remedial Services	69,817	76,881	10.1	4,494	4,664	3.8
Educational Services	92,793	86,673	−6.6	7,002	7,335	4.8
Healthcare and Social Assistance	92,470	87,752	−5.1	6,805	6,980	2.6
Arts, Entertainment, and Recreation	4,644	3,852	−17.1	5,312	5,753	8.3
Accommodation and Food Services	76,953	70,224	−8.7	3,492	3,491	0.0
Other Services (except Public Adm)	15,107	14,032	−7.1	4,895	5,143	5.1
Public Administration	131,054	125,826	−4.0	6,950	7,233	4.1

Note: Wages include bonuses, stock options, severance pay, profit distributions, cash value of meals and lodging, tips and other gratuities.
Source: Puerto Rico Quarterly Census of Employment and Wages.

given Hurricane Maria's catastrophic destruction), and arts, entertainment, and recreation, with a 17.1 percent decline, consistent with the loss of tourism the island encountered. The largest number of jobs lost occurred in industries related to the tourism, accommodation and food services, where employment decreased by 6,729 jobs, and in retail trade, where it declined by 5,964.

Not all the job losses can be attributed to Hurricane Maria. Some of the reductions in jobs related to the economic crisis and fiscal austerity measures that were ongoing before the hurricane as discussed in the previous chapter. For example, public administration lost 5,228 jobs, education services lost 6,120 jobs, and healthcare services lost 4,718 jobs. Many, but not all, jobs lost in education and healthcare services were in the public sector. The exodus of the population through the economic and financial crises, the rapidly aging population, the decrease in fertility rates, and the government's need to reduce expenditures all may have played a role. According to the Center for Puerto Rican Studies (2018), Puerto Rico closed 265 elementary and middle schools (or 24% of the total) after the hurricane. Nevertheless, the findings presented in tables 3.1 and 3.2 demonstrate that Hurricane Maria was an important factor in exacerbating job losses. The number of people who left Puerto Rico for the U.S. mainland, which spiked after Hurricane Maria (discussed in chapter 1), is another indication of the dearth of employment opportunities.

At the same time, table 3.2 shows that after the hurricane some industries in Puerto Rico experienced job growth. These industries were typically in hurricane recovery and reconstruction sectors. The construction industry had the largest percentage increase in jobs, 26 percent or 5,424 jobs, and waste management and remediation services had the second largest, 10.2 percent or 7,064 jobs. Note, however, that while there was an increase in jobs owing to the recovery and reconstruction, the 50,211 lost jobs initially attributed to Hurricane Maria in the third and fourth quarters of 2017 were not fully replaced a year and three months after the hurricane's landfall. By the end of the fourth quarter of 2018, my estimates reveal that 29,454 net jobs had yet to be recreated. This finding is consistent with the previous chapter that Hurricane Maria had reduced employment in Puerto Rico on net 19 months after making landfall despite the aid that flowed into the island.

THE IMPACT OF THE DISTANCE OF HURRICANE MARIA'S EPICENTER ON LABOR MARKETS

I now investigate the impact of Hurricane Maria on Puerto Rico's municipalities, comparing labor market outcomes of the municipalities closer to the path of the epicenter of the hurricane with those that were further away.[3] The main goals are to understand how long it took for municipalities in the path of the hurricane to begin recovering employment relative to municipalities farther

Table 3.3 Impact of Hurricane Maria on Employment in Puerto Rico's Municipalities Based on Distance from Maria's Epicenter: 1–18 Months after Landfall

	Change in Log(Employment) from Prior Year Based on Time after Hurricane Maria's Landfall					
Municipality Characteristics	*1 month*	*2 months*	*3 months*	*6 months*	*12 months*	*18 months*
Distance from epicenter	0.0005* (0.0003)	0.0004* (0.0003)	−0.0009** (0.0003)	−0.0014** (0.0004)	−0.0026** (0.0006)	−0.0005 (0.0005)
San Juan Metro	−0.004 (0.011)	−0.003 (0.009)	0.004 (0.010)	0.030 (0.013)	0.030 (0.022)	0.007 (0.018)
R-Squared	0.01	0.02	0.09	0.12	0.19	0.01

*, ** Statistically significant at the five or ten percent level.

Notes: See note 3 for details on the empirical methodology. The number of observations for each model is 78. The San Juan metropolitan area includes the municipalities of San Juan, Bayamón, Carolina, Cataño, Guaynabo, and Trujillo Alto.

Source: Authors' estimates using data from the Quarterly Census of Employment and Wages (QCEW), Puerto Rico Department of Labor, U.S. Bureau of the Census, and Center for Puerto Rican Studies (2018).

away from the hurricane's eyewall, and when growth in employment in the most affected municipalities slowed relative to less affected municipalities.

Table 3.3 shows the results for how percentage changes in employment from the previous year related to distance from the epicenter 1 month, 2 months, 3 months, 6 months, 12 months, and 18 months after Hurricane Maria. As expected, municipalities near the epicenter of the hurricane experienced greater job losses than municipalities farther away from the epicenter in the first two months after Hurricane Maria landed. This is shown by the estimated positive relationship between distance from the epicenter of the hurricane and employment growth. However, this relationship is small and may be interpreted as empirically weak.[4] Areas near the epicenter had an estimated employment growth that was 1 percent lower than those 20 miles away.

The recovery of employment in municipalities close to the epicenter of Hurricane Maria began three months after landfall. My estimates show that areas closer to the epicenter experienced greater employment growth than those farther away starting in the third month after the hurricane and continued to be higher up to a year after Hurricane Maria's landfall. A year after the hurricane, municipalities that were 20 miles away from the epicenter had 5 percent lower employment growth than those located near Hurricane Maria's eyewall. This difference likely reflects increases in resources and reconstruction in the areas that needed them the most—those most devastated by the hurricane. However, table 3.3 shows that this difference soon dissipated; 18 months after Hurricane Maria, municipality employment growth rates no longer related to the distance its epicenter. Thus, employment growth due to reconstruction seems to have occurred up to a year after Hurricane Maria.

I also conduct a similar analysis for how distance from Hurricane Maria's eyewall related to the change in log quarterly wages from a year earlier, starting with the quarter Hurricane Maria landed and ending five-quarters later, 15 months after the hurricane. None of these results (not shown to conserve space) revealed significant differences in wage growth between municipalities closer to Hurricane Maria's epicenter and those further away. (Contact the author for details.)

Similarly, I analyze how changes in log employment nine months after Hurricane Maria landed related to distance from the epicenter for specific industries: hotels and restaurants, manufacturing, construction, and retail trade (results available from the author).[5] Unlike the findings for overall employment, this analysis did not reveal a significant relationship between distance from Hurricane Maria's epicenter and employment growth for these specific industries. Still, this analysis may have been compromised by missing and suppressed data on industry employment by municipality.

DISCUSSION AND CONCLUDING REMARKS

Hurricane Maria was responsible for the loss of approximately 50,211 jobs on net in the private sector in Puerto Rico during the third and fourth quarters of 2017. While there was a subsequent increase in jobs due to the recovery and reconstruction, the initial jobs lost were not fully replaced 15 months after Hurricane Maria. By the end of 2018, close to 30,000 jobs had yet to be recreated. Industries hardest hit by the hurricane were in agriculture and those that rely on tourism such as entertainment and recreation as well as accommodation and food services.

My findings also show the timing of the labor market recovery in the municipalities. Municipalities in the path of Hurricane Maria experienced the largest job losses in the first two months after the hurricane landed. However, employment recovery in these municipalities began in the third month and lasted up to a year after the hurricane. Damage to roads, lack of electricity and water in areas where the hurricane brought more destruction, and the slow response by the government may have contributed to the slow recovery of these labor markets.

The large impact of Hurricane Maria on labor markets in Puerto Rico is due to many factors, including government readiness, government response, the economic crisis in the island, austerity measures (including those under PROMESA's Oversight Board mentioned in chapter 1), and the large net out-migration that spiked after the hurricane. It is not possible to fully isolate all of these confounding factors.

Policymakers were not prepared for a natural disaster like Hurricane Maria, which contributed to the large magnitude of labor market losses. While a hurricane is an act of nature and cannot be controlled, readiness and response to acts of nature are in the hands of policymakers. Moving forward, resources need to be invested to build disaster readiness and the government needs to develop robust resilience planning, recovery, and business continuity plans in preparation for future hurricanes and other natural disasters.

NOTES

1. For example, Sharon Brown, Shannon Mason, and Brandon Tiller (2006) found that Hurricane Katrina was responsible for increasing unemployment in Louisiana from 5.8 to 11.5 percent between August 2005 and November 2005, only to revert back to pre-hurricane levels three months later. Ariel Belasen and Solomon Polachek (2008) also found that while employment initially fell in Florida counties hit by hurricanes, employment in these areas recovered within three months of being hit and average earnings rose by more than 4 percent compared to other counties. A more detailed discussion on the literature on hurricanes and labor markets is provided in the previous chapter.

2. This empirical analysis is based on regressions of net employment changes in Puerto Rico on the U.S. annual GDP growth rate as well as a time trend between Quarter I 2008 and Quarter II 2017. The coefficients (standard deviations) from this analysis based on 38 observations were 774.31 (359.66) on the GDP growth rate variable and 107.45 (86.36) on the time trend variable; the R-squared was 0.18. Contact the author for more details.

3. Specifically, using the empirical methodology of ordinary least squares, I estimate the following model: $\log(Employment_{i,t}) - \log(Employment_{i,t-1}) = \alpha + \beta_1 Epicenter_i + \beta_2 Metro + \varepsilon_{i,t}$, where $Employment_{i,t}$ is the employment in municipality i during time t. The left-hand side approximates the percentage change in employment, where time t includes 1 month, 2 months, 3 months, 6 months, 12 months, and 18 months after Maria's landfall. In the cases where this model is estimated one year after Hurricane Maria's landfall, the reference year is August of the previous year since employment data for September 2017 are not available. *Epicenter* is the distance of municipality i from the Maria's epicenter in miles, classified in the categories of 1, 5, 10, 15, 20, 25, 30, and 35 or more miles. *Metro* is a binary variable that equals one if the municipality is in the San Juan metropolitan area (which includes a quarter [26%] of the island's population and covers the municipalities of San Juan, Bayamón, Carolina, Cataño, Guaynabo, and Trujillo Alto) and equals zero otherwise. The terms α, β_1, *and* β_2 represent coefficients to be estimated, and ε denotes the error term.

4. The estimated coefficient is statistically significant at the 10 percent level.

5. These four industry groups are classified as 72, 31–33, 23, and 44–45 in the North American Industry Classification System. Data by industry within each municipality are available quarterly.

Chapter 4

Hurricane Effects on Industry Employment

Evidence from Puerto Rico

José Caraballo-Cueto

ABSTRACT

This chapter constructs an alternative method to approximate the level of employment in key industries in Puerto Rico that would have been expected in the absence of Hurricane Maria. Comparing expected employment (based on pre-hurricane conditions) with actual employment in the industry sector reflects the hurricane's impact on employment. The findings suggest that the short-term economic consequences related to Hurricane Maria were beneficial for some economic sectors, especially construction and retail trade, but detrimental to others such as transportation, communications, and agriculture.

Natural disasters such as hurricanes are known to disrupt markets, including labor markets as discussed in the previous two chapters by Maria E. Enchautegui and Zadia M. Feliciano (see also Belasen and Polachek 2008; Groen et al. 2020; Guimarães et al. 1993). According to Hallegatte and Ghil (2008), economies in recessions better counteract the economic impact of natural disasters than economies during expansionary phases. Enchautegui and Feliciano examined Hurricane Maria's consequences on employment and wages in a depressed economy that existed in Puerto Rico. I complement those chapters by constructing an expected (or synthetic) series to project employment in key industry sectors that should have been observed in Puerto Rico had Hurricane Maria not made landfall. The findings suggest that the economic consequences related to Hurricane Maria were beneficial for some industry sectors, especially construction and retail trade, but detrimental to others, including transportation and communications and agriculture, at least in the short run.

ANALYSIS OF EXPECTED VERSUS ACTUAL EMPLOYMENT

The literature on how hurricanes affect markets usually compares counties hit by hurricanes vis-à-vis nonaffected counties (e.g., Belasen and Polacheck 2009). I am unable to apply such a border analysis to Puerto Rico because Hurricane Maria impacted the whole island. Thus, I construct a synthetic or expected series to project the employment in key industry sectors that should have been observed without hurricanes.[1]

At the time the main part of this analysis was conducted, administrative data were only published through April 2018. Thus, the data used here for sectoral employment come from the labor force survey administered by the Puerto Rico Department of Labor, under the supervision of the U.S. Bureau of Labor Statistics.

From January 2007 to August 2017 (the month before the arrival of Hurricane Maria), the estimates predict sectoral employment within an average difference of −0.02 to −7.0 percent of the actual employment in the major industries. In particular, as shown in the first column of table 4.1, expected employment was higher on average than actual employment in only three (one-third) of the nine industry sectors: government sector by 2 percent, services by 0.2 percent, and transportation and communication by 2.3 percent. In this model, lower employment is predicted than what existed in the other six sectors: by 1.5 percent in the finance, insurance, and real estate (FIRE) sector; 3.4 percent in manufacturing; 1.0 percent in retail and wholesale trade (henceforth, trade); 7.0 percent in construction; 3.1 percent in

Table 4.1 The Average and Absolute Deviation of the Percentual Difference between the Industry Synthetic Series and Actual Series, 2007–2017, and Employment Shares by Industry Sector, August 2017 and 2018

Sector	*Average Percentual Differences: 2007–2017*	*Mean Absolute Deviation of Percentual Differences*	*Employment Share: August 2017*	*Employment Share: August 2018*
Government	2%	3.3	17.0%	16.1%
Services	0.2%	2.9	29.6%	30.6%
Transportation and Communications	2.3%	8.0	4.4%	3.9%
FIRE	1.5%	11.3	3.4%	2.0%
Manufacturing	3.4%	6.5	7.7%	8.2%
Trade	1.0%	3.5	19.4%	20.5%
Construction	7%	11.6	2.6%	4.0%
Self-employment	1.2%	4.3	13.8%	14.0%
Agriculture	3.1%	18.4	2.0%	1.0%

Source: Author's calculations based on data from the Labor Department of Puerto Rico (2019).

agriculture; and 1.2 percent in self-employment.[2] Table 4.1 (second column) also shows that services, FIRE, and agriculture were the three industry sectors with the highest deviations from their means.

HOW INDUSTRY EMPLOYMENT FARED AFTER HURRICANE MARIA

In this section, I present the actual industry sectoral employment vis-à-vis the expected (synthetic or counterfactual) employment levels that should have been observed had Hurricane Maria not landed in Puerto Rico. These synthetic employment levels were estimated using the methodology described in note 1.

Construction

Construction is the first sector expected to benefit from reconstruction following Hurricane Maria. Figure 4.1 illustrates the actual employment versus the synthetic (expected) employment in construction; the period after Hurricane Maria shows the reconstruction period. As expected, employment in construction was higher after Hurricane Maria than the counterfactual

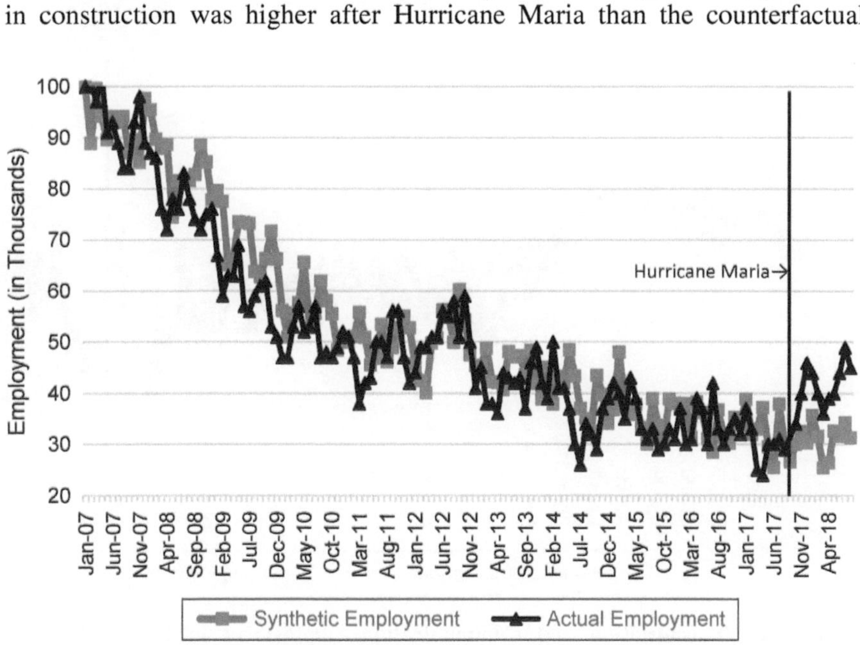

Figure 4.1 Construction Employment in Puerto Rico (in Thousands): 2007–2018. *Note*: The synthetic estimate is the employment approximation based on note 1. *Source*: Author's calculations based on data from the Labor Department of Puerto Rico (2019).

levels. It is important to point out that such counterfactual levels are conservative estimates as they were higher than the actual employment levels in the recent period.

Because there is a positive correlation between employment and economic production (e.g., Okun 1963), the increase in construction employment likely indicates an increase in economic activity in that sector. Thus, workers and investors related to the construction sector likely achieved economic gains after Hurricane Maria than beforehand, at least within the first several months after landfall.

Transportation and Communication

In the transportation and communication industry, the synthetic or expected employment series is relatively close to the actual series, showing low forecasting errors in figure 4.2. Based on these findings, a few months after the landfall of Hurricane Maria, the employment in this sector was at a similar level that one could have expected. This can be explained by the relatively large scale of reconstruction activities needed to restore the transportation and communication infrastructure. However, this tendency changed by mid-2018,

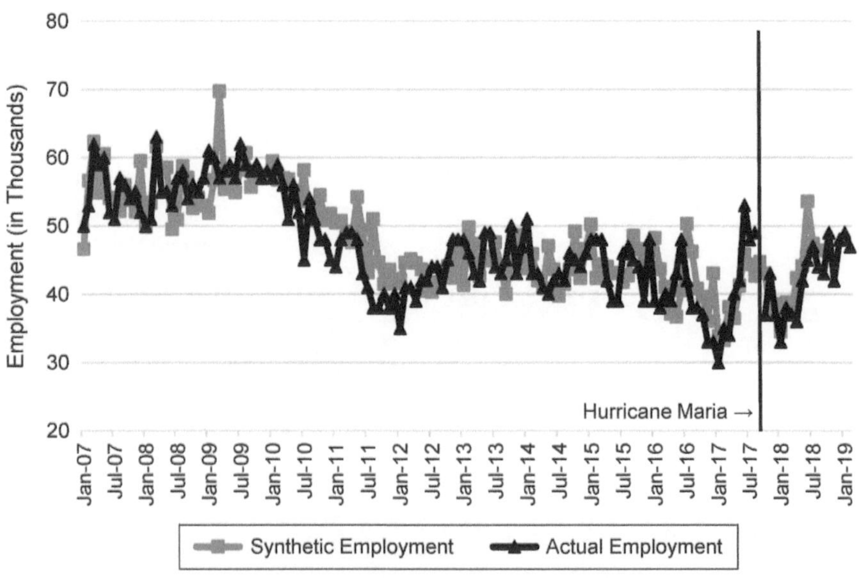

Figure 4.2 Transportation and Communication Employment in Puerto Rico (in Thousands): 2007–2018. *Note*: The synthetic estimate is the employment approximation based on note 1. *Source*: Author's calculations based on data from the Labor Department of Puerto Rico (2019).

as the expected employment in this sector exceeded the employment level observed after the impact of the hurricanes. Thus, the transportation and communication appeared to have lost ground as the island recovered from Hurricane Maria.

Retail and Wholesale Trade

In figure 4.3, the actual and the counterfactual employment in the retail and wholesale trade sector is presented before and after Hurricane Maria. Seasonality (variations that depend on the particular month of the year) in this sector is common, as sales increase during specific periods, especially in December, and decrease in others, such as January. Before Hurricane Maria, the synthetic employment series matched closely with the seasonality of the actual data. Thus, the expected employment levels without the reconstruction were lower than the actual employment levels observed after Maria. In fact, employment in trade reached a peak in January 2018 which was its highest level since 2007.

One might have expected that immediately after Hurricane Maria made landfall, the increase in demand for basic necessities, rebuilding supplies, and goods to replace those damaged or lost during the storm led retailers to temporarily increase their workforce for a few months. However, as observed

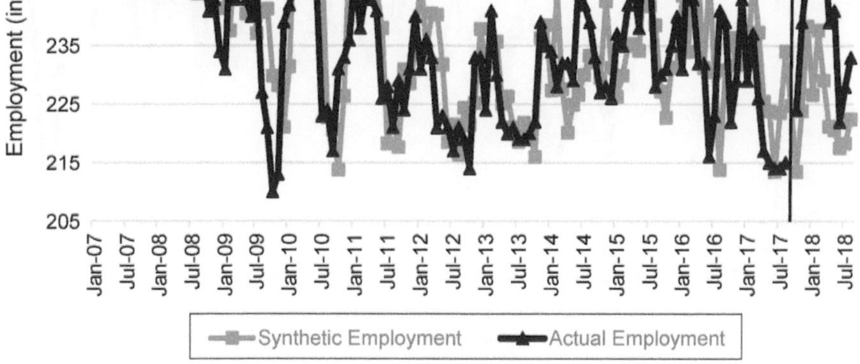

Figure 4.3 Trade Employment in Puerto Rico (in Thousands): 2007–2018. *Note:* The synthetic estimate is the employment approximation based on note 1. *Source*: Author's calculations based on data from the Labor Department of Puerto Rico (2019).

in figure 4.3, the increase in employment relative to the counterfactual levels persisted during the whole reconstruction period considered. Beyond the recovery phase, this finding could result from the extension in the emergency benefits associated with programs that have a direct impact on consumption, such as Puerto Rico's Nutrition Assistance Program (NAP), the local version of the U.S. Supplemental Nutrition Assistance Program. In fact, from August 2017 to August 2018 the average NAP benefits per family in Puerto Rico grew by 50 percent, and the percentage of the population participating rose by 13 percent, signaling the economic cycles during the post-Hurricane Maria recovery period did not equally improve the livelihoods of Puerto Ricans on the island. Still, the higher NAP participation and higher NAP benefits per family mixed with a higher demand for construction materials also meant higher consumption demand for goods in the retail sector. This increased demand seemingly related to reconstruction activities and might have benefitted those employed in the trade sector.

Services

Employment in the services sector shown in figure 4.4 appeared to have sharply deteriorated after Hurricane Maria relative to the expected

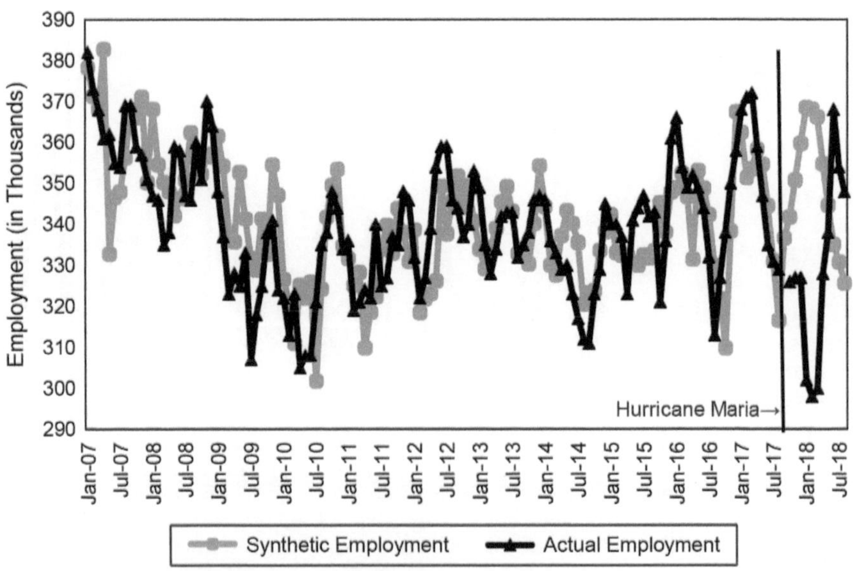

Figure 4.4 Service Employment in Puerto Rico (in Thousands): 2007–2018. *Note*: The synthetic estimate is the employment approximation based on note 1. *Source*: Author's calculations based on data from the Labor Department of Puerto Rico (2019).

employment. This employment decline was especially the case in the last quarter of 2017; the expected employment level in this sector without Hurricane Maria was close to 330,000, considerably larger than the reported observed level. However, in the first quarter of 2018, this sector appeared to undergo a countercyclical change not observed in the previous two years. At the end of the period observed, jobs in the services sector appeared to have stabilized relative to the pre-Hurricane Maria period.

Self-Employment

Previous studies have found that the incidence of self-employment tends to increase after hurricanes because evacuees and displaced small business owners shift toward this sector to survive (Zissimopoulos and Karoly 2010). The evidence provided in figure 4.5 following Hurricane Maria suggests that Puerto Rico is no exception. After a short drop in self-employment in October 2017, self-employment recovered in November 2017 and afterward it remained over the expected level. By the end of the period under study, the self-employment sector approximately had 7,000 more workers than expected in the absence of Hurricane Maria.

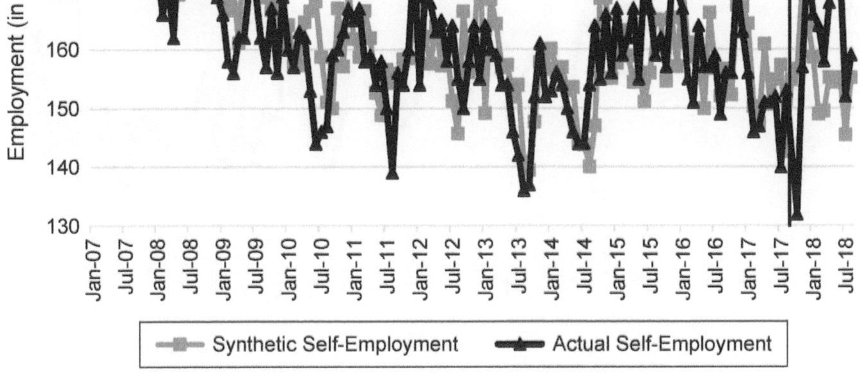

Figure 4.5 Self-Employment in Puerto Rico (in Thousands): 2007–2018. *Note*: The synthetic estimate is the employment approximation based on note 1. *Source*: Author's calculations based on data from the Labor Department of Puerto Rico (2019).

Manufacturing

Most of the exports from Puerto Rico to the U.S. mainland are made by multinational corporations that manufacture chemical and medical products on the island. While exports to foreign countries in November and December of 2018 reached a similar level than in November and December of 2016, exports to the U.S. mainland were still below the pre-Hurricane Maria levels over a year following Hurricane Maria. According to the Puerto Rico Planning Board, exports to the U.S. mainland in November and December of 2018 were 18 and 35 percent below their respective levels two years beforehand. On the surface, these numbers suggest that multinational manufacturing on the island had not recovered over a year after Hurricane Maria.

Why, then, are we observing an increase in manufacturing employment vis-à-vis the synthetic employment series in figure 4.6? Perhaps local manufacturers were the "winners" in this sector during the reconstruction period, as the production of construction materials such as cement and windows is mostly made locally and increased significantly following Hurricane Maria as rebuilding got underway. In fact, the production of cement bags was 45 percent higher in 2018 than in 2016. More research on particular manufacturing subsectors is needed, especially as more data become available to determine

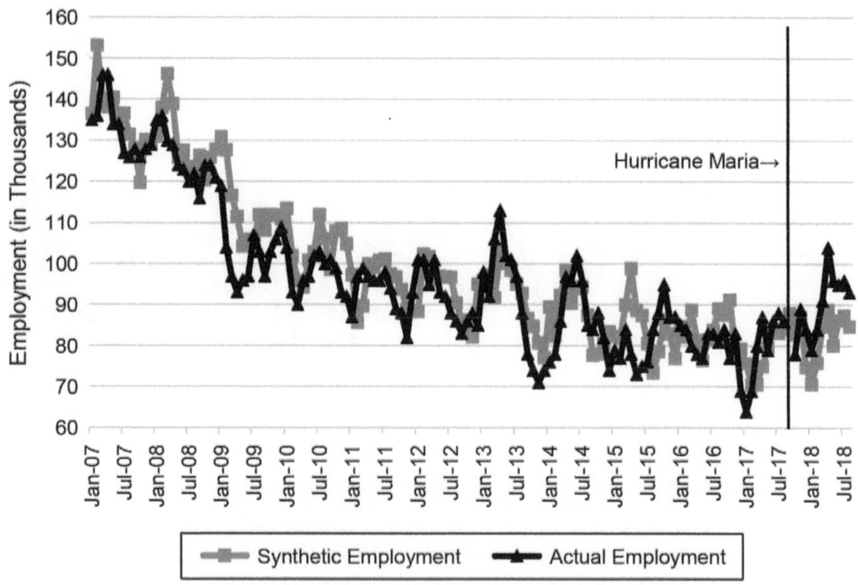

Figure 4.6 Manufacturing Employment in Puerto Rico (in Thousands): 2007–2018. *Note*: The synthetic estimate is the employment approximation based on note 1. *Source*: Author's calculations based on data from the Labor Department of Puerto Rico (2019).

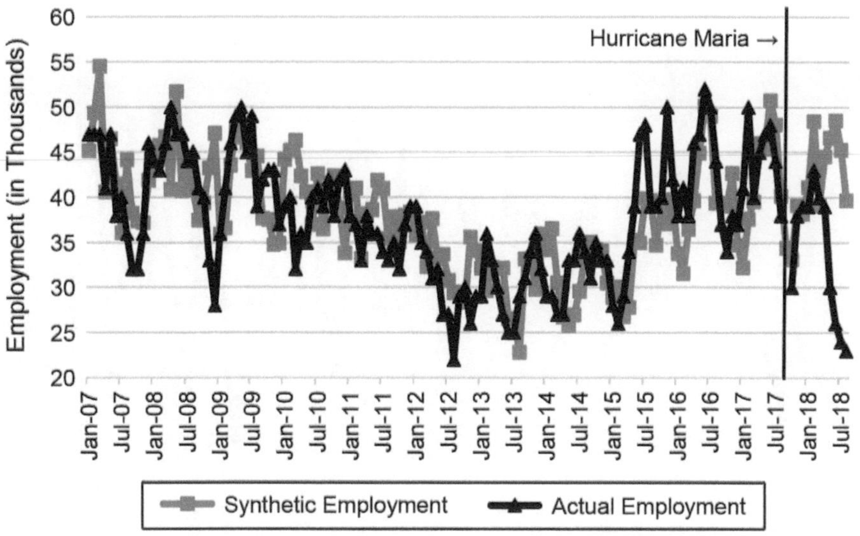

Figure 4.7 FIRE Employment in Puerto Rico (in Thousands): 2007–2018. *Note*: The synthetic estimate is the employment approximation based on note 1. *Source*: Author's calculations based on data from the Labor Department of Puerto Rico (2019).

the relative employment gains for local versus multinational manufacturers over time.

The FIRE Industry

Employment in the FIRE industry is shown in figure 4.7. After the unexpected shock from Hurricane Maria in September 2017, the employment levels in this sector followed closely the expected levels throughout the remainder of the year. However, during 2018, employment in this sector slumped. By July 2018, this sector had 47 percent lower employment levels than the levels projected without Hurricane Maria. The impact received by the insurance subsector is a likely major explanatory factor behind this reduction, but more detailed data pertaining to the disaggregation of specific subsectors of the FIRE industry were not available when this analysis was conducted.

Agriculture

Employment in agriculture has tended to be the most volatile of all the sectors over the years. As figure 4.8 indicates, there have been specific seasonal cycles: upswings start in the first quarter of the years and downswings begin at the end of the years. Considering that the synthetic employment series

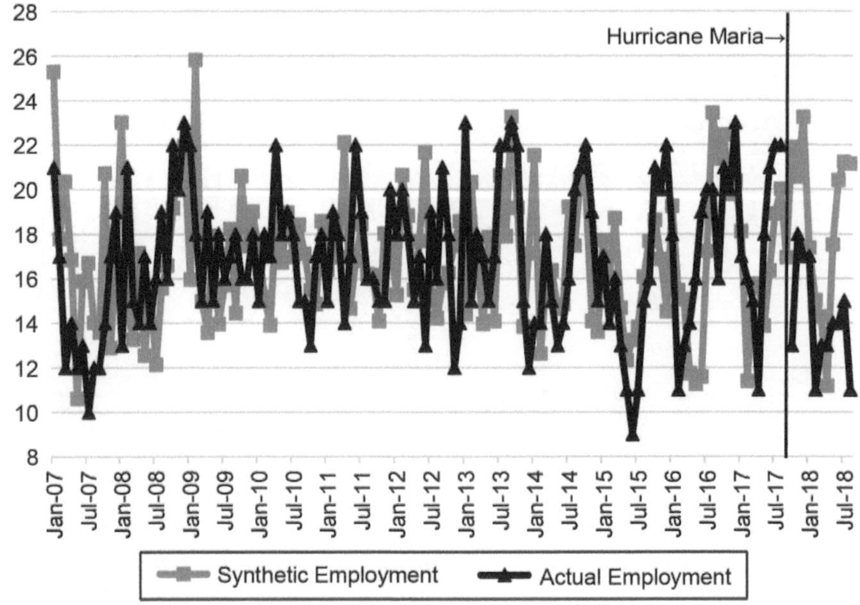

Figure 4.8 Agriculture Employment in Puerto Rico (in Thousands): 2007–2018. *Note*: The synthetic estimate is the employment approximation based on note 1. *Source*: Author's calculations based on data from the Labor Department of Puerto Rico (2019).

followed a similar pattern before Hurricane Maria, this figure shows that employment in agriculture after Hurricane Maria was negatively affected; except for April 2018, all the months after the hurricane showed a lower level of employment than expected without the hurricane. This finding is not surprising in light of the devastation and destruction that Hurricane Maria caused to the island's agricultural infrastructure.

CHANGES IN SECTORAL EMPLOYMENT SHARES AFTER HURRICANE MARIA

Another way of evaluating the sectoral gains and losses from Hurricane Maria in Puerto Rico is by evaluating changes in the representation of employment in each industry out of total employment before and after the storm. The last two columns of table 4.1 present these shares for August 2017 (the month before Hurricane Maria's landfall) and August 2018 (nearly a year after Hurricane Maria). These columns show similar phenomena to those presented in figures 4.1 through 4.8. To illustrate, the employment shares of services, manufacturing, trade, self-employment, and construction among total employment on the island grew from August 2017 to August 2018. Consider also the government sector, agriculture, FIRE, and transportation and communication lost ground with respect to their sectorial representation among total employment.

Regarding the government sector, it should be noted that the public workforce has been undergoing a series of reductions that started over a decade before Hurricane Maria, as Puerto Rico's severe economic crisis got underway (e.g., Caraballo-Cueto and Lara 2018; Mora, Dávila, and Rodríguez 2017a). Thus, the reduction in the relative share of government employment from 17.0 to 16.1 percent between August 2017 and August 2018 was not surprising, and the longer-term trend makes it difficult to assess how much of the loss in its employment share was specifically related to Hurricane Maria. For example, the reduction in this share by 0.9 percentage points during the time period in question was only 0.1 percentage points larger than the corresponding reduction in the same months between 2016 and 2017.

DISCUSSION AND CONCLUDING REMARKS

The consequences that Hurricane Maria had on the Puerto Rico economy benefitted those involved in certain economic sectors and impacted others, at least in the short term. Using monthly data, I compare expected employment levels within industry sectors in the absence of Hurricane Maria with the actual employment levels in these sectors. I find the agriculture, FIRE, and transportation and communication industries lost ground relative to expected employment levels following the hurricane, while other industries including construction, trade, and manufacturing appear to have gained in employment. Employment in services, while initially hit hard by Hurricane Maria, recovered late in 2018.

Of course, more research is needed in terms of analyzing changes in employment and wages in specific subsectors (such as insurance) as well as over longer time periods, as more data become available. For instance, it is possible that the increase in the manufacturing activity related more to local producers (such as in the production of cement) than to multinational manufacturers.

In terms of policy implications, perhaps asymmetrical employment outcomes following natural disasters can be smoothed out by public policies. For example, training programs could be designed to facilitate the transition of workers from one sector to another as relative demand changes. Moreover, a better integration of the self-employed into the formal economy might be attained by eliminating penalties for not filing taxes and allocating more personnel to regional permit offices, among others. Similarly, tax transfers from the benefited sectors to negatively impacted sectors (e.g., raising payroll taxes of firms by the sales growth observed after the disaster, to fund higher unemployment insurance benefits for displaced workers) could alleviate these sectoral asymmetries. Such tax transfers could be designed such that the industries that gain from natural disasters are still better off with the reconstruction activities brought about by disasters than otherwise.

These types of policies could be incorporated as resiliency measures that result in a more equitable recovery for workers across industries. Moreover, other jurisdictions located in hurricane zones such as Florida, Texas, and the U.S. Virgin Islands can learn from the experiences of Puerto Rico with Hurricane Maria to plan a better mitigation to these sudden natural events. A natural event does not necessarily imply an economic disaster if effective and targeted policies are implemented in a timely manner.

NOTES

1. Specifically, I construct this synthetic series through estimating the following equation, $\sqrt[5]{E_{t-12}E_{t-24}\left(\frac{E_{t-1}}{E_{t-13}}E_{t-12}\right)^2\frac{E_{t-2}}{E_{t-14}}E_{t-12}} = \sqrt[5]{E_{t-12}{}^4E_{t-24}\frac{E_{t-2}}{E_{t-13}{}^2E_{t-14}}E_{t-1^2}}$ where E stands for employment in a given sector and t represents months. This equation is the geometric mean of the following components (from left to right): employment in the same month a year ago, employment in the same month two years ago, projected employment if the growth observed in the previous month would hold for the current month (double weighted), and the projected employment if the growth observed two months ago would have held for the current month. We forecasted sectorial employment up to a year after Hurricane Maria by substituting figures of $t-1$ and $t-2$ with the projections of the synthetic series.

2. Had we detrended and seasonally adjusted each series, it should be noted that the accuracy of the empirical model described in note 1 grows exponentially. For instance, in the case of trade, the average percentual difference between the synthetic series and the detrended and seasonally adjusted employment would have been 0.2 percent instead of 1 percent. However, because we are studying short-term impacts of Hurricane Maria on industry employment in Puerto Rico, the noise in each series is information that cannot be discarded.

Chapter 5

Understanding Hurricane Maria through Puerto Rico's Electrical System

Disaster Response as Transition Management

Marla D. Pérez-Lugo, Cecilio Ortiz-García, and Didier Valdés

ABSTRACT

This chapter contextualizes one of the most pressing issues during the response and recovery phases in the aftermath of Hurricane Maria—the collapse of Puerto Rico's electrical grid. Maria's powerful winds destroyed essentially the island's transmission and distribution system. Following this catastrophic event, many stakeholders saw a window of opportunity to create a more sustainable and resilient system. However, it appears Puerto Rico's electrical system is being rebuilt as it was before Hurricane Maria, potentially reproducing the vulnerabilities that created the disaster. This chapter provides insights into explanations as well as potential consequences from these decisions.

As discussed throughout this volume, the catastrophic impact of Hurricane Maria on Puerto Rico in 2017 has been labeled as one of the most devastating and deadliest disasters in U.S. history. The storm led to economic losses and rebuilding estimates, when combined with Hurricane Irma, are in the range of $132 billion. As noted in other chapters, the official death toll estimate stands at 2,975 in Puerto Rico, but the number of deaths has been estimated between 1,000 and almost 5,000, depending on the data source and the methodology used (Santos-Lozada and Howard 2018; Kishore et al. 2018).

In the aftermath of Hurricane Maria, one of the most pressing issues for the disaster response and recovery was the collapse of Puerto Rico's electrical grid. Other chapters in this volume have noted that nearly 3.3 million American citizens in Puerto Rico were left without electrical power resulting from the almost complete destruction of the electrical grid (also see Kwasinski et al. 2019). The lack of electricity has been singled out as one of the main contributing factors to the high death toll associated with the hurricane (discussed in upcoming chapters), mostly because of the interdependencies between the electrical and the water systems, health services, telecommunications, transportation, and so on, and their interconnections with the documented socioeconomic and other vulnerabilities of the Puerto Rican population (Garcia-Lopez 2018; Cruz-Cano and Mead 2019).

Aside from the attention that has been rightly placed on the well-documented adverse impact on human resources and the loss of human lives, this natural disaster also led scholars and policymakers to debate and discuss whether the collapse of the electric infrastructure created a window of opportunity to establish a more sustainable and resilient system (Perez-Lugo and Ortiz-Garcia 2018). Many energy policy stakeholders inside and outside the island believe that the collapse was a critical moment in Puerto Rico's energy history, providing the opportunity to re-envision the entire system for the transition toward renewable energy sources and energy democracy. However, when writing this chapter, that expectation had not yet materialized. Puerto Rico's electrical system was being rebuilt as it was before Hurricane Maria, centered on the use of fossil fuels and centralized energy generation, reproducing all the vulnerabilities that contributed to the disaster in the first place (IEEE 2019).

Perhaps disaster research and disaster management are entrenched in a way that focus is lost on how a society addresses key response and vulnerabilities following a disaster. We propose in this chapter that a myopic view of disasters creates "windows of opportunity" for powerful actors to advance their interests and vision of the future, sometimes without necessarily focusing on the protection of the most vulnerable groups impacted by these events.

The next section of this chapter develops our thesis by describing the sociotechnical nature of Puerto Rico's electrical system. We will focus on how social dimensions of the electrical system have influenced its physical infrastructure and vice versa. We will also describe the ways in which energy governance is configured in Puerto Rico and the rhetoric that was used before and during the reconstruction period to seemingly carry a specific agenda forward.

PHYSICAL AND SOCIAL VULNERABILITIES OF PUERTO RICO'S ELECTRIC GRID

The 2017 State of Energy Report for Puerto Rico (2018), produced by the University of Puerto Rico's National Institute for Energy and Island

Sustainability, states that Maria's powerful winds destroyed almost all of the island's transmission and distribution system, including 2,478 miles of transmission and subtransmission lines, 48 transmission centers, 31,446 miles of aerial lines, 1,723 of underground lines, 293 substations, and 27 technical offices (National Institute for Energy and Island Sustainability, 2018). Research conducted by Castro-Sitiriche et al. (2018) shows that the blackout lasted more than 329 days, and there were 2.8 billion customer hours of electrical service lost in the mountainous center region and the southeastern corner of the main island (Castro-Sitiriche, Cintrón-Sotomayor and Gómez-Torres 2018). Castro-Sitiriche et al. (2018) further identified the "Maria Blackout" as the longest in Puerto Rico's history and one of the largest ever recorded worldwide.

The design of Puerto Rico's electrical system made it highly vulnerable to meteorological hazards such as hurricanes. Puerto Rico's main electrical infrastructure includes six big generation facilities, a transmission, and a distribution system (INESI, 2016). Most of the generation, four out of the six plants, are located on the southern coast of the main island while most of the consumption of the output of these plants is by the northern coast. This configuration requires a complex electrical grid. To move the electricity from the south to the north of the island requires a transmission and distribution system that crosses across the irregular and unstable terrain of the central mountain range, leaving long lines exposed to the natural elements.

Puerto Rico's Electrical System as a Sociotechnical System

Sociotechnical systems represent a framework to understand the recent history of Puerto Rico's electrical system. According to Borrás and Edler (2014), sociotechnical systems are "articulated ensembles of social and technical elements which interact with each other in distinct ways, are distinguishable from their environment, have developed specific forms of collective knowledge production, knowledge utilization, and innovation, and which are oriented towards specific purposes in society and economy."

The Puerto Rico Electric Power Authority (PREPA) is the public corporation created by the Government of Puerto Rico to administer the electric infrastructure of the archipelago (O'Neill-Carrillo 2010). When created, PREPA was the backbone to "Operation Bootstrap," the economic development model adopted by the Puerto Rican government since the creation of the Commonwealth in 1952 (e.g., O'Neill-Carrillo 2010). This model was based on attracting U.S. investment in the heavy manufacturing sector with the goal of eradicating poverty, by industrializing the island's economic base from agriculture to manufacturing, and modernizing Puerto Rico (Goldsmith and Vietorisz 1979). For that to happen, the government needed to develop a strong and robust electric grid that sustained the electricity generation demanded by heavy industry as well as supply electricity to all corners of the archipelago (O'Neill-Carrillo 2010).

At that time, only a few stakeholders had the influence to make energy policy decisions, and they agreed on the PREPA model (O'Neill-Carrillo 2010). Because of the technical complexity of the task, PREPA had complete control of the decision-making processes. In fact, until 2014, PREPA was the sole entity responsible for the electric energy sector in Puerto Rico. It decided what energy sources were to be used, who could generate energy, and the rules and structure regarding electricity production and distribution across Puerto Rico (O'Neill-Carrillo 2010).

After achieving total rural electrification in the early 1980s, and after the decline of the manufacturing sector as an engine for economic development (Feliciano 2018), PREPA was not given a new mission (Nieves et al. 2018). Since then, PREPA's goal has been described by some as self-preservation (O'Neill-Carrillo 2010). Because of its power to control energy decision-making processes, it was able to stay at the center of Puerto Rico's energy policy. The only two stakeholders that penetrated PREPA's defenses were the two political parties that had been alternating in power since 1952 (Institute for Energy Economics and Financial Analysis 2018). Consequently, it came with little surprise when former PREPA's executive director Ricardo Ramos stated in congressional hearings that political party affiliation was one of the main criteria in the organization's human resource management strategies (Ramos 2017). PREPA had thus become a highly centralized and politicized entity, where power (both political and electrical) was concentrated.

According to Smith-Nonini (2019), as a multimillion dollar industry, PREPA had developed a complicated Ponzi scheme allowing political parties to use electricity prices to fund elections and the corporation's monies for infrastructure maintenance to control the local regime. This political behavior arguably led to PREPA's bankruptcy at the beginning of the 2000s (Smith-Nonini 2019).

According to investigative reports, PREPA's financial situation had a dramatic impact on the levels of grid vulnerability. During its debt restructuring process, and before Maria's landfall, the physical infrastructure deteriorated as PREPA had lost most of its trained personnel, privatized some of its essential operations, and significantly decreased inventory of fuel and replacement parts (Brown, Respaut and Resnick-Ault 2017). Therefore, the recovery after PREPA's economic collapse depended on external factors, such as the speed of manufacturing, importing new parts, and subcontracting with external companies to reconstruct the grid in an unfamiliar terrain.

A NARRATIVE OF EXCLUSION

During the immediate response phase following Hurricane Maria, the Puerto Rican government developed a narrative portraying Puerto Rico as a blank canvas, as a laboratory for technological innovation and experimentation (Government of Puerto Rico 2018). Puerto Rico, at least regarding energy production, was described as waiting for a new "Picasso" to draw in it the masterpiece of a new electric system (Ortiz-García 2018). This narrative also emphasized Puerto Rico was "open for business," which was an opportunity for external agents and organizations to invest and build a new system from scratch. The implication was the lack of resources and agency on the island necessary for a successful and speedy reconstruction among internal stakeholders.

For example, three months after Hurricane Maria's impact, Puerto Rico's then-governor Dr. Ricardo Rosselló referred to the Caribbean archipelago as "a blank canvas where we can start thinking anew, where we can take bold steps into investment and innovation and rebuild Puerto Rico much more effectively" (Bonilla 2018). The president of the Smart Electric Power Alliance echoed these words by stating: "Here we are, sadly, in a position where Puerto Rico is as close to a blank slate as we ever thought realistically would come to pass" (Ferris and Behr 2017). More than two years after the impact, the commonwealth government still reaffirmed the idea of the blank canvas through investors meetings and radio and internet marketing campaigns (Government of Puerto Rico 2018).

Disasters as Windows of Opportunity

In her seminal book, *The Shock Doctrine: The Rise of Disaster Capitalism*, Naomi Klein explains how disasters, both technological and those triggered by the impact of a natural event, are windows of opportunity for exploitation of the most vulnerable (Klein 2007). She argues sociopolitical actors consistently promote plans for privatizing essential services and defrauding public funds. However, they are faced with public opposition. A disaster, the "shock," serves as the ideal opportunity to implement those policies because citizens are in a collective trauma. Disaster managers at the federal level, such as the U.S. Corps of Engineers and Federal Emergency Management Agency (FEMA), seemingly found themselves embedded in these local "shock-and-awe" political structures while trying to reconstruct the electrical system.

According to media accounts and government documents, Puerto Rico's then-governor Ricardo Rosselló took advantage of the crisis and announced the system's privatization (Aronoff 2018). The most recent privatization attempt, before 2017, was in 2014 with the passing of Law 57 (O'Neill-Carrillo and Rivera-Quiñones 2018), described later in this section. The post-Maria privatization strategy was different than prior attempts: The federal money and the labor of government entities being used for the reconstruction were a potential subsidy to the private companies interested in buying PREPA's assets. As described by Campoy (2017):

> Before the storm, PREPA [owed] more than $9 billion—$2.7 billion more than what its rickety system was worth. In a single day, even that value was wiped out as the hurricane turned much of the company's infrastructure from assets into scrapyard material. The cost of repairs is [was] unclear—PREPA had said it was in need of a $4.6 billion upgrade even before the storm—but officials supervising its bankruptcy proceedings say both federal aid and private funds will be needed.

These discussions involved little input from the communities most affected by the lack of service nor did they focus on addressing why Puerto Rico's electrical infrastructure was in a weakened state *before* the storm. In fact, according to the public hearings held by Puerto Rico's Senate on November 8, 2018, the deaths related to the lack of electricity in rural and isolated areas and the cascading effects of the blackout into health services, telecommunications, and food security were absent from the discussion on how to rebuild the electrical system (EFE 2018). The voices heard throughout the process were the ones coming from the manufacturing and the tourism sectors. In the first congressional public hearings regarding the reconstruction of Puerto Rico's electrical system, the senator presiding, Lisa Murkowski, asked: "as in right now, who is in charge of the electrical system in Puerto Rico?" Only one voice broke the silence—Rodrigo Masses, the president of the Puerto Rico Manufacturers Association, who said "I don't know who is in charge but I do know who should be . . . us" (Masses 2018).

Historically, important stakeholders, such as community leaders and the health services' sector, have been systematically excluded not only from PREPA's decision-making processes but also from energy policy in general. For example, Law 57 of 2014 established three representatives of the consumers elected by PREPA's clients in PREPA's board to balance the power of the governor over the administration of the public corporation (O'Neill-Carrillo and Rivera-Quiñones 2018). It also established the professional qualifications of the candidates as a criterion for the selection of all its members: the appointments could be either political or merit based. That polarized view of the board's composition missed the main point of the need for increased representation of Puerto Rico's energy stakeholders.

Although this redistribution of power might seem capable of destabilizing the nonphysical dimension of the electrical system, the hard political capture of PREPA's decision-making structures has allowed major Puerto Rican parties in power to manufacture the illusion of governance changes. In fact, the board's representation was reduced even more after Governor Rosselló came to power. New legislation, Law 83, was passed to change again the composition of PREPA's Board of Directors, to include only one member selected by PREPA's clients to represent the consumer's interest (O'Neill-Carrillo and Rivera-Quiñones 2018). The result was that the representation of the governor and its political party increased at the expense of the consumers' interest, representation that was reduced by 67 percent. In fact, the leadership's political capture of all public corporations has increased in recent years, through an executive order stating that members of the boards of public corporations had to be in "complete alignment" with the governor's policies for them to remain in their positions (De Jesus Salamán 2017).

After the hurricane, the systematic decrease in stakeholder participation in energy decision-making processes has brought other subtler but also more pervasive forms of exclusion. These are based on geography, language, and income, among other factors. For example, events focused on the future of Puerto Rico's energy policies and practices are coordinated by nongovernmental organizations (sometimes with government funding and often with government participation). In all 12 events held between January 2017 and March 2019, the main language used was English, even though according to the U.S. Census Bureau, only 22 percent of the population in Puerto Rico speaks English fluently. Seven of those events were held outside of Puerto Rico, and the rest occurred in the capital city of San Juan. Nine of the twelve events required an entrance fee ranging between $50 and $1,500 per person, even though according to U.S. Census Bureau data, the median annual income in Puerto Rico was $19,343. Attendance to the other three events was by invitation only.[1]

In our view, the result of a governance model that was seemingly without transparency, accountability, and stakeholder representation paved the road for a reconstruction process that has jeopardized the long-term future and sustainability of energy in Puerto Rico.

TRANSITION MANAGEMENT AS A NEW DIRECTION FOR DISASTER MANAGEMENT AND RESEARCH

Energy transitions are fundamental structural changes in the energy sector that can differ in terms of motivations and objectives, and their drivers and governance provide a diverse set of challenges and opportunities (Weltenergierat-Deustchland 2010). According to extant literature, energy transitions are not necessarily about technological changes but about changes in purpose (Fouquet and Pearson 2012). Changing from fossil fuels to solar energy would not necessarily mean a transition to a different electrical system. What marks a transition are the social changes that trigger a different purpose to generate and consume electricity.

However, according to Unruh (2000) and Walker (2000), sociotechnical systems are characterized by "path dependence" and "lock-in," resulting from stabilizing mechanisms on those two dimensions in conjunction with the systems' material and technical elements. According to Nieves et al. (2018), the purpose for generating electricity has not changed, even after Hurricane Maria's island-wide blackout and slow restoration.

Rethinking How We Frame Disasters

Governmental response has been described as inadequate at both levels, commonwealth and federal. In most media accounts (e.g., Sullivan and Swartz 2018), as well as federal and congressional reports (e.g., Democratic Staff Report 2008), the severity of the disaster was portrayed as a direct consequence of an unexperienced and ill-prepared commonwealth government and a Federal Emergency Management Agency that has been described as ignorant of the cultural and structural characteristics of the Puerto Rican society (Robles 2018). At a minimum, there is vast agreement about the dramatic differences between the treatment given to Puerto Rico by federal emergency management agencies when compared to similar events in the mainland (Willison, Singer and Creary 2019).

The governmental response to Hurricane Maria provides an opportunity to examine various basic premises behind the current disaster response paradigm. The disaster response and recovery in Puerto Rico reveals the multilevel complexities of disasters that transcend the typical organizational misalignments often documented in the disaster literature, from the classic Charles Perrow's Normal Accidents (1984) to more recent applications of the aforementioned Naomi Klein's shock doctrine and disaster capitalism to climate change-related events (Klein 2015).

Disaster response, when it fails to restore normalcy to everyday life quickly, is perceived as defective (Lester 2018). The tendency is to treat disasters as disturbances. In that context, disaster response means restoring society back to its predisaster state. The literature on resilience calls this the ability to bounce back (Walker, Holling, Carpenter, and Kinzig 2004). However, the analysis of the root social causes and the dynamic political pressures offered in this chapter suggests this view is insufficient. The case of Puerto Rico, when confronted with this myopic view of disasters, begs the question, "bouncing back to what?" While we continue considering disasters as discrete events to which governmental and societal institutions must respond, we will be unable to address the longer-term and/or chronic socioeconomic vulnerabilities that yielded disaster outcomes following natural events. A new definition of resilience will be the ability to bounce forward to a more adaptable and sustainable state (Manyena, O'Brien, O'Keefe, and Rose 2011; Houston 2015; Sudmeier-Rieux 2014).

Resilience thinking becomes particularly important for rebuilding in the climate change era. However, limiting our definition of resilience to the hardening of physical infrastructure blinds us to one of Hurricane Maria's biggest lessons: electrical systems as well as any other critical infrastructure system are sociotechnical. That means that while the storm's 155 miles per hour winds destroyed the electrical grid, in our view the fragmented, bureaucratic, and politically captured social structures of the electrical system served as a faulty foundation on which to construct it in a more resilient way. The long-term effective recovery and reconstruction of Puerto Rico will depend not only on rebuilding the physical components to these systems but also accounting for the values, beliefs, purposes, perceptions, and knowledge embedded within them.

Natural hazards (e.g., hurricanes, earthquakes, etc.) become disasters (e.g., events leading to loss of life, prolonged suffering) because of the vulnerable socioeconomic conditions of the impacted community. Societies can experience disaster because they are also socioeconomically, politically, culturally, and ecologically vulnerable. As the case of Puerto Rico post-Hurricane Maria suggests, bouncing back and restoring normalcy reproduces the same conditions that created the crises in the first place (Manyena, O'Brien, O'Keefe, and Rose 2011; Cannon 2008). This distinction will become increasingly crucial as we face climate change. As argued by O'Keefe et al. (2008), "dealing with a plethora of complex problems using existing techniques lead to inadequate and inappropriate measures."

The collapse and reconstruction of Puerto Rico's electrical system also suggests that while managers and practitioners on the island may have developed a myopic view of disasters, other actors such as political parties and the private sector may have a farsighted view with a vision and clear objectives for the future, potentially using disasters as windows of opportunity to advance their own agendas. As we argue here for the case of Puerto Rico, when societies lack open and strong governance structures, the most powerful stakeholders capture the processes, creating a new future for all not necessarily based on the common good (O'Keefe 2008).

DISCUSSION AND CONCLUDING REMARKS

Transitions are political. Transitions often bring about structural regime transformations, in which government officials and managers need to adapt with the process or fall out of the system. As transitions are ultimately shifts in power, transition management and subsequent rebuilding supports niche actors or communities on their innovative journeys by providing the necessary instruments, strategies, and networks. Empowering communities is therefore a crucial part of transition management. As Puerto Rico continues to rebuild years after Hurricane Maria's landfall, local communities should have a voice in the nature and sustainability of key components of its infrastructure.

The case of Hurricane Maria demonstrates that disaster response and recovery should change this focus by adopting a new paradigm based on managing the transition. A transition management model, using the concept of sustainable development as a normative frame to develop the future orientation or vision, can help us design policy interventions that mitigate vulnerabilities resulting from and contributing to disasters. It can also empower disaster managers to embrace uncertainty and focus on governance to improve society through rebuilding instead of maintaining the status quo. In doing so, we should be able to deal with the inherent complexity of the modern society and its associated problems (Loorbach 2007).

In the case of Puerto Rico, following a narrow approach to disaster response by simply returning Puerto Rico to pre-Hurricane Maria conditions (which, as discussed throughout this volume, was already in a socioeconomically vulnerable state with a weakened infrastructure) does not bode well when another natural disaster strikes the island. Moving Puerto Rico forward will involve rebuilding the electrical, transportation, telecommunication, and other infrastructures through the active engagement and empowerment of the affected communities. It will also involve accepting that electrical systems, as well as other basic infrastructures, have no intrinsic value. Their value relies on the services they provide to a society that strives to be resilient and sustainable.

NOTE

1. See, for example, the Puerto Rico Energy Summit, organized by the Solar and Energy Storage Association (SESA) of Puerto Rico, an affiliate of the Solar Energy Industries Association (SESA, n.d.). The event was held at the Intercontinental Resort in Isla Verde on June 25, 2018. The minimum entrance fee was $100 per person. Another example is the Solar Power Puerto Rico Event held also at the Intercontinental Resort on April 30, 2019, which too was organized by SESA of Puerto Rico; its minimum entrance fee was $200 per person.

Chapter 6

Health and Healthcare Delivery in Puerto Rico before and after Hurricane Maria

Jose M. Fernandez

ABSTRACT

This chapter examines how the healthcare sector of Puerto Rico was adversely affected by Hurricane Maria. The evidence describes an aging population in need of more healthcare workers, but when comparing healthcare establishments between Puerto Rico and the U.S. mainland, Puerto Rico is both under supplied and underpaid for healthcare services. Moreover, both healthcare employment and the number of establishments significantly declined in Puerto Rico in the last two quarters of 2017—during and immediately after Hurricane Maria, with the largest changes occurring along the eastern coast and within the center of the island, essentially along Hurricane Maria's path.

Puerto Rico is experiencing both an economic and a public health crisis. The commonwealth sought debt relief in May of 2017 through the approval of the Oversight Board created by the 2016 Puerto Rico Oversight, Management, and Economic Stability Act (PROMESA, discussed in chapter 1) when it was unable to make a debt payment on publicly issued bonds, effectively declaring bankruptcy. The island's financial crisis was compounded by the devastating effects of Hurricane Maria, which when it made landfall in September 2017 as a strong Category 4 hurricane, wiped away most of the island's agriculture and decimated its already weakened infrastructure, including the electrical grid (discussed in the previous chapter). However, as Marie T. Mora, Havidán Rodríguez, and Alberto Dávila (chapter 1) highlighted, the difficulties facing Puerto Rico predated these events. Previous chapters focused on how these events affected labor markets in Puerto Rico. In this chapter, I discuss how Puerto Rico's healthcare was affected by both

Table 6.1 Health Disparities between Puerto Rico and the U.S. Mainland in 2017

	Puerto Rico	*U.S. Mainland*
Health indicators		
Diabetes	17.2%	10.5%
Depression	18.1%	20.5%
Currently smoking	11.3%	17.1%
Obese	32.9%	31.3%
Overweight	35.4%	35.3%
High cholesterol	36.7%	33.0%
Hypertension	44.7%	32.3%
Fair or poor health	37.1%	17.6%
Drinking and driving	7.4%	3.9%
Health insurance		
Private	32%	56%
Public	62%	36%
- Medicaid	47%	21%
- Medicare	14%	14%
- Other	1%	1%
No Insurance	7%	9%

Source: Author's estimates from the 2017 Behavioral Risk Factor Surveillance System (for health indicators) and the 2017 American Community Survey (for health insurance).

the more-than-decade's long economic downturn and the devastating effects of Hurricane Maria.

The healthcare sector constitutes slightly over 10 percent of Puerto Rico's economy, in contrast to 17.4 percent of the United States' economy (ASPE Issue Brief 2017). According to the 2017 American Community Survey, 94 percent of Puerto Rico's residents had health insurance, which was slightly higher than the 91 percent on the mainland, but as seen in table 6.1, the composition of health insurance types varies greatly between Puerto Rico and the mainland (U.S. Census Bureau). Only 32 percent of Puerto Ricans had private health insurance policies, compared to 56 percent in the U.S. mainland. Of the 62 percent of Puerto Ricans using public health insurance, nearly half (47%) received Medicaid. This rate was more than twice the U.S. average where the highest percentage of the population covered by Medicaid was 33 percent in New Mexico that year.

Since most of Puerto Rico's population is covered by some form of government health insurance, which tends to have lower reimbursement rates than private plans, health expenditures per capita tend to be much lower in Puerto Rico relative to the United States overall. The Office of Health Policy of the Assistant Secretary for Planning and Evaluation (ASPE Issue Brief 2017) reported the health expenditures per capita in Puerto Rico were $3,065 compared to $9,515 in the United States. Puerto Rico had the lowest expenditures per capita when compared to individual states with the closest being Utah at $5,982 (Lassman et al. 2017).

There is a strong reliance on publicly funded health insurance fueled by the poor state of the economy. In 2016, median household income in Puerto Rico was approximately $20,007, which was about one-third the amount of the average American household ($57,617). Nearly half of the island's population lived in poverty (44.9%) compared to 14 percent on the U.S. mainland, while unemployment was more than double the U.S. national average, at 7.8 percent versus 3.6 percent in 2019. The poverty rate in Puerto Rico was more than double either Mississippi (19.7%) or Michigan (19.5%), which had the highest rates of poverty among U.S. states. (See chapter 1 for additional details on the poverty rates among recent Puerto Rican migrants in the states.)

These differences are projected to grow. As noted in previous chapters, the population of Puerto Rico steadily decreased from 3.8 million in 2006 to 3.2 million in 2019. As Mora and colleagues (chapter 1) point out, Puerto Rico's shrinking population is also rapidly aging. For example, the median age in Puerto Rico increased by three years in less than a decade, from 36 in 2010 to 39 in 2017. A large reason is that the net out-migration outflows are comprised of younger Puerto Ricans headed for the mainland. Their departure leaves an aging society behind in need of social programs with a shrinking of the tax base.

The good news is that the out-migration has not induced a "brain drain" from the island. For example, Jason Adel and Richard Deitz (2014) find the proportion of college-educated residents leaving the island is nearly equivalent to those that remain on the island. This relationship has been virtually unchanged since the 1980s. If anything, the share of high school graduates among out-migrants has been higher in recent years than the share remaining in Puerto Rico.

The debt crisis also leaves many government employees uncertain about their retirement and health insurance benefits. The government sector employs 22 percent of workers (compared to the 15% U.S. average), although the share has been falling, as discussed in chapter 4 by José Caraballo-Cueto. At this percentage, Puerto Rico would be ranked fourth among all states behind New Mexico, Alaska, and Wyoming. These have traditionally been typically good-paying secure jobs. Government workers also participate in *Mi Salud*, a publicly funded health insurance plan. However, the debt settlement requires the Puerto Rican government to pay foreign entities first before covering the pension liability to these workers. Failure to cover these pension liabilities may increase the percentage of elderly living in poverty and requiring further government assistance. Additionally, the Puerto Rican government adopted strong austerity measures in 2016 as a part of PROMESA to combat its debt crisis, which led to further reductions in government spending and employment.

MEDICAID, MEDICARE, AND THE AFFORDABLE CARE ACT (ACA)

In 2014, the ACA was enacted to allow states to expand Medicaid coverage and create health insurance exchanges to reduce the number of uninsured individuals in the United States. As part of the ACA, states could expand Medicaid coverage to families living at 133 percent of the federal poverty line, and these additional costs would be paid for by the federal government instead of by the state. Additionally, individuals could purchase health insurance plans using either a federal or state-run exchange and receive subsidies to help offset the cost.

However, the U.S. Department of Health and Human Services declared that given its status with the United States, Puerto Rico does not fit the definition of a state under Title I of the ACA; therefore, the Commonwealth of Puerto Rico was excluded from many parts of the reform, including the individual mandate, employer mandate, small business tax credits, and premium tax credits for purchasing private health insurance on the federal exchange (Mach et al. 2016; Portela and Sommers 2015). Puerto Rico also could not create its own health insurance exchange. Moreover, Puerto Rico needed to adopt a local measure of poverty for families to qualify for Medicaid. The commonwealth determined that families living at 133 percent of the Puerto Rican poverty line would qualify, which is the equivalent of $850 a month for a family of four or 42 percent of the federal poverty line on the mainland.

Further, Puerto Rico received a block grant for Medicaid expansion instead of the per enrollee subsidy that other expansion states received. The block grant, totaling $6.9 billion, provided the Puerto Rican government with a fixed amount of funds adjusted for inflation to finance the Medicaid expansion from 2011 through 2019 independent of the number of new enrollees. After this time period, Puerto Rico would return to the statutory level, which is capped to slightly less than $400 million. While the government was given much flexibility with how these funds could be used, the funds were insufficient to provide the same level of service for each Medicaid enrollee in Puerto Rico. The island's statutory allotment in 2018 was $359.5 million but it spent $2.49 billion (Solomon 2019). These expenditure amounts are despite meeting only 10 of Medicaid's 17 mandatory benefits. Without additional funds, 900,000 Medicaid enrollees in Puerto Rico may lose healthcare coverage (ASPE Data Point 2017).

"You've got this extreme poverty, extreme deprivation, high dependence on public programs, gross underfinancing of public programs to the point that the underfunding of the health care system is one of the major factors associated with their economic crisis before the hurricane," said Sara Rosenbaum, a professor of health law and policy and one of the authors of a George Washington University report on Puerto Rico published in November 2017.

Medicare faces similar financing problems. Puerto Rico receives less federal funding for healthcare than any of the 50 states (including the 21 states with smaller populations), even while paying Medicare taxes. Roman (2015) states the Medicare reimbursement rate in Puerto Rico is 70 percent less than that in the 50 U.S. states and the District of Columbia. Total enrollment in Medicare programs in Puerto Rico is equal to the U.S. average of 14 percent. However, Medicare Advantage enrollment is higher in Puerto Rico than in any U.S. state at 89 percent, but Medicare Advantage reimbursement in Puerto Rico is only 43 percent of that on the mainland (Richman 2018).

These changes to Medicaid, Medicare, and the government-adopted austerity measures have affected access to healthcare. The reduction in the government spending likely forced some individuals into unemployment or outside of the labor force altogether. Other individuals have lost Medicaid benefits because they earn too much to be at the Puerto Rican poverty level but are still below the federal poverty level. In these cases, there is an incentive to leave the island in favor of one of the Medicaid expansion states where the same family can now receive Medicaid benefits. Remaining on the island implies seeking care without a method to pay. These individuals turned to community health centers to seek care. Community health centers are a critical part of the healthcare system—20 federally funded health centers provide primary and preventive care services at 98 urban and rural sites across the island (Sharac et al. 2018). About 10 percent of Puerto Rico's population uses community health centers for their care, as compared to 7.1 percent on the mainland.

Given these low reimbursement rates for both Medicare and Medicaid, physicians are among the net out-migrants leaving the island because it is simply not profitable to stay. To illustrate, based on data from the U.S. Bureau of Labor Statistics in 2016, physicians and surgeons in Puerto Rico earned an average hourly wage of $41.45, less than half the U.S. average hourly wage of $99.48. Reimbursement rates for a primary care visit from Medicaid were reported as low as $10 (Torres 2019).

From 2006 to 2016, over one-third (36%) of physicians left the island for the mainland, a drop of 5,000 physicians (Arroyo 2016). As with the rest of Puerto Rico's population, those that have stayed behind are rapidly aging (Mora, Dávila, and Rodríguez 2017a), leading to the "graying of Puerto Rico's doctors" (*New York Times* 2017). Moreover, an estimated 500–600 physicians and surgeons out of roughly 10,000 on the island left in the first year following Hurricane Maria (Medical Schedule Inc. 2018).

According to the Area Health Resource File, Puerto Rico has less than half the population coverage rates of emergency physicians; neurosurgeons;

orthopedists and hand surgeons; plastic surgeons; and ear, nose, and throat specialists, compared to the availability of these providers on the U.S. mainland. In 2015, the island had only one pediatric anesthesiologist, two pediatric allergists, six hand surgeons, and eight colorectal surgeons covering a population of then 3.4 million residents. Moreover, the Health Resources and Services Administration (HRSA) deemed 72 of Puerto Rico's 78 municipalities as medically underserved areas (U.S. Department of Health and Human Services 2019). HRSA has also identified 39 Health Professional Shortage Areas on the island where less than 2 percent of the healthcare need is met. For example, only 90 obstetricians/gynecologists assist in childbirths, resulting in an estimated ratio of 400 births per obstetrician each year, or more than one birth per doctor per day, which is double the U.S. average (Arroyo 2016). In order to remove these designations, Puerto Rico needs 98 mental health practitioners, 4 dentists, and 554 primary care physicians (U.S. Department of Health and Human Services 2019).

To stem the exodus of healthcare professionals from Puerto Rico, then-governor Ricardo Rosselló signed into law Act 14-2017 on April 22, 2017, which is known as the "Incentives Act for the Retention and Return of Medical Professionals." The law provides tax incentives for physicians to remain or relocate to Puerto Rico. The law allows for qualified physicians to be subject to a 4 percent flat income tax on medical services, up to $250,000 of corporate dividends would be exempt from income tax, and physicians contribute up to 25 percent of after-tax income into retirement plans. These benefits are extended for 15 years with the possibility for renewal for an additional 15 years. A qualified physician is defined as a healthcare professional who is authorized to practice medicine, podiatry, or any specialty in odontology and works at least 100 hours per month on these activities. Medical residents attending an accredited program in Puerto Rico are considered qualified physicians by this definition. These tax incentives are in addition to the physician bonus program already in place for HRSAs where physicians received an additional 10 percent reimbursement for Medicare patients.

THE HEALTH STATUS OF PUERTORRIQUEÑOS

As this chapter was finalized, life expectancy in Puerto Rico was 81 years from birth, which was higher than the U.S. average of 78.6 years (Xu et al. 2018; World Bank 2019). In terms of the rankings of states and territories, Puerto Rico only trails California and Hawaii with the longest average life expectancy in the United States. This life expectancy advantage over non-Hispanic whites is shared with other Hispanic groups in the United States and is known as the "Hispanic Paradox." Hispanic women in the United States in particular have gained the most additional life years since the 1990s. The primary driver of the life expectancy advantage is difference in smoking preferences, which explains about 40 percent of the variation (Fenelon and Blue 2015). (More will be discussed on how Puerto Ricans fare relative to other U.S. Hispanic groups in the following chapter by Fernando I. Rivera and his colleagues.)

However, longer life does not necessarily equate to better health. The inhabitants of the island experience significant health concerns. The Behavioral Risk Factor Surveillance System (BRFSS) is a nationally represented annual telephone survey of over 400,000 U.S. citizens living in all 50 states and three U.S. territories including Puerto Rico. The survey collects data associated with health-related risky behaviors, chronic health conditions, and utilization of preventive health services. In 2017 (but before Hurricane Maria), BRFSS found that individuals in Puerto Rico were more likely to report having "fair or poor" health with 37 percent responding in this way compared to just 17.6 percent of those in the U.S. mainland. This rate is the highest across all states. Similar responses could only be found in the U.S. southern and Bible belt states with an average response of 23 percent.

BRFSS also found higher incidence rates of diabetes, hypertension, high cholesterol, obesity, as well as drinking and driving among Puerto Rico's residents than U.S. mainland respondents. Over 17 percent of respondents reported receiving a diagnosis of diabetes relative to only 10 percent of respondents in the U.S. mainland. West Virginia and Mississippi have the highest rates in the United States with rates of 15.2 and 14.2 percent, respectively. Similarly, 44.7 percent reported having hypertension in comparison with 33.2 percent in the United States. Puerto Rico has similar rates to Alabama, Arkansas, Mississippi, and West Virginia, which all have rates above 40 percent. Both groups of respondents had similar levels of drinking and depression, but Puerto Rican respondents admitted to driving while intoxicated 7.4 percent of the time, approximately twice the rate of respondents living stateside at 3.8 percent. Moreover, basic health statistics collected before Hurricane Maria reveal that Puerto Rico had higher rates of low birth weight, infant mortality, and HIV mortality in comparison to the U.S. average (Michaud and Kates 2017). In contrast, smoking rates are lower in Puerto Rico at 11.3 percent than the 17.1 percent in the 50 states plus DC.

Diabetes is a disease in which a person's blood sugar level is elevated due to the inability to produce enough insulin. Over time, elevated blood sugar levels damage the eyes, kidneys, and nerves. Diabetes is also associated with cardiovascular disease and can lead to skin ulcers that may progress to deeper bone infections requiring amputation of a limb. According to Puerto Rico's Departamento de Salud in 2010, diabetes-related mortality was equal to 81.6 per 100,000 people in Puerto Rico, but only 23.6 per 100,000 in the

U.S. mainland. Compared to all OECD countries, only Mexico had a higher diabetes incidence rate (152.1 diabetes-related deaths per 100,000) than Puerto Rico.

Because of these factors, the additional life longevity enjoyed by Puerto Ricans comes at the expense of additional years of experiencing chronic diseases. Island-born female Puerto Ricans and mainland-born male Puerto Ricans spend more years with morbidity than non-Hispanic whites (Garcia et al. 2018). This result partially reflects considerably higher rates of obesity and diabetes in these subpopulations coupled with longer life expectancy. More details on the health indicators among Puerto Ricans will be discussed by Rivera and colleagues in the following chapter.

HEALTHCARE ACCESS IN PUERTO RICO FOLLOWING HURRICANE MARIA

We have highlighted diabetes, obesity, and hypertension among Puerto Ricans as these diseases were most adversely affected by Hurricane Maria. A chronic illness needs frequent maintenance and access to healthcare providers. In the aftermath of Hurricane Maria, as discussed by Bill Chapell (2017), these patients could not receive the care they needed with the loss of communication systems, electricity (which as noted in previous chapters, took nearly a year to restore in some areas), and roadways (approximately 3 percent of which were drivable immediately following Hurricane Maria, according to the Government of Puerto Rico [2018]). Diabetes is a major risk factor for end-stage renal failure that requires dialysis to remove the toxins from the flood when a person's kidneys are incapable. Almost all of the island's 47 dialysis centers lost power as a result of Hurricane Maria and many had to rely on generators to operate during the recovery period (Michaud and Kates 2017).

As this chapter was finalized, the official government death count related to the hurricane stood at 2,975 deaths, but as Zadia M. Feliciano (chapter 3) pointed out, an official list of the names of the victims had yet to be released. Several reports placed the number of storm-related deaths even higher, including up to 4,645 people (Kishore et al. 2018; Santos-Lozada and Howard 2017, 2018). The excess number of deaths occurring after the hurricane related to the loss of electricity, clean water, food, medications, and housing—not from the direct impact when Hurricane Maria initially made landfall. In their estimates of the causes of the excessive deaths due to the hurricane, Raul Cruz-Cano and Erin Mead (2019) found that over 85 percent were people over the age of 60 years old. The three major disease-related deaths from Hurricane Maria were heart disease (21%), diabetes (16.2%), and Alzheimer's disease (10.1%). More will be discussed on the conditions that healthcare providers encountered after Maria in the following chapter by Fernando I. Rivera and colleagues.

HEALTHCARE SUPPLY IN PUERTO RICO AFTER HURRICANE MARIA

After the storm, most efforts on the island were concentrated on safety and recovery. Many hospitals operated on generators and virtually all the community centers were without power. Much of the data collection on health outcomes or healthcare units on the island entirely ceased. For this reason, the data available at the time this analysis was conducted were limited.

One reliable and available measure of healthcare supply in Puerto Rico is the number of healthcare establishments. These data are a panel of quarterly municipal-level observations from Puerto Rico between 2015 and 2018. For each quarter, we observe the average number of healthcare establishments as defined by the North American Industry Classification System (NAICS) in each municipality (*municipios* as they are known in Spanish). The NAICS code 62 refers to the Healthcare and Social Assistance industry sector, which is comprised of establishments providing healthcare and social assistance for individuals. Both healthcare and social assistance are included because it is sometimes difficult to distinguish between the boundaries of these two activities. The establishment count data are supplied by the Bureau of Labor and Statistics through the Quarterly Census of Employment and Wages (QCEW) database (the same database used in chapters 2 and 3). In addition, we collect data on total employment and average wages by sector.

The Healthcare and Social Assistance industry can be disaggregated into four major subgroups: (1) Ambulatory Services, (2) Hospitals, (3) Nursing and Residential Care, and (4) Social Assistance. The bulk of Ambulatory Services establishments is comprised of offices for primary care physicians, specialists, and dentists. However, Ambulatory Services also includes chiropractors, optometrists, mental health professionals, podiatrists, family planning offices, mental health and substance abuse centers, medical imaging and diagnostic laboratories, home healthcare services, physical therapists, occupational therapists, speech pathologist, blood/organ banks, and ambulances.

The Hospital sector includes general hospitals, psychiatric and substance abuse hospitals, and specialty hospitals. Nursing and Residential care includes skilled nurse facilities, assisted living and continued care communities, residential care for mental health and substance abuse patients, and residential care for individuals with intellectual disabilities or development disabilities. Finally, the Social Services sector covers a wide range of services for vulnerable groups but does not include medical services

Table 6.2 Healthcare Supply: United States and Puerto Rico in 2018

	Avg Weekly Wage		*Employees per 10,000 people*		*Establishments per 10,000 people*	
Industry	*U.S. Avg*	*PR*	*U.S. Avg*	*PR*	*U.S. Avg*	*PR*
Healthcare and Social Assistance	$1,075.44	$591.00	679.65	270.04	38.94	23.48
Ambulatory Services	$1,055.02	$589.00	226.85	117.62	18.56	19.55
Hospitals	$1,079.08	$625.67	208.37	102.40	0.48	0.30
Nursing and Residential Care	$589.76	$133.00	116.26	19.26	2.80	1.76
Social Assistance	$597.12	$443.75	121.87	34.63	17.10	1.87
Pharmaceutical Mfg.	$1,508.74	$1,169.00	7.66	44.22	0.14	0.16

Source: Author's estimates from the 2018 Quarterly Census of Employment and Wages from Bureau of Labor Statistics.

or long-term accommodations. The establishments provide food shelters, homeless shelters, soup kitchens, vocational training, childcare, senior citizen programs, adoption agencies, youth centers, and foster care placement services.

When comparing healthcare establishment between the U.S. mainland and the Commonwealth of Puerto Rico, we find Puerto Rico is both under supplied and underpaid (see table 6.2). Average pay across all healthcare sectors is nearly half (55%) of those in the United States. On average, a healthcare employee has a weekly pay of $591 compared to $1,075 (in 2017 dollars) on the U.S. mainland. The largest discrepancy is in Nursing and Residential care where the pay is 23 cents to the dollar. Consistent with the discussion earlier in this chapter on the island's healthcare undercoverage, these data also indicate that Puerto Rico has 60 percent of the number of establishments per 10,000 people (23.38 vs 38.94) and 40 percent of the number of employees per 10,000 people (270.04 vs 679.65) in healthcare compared to the U.S. mainland. Interestingly, Puerto Rico has about the same number of ambulatory services per capita as the mainland at 19 per 10,000, but only half (52%) of the staff. This statistic indicates sufficiency in the number of facilities, but these facilities are woefully understaffed.

There exist two challenges in identifying the effects of Hurricane Maria on healthcare supply in Puerto Rico. First, there is a concurrent downward trend of healthcare employment because of Puerto Rico's severe economic crisis and its debt crisis. Second, the timing of the hurricane in September 2017 makes annual data an unreliable measure. An advantage of using the QCEW database is that it contains quarterly data on these establishment counts. Therefore, the pre-hurricane period can be defined as up to the second quarter of 2017, the hurricane period as the third and fourth quarter of 2017, and the

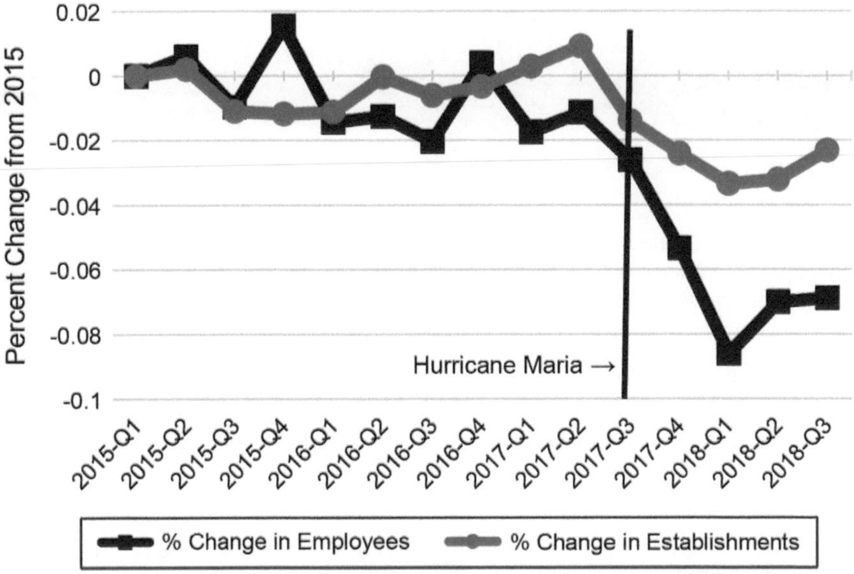

Figure 6.1 Effect of Hurricane Maria on Healthcare Supply in Puerto Rico: Employment and Establishments QI 2015–QIII 2018. *Source*: Author's estimates using the Quarterly Census of Employment and Wages 2015–2018.

post-hurricane period as the first quarter of 2018 and onward. These data help isolate the effect of the storm.

In figure 6.1, the percentages of the number of establishments and employment of the healthcare sector within Puerto Rico are presented relative to the base year of 2015. Immediately before Hurricane Maria, employment was down by 1 percent and the number of establishments was up 1 percent relative to 2015. However, both employment and establishments experienced a strong decrease in the latter two quarters of 2017—during and immediately after the hurricane. The number of establishments fell by 4.2 percent and employment fell by 7.2 percent.

The effects are disaggregated by subsector in table 6.1. Ambulatory Services demonstrate the same decreases as the overall healthcare sector with a 7.7-percent drop in employment and a 4.1-percent decrease in establishments. Nursing and Residential Care experienced a similar 7.7-percent drop in employment. Ironically, the sector most affected by the Hurricane Maria was the Social Assistance sector, which provides services when people are most in need. Employment in the social assistance sector fell by 12.1 percent and the number of establishments fell by 6.6 percent following Hurricane Maria. The number of healthcare establishments had yet to rebound after the hurricane, at least through 2018, but employment in this sector increased slightly by 2 percent.

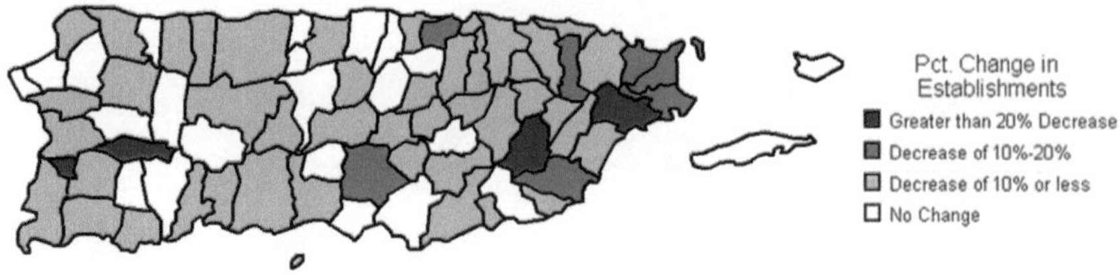

Figure 6.2 Percentage Changes in the Number of Healthcare Establishments by Municipality in Puerto Rico: Effect of Hurricane Maria. *Source*: Author's estimates using the Quarterly Census of Employment and Wages 2015–2018.

Next, the geographic effects of the Hurricane Maria on the supply of healthcare are considered. In figure 6.2, we map the change in establishment counts by municipality immediately before and after the hurricane. The largest changes occur all along the eastern coast, particularly around Yabucoa where the hurricane entered, and small areas within the center of Puerto Rico essentially along the path of the storm as the hurricane diagonally moved across the island before exiting in the northwest (recall figure 1.1). The San Lorenzo municipality lost over 30 percent of its healthcare establishments. The municipalities of Hormigueros, Luquillo, Maricao, and Naguabo each lost about 20 percent, and the municipalities of Canóvanas, Ceiba, Coamo, Fajardo, Toa Baja, and Yabucoa lost over 10 percent. In total, 33 of Puerto Rico's 78 municipalities lost 5 percent of their healthcare establishments or more.

Lastly, consider the pharmaceutical industry. In 2017, Puerto Rico had 50 pharmaceutical manufacturing plants and 30 medical device companies (Isidore, Kopan, and Horowitz 2017). The pharmaceutical industry comprised 30 percent of Puerto Rico's GDP, more than 50 percent of all manufacturing in Puerto Rico, and 25 percent of all U.S. pharmaceutical exports in 2016 (Puerto Rico Planning Board 2017). The pharmaceutical industry blossomed in Puerto Rico owing to a tax incentive known as Section 936 put into place in 1976, which allowed companies to send profits back to the U.S. mainland with zero federal tax liabilities. President Clinton signed a bill in 1996 that phased out Section 936 over 10 years, which, as discussed in chapter 1, was one of the causes of Puerto Rico's severe economic crisis and may have been the leading edge to the debt crisis (e.g., Schoen 2017). Recall it had the unintended consequence of reducing manufacturing labor in Puerto Rico by up to 40 percent and manufacturing wages (relative to the those on the U.S. mainland) by nearly 17 percent, among other outcomes (e.g., Feliciano and Green 2017; Schoen 2017; Caraballo-Cueto and Lara 2018).

Table 6.3 reports changes in pharmaceutical employment and establishments as a result of Hurricane Maria. Although the pharmaceutical

Table 6.3 The Effect of Hurricane Maria on Healthcare Employment and Establishments in Puerto Rico

	Employment			*Establishments*		
Industry	*2017 Q2*	*2017 Q4*	*Percent Change*	*2017 Q2*	*2017 Q4*	*Percent Change*
Healthcare and Social Assistance	91,390	84,821	−7.2%	7,749	7,426	−4.2%
Ambulatory Services	39,930	36,860	−7.7%	6,458	6,193	−4.1%
Hospitals	33,932	32,493	−4.2%	98	97	−1.0%
Nursing and Residential Care	6,580	6,072	−7.7%	554	539	−2.7%
Social Assistance	12,107	10,623	−12.3%	639	597	−6.6%
Pharmaceutical Mfg.	14,321	14,261	−0.4%	53	52	−1.9%

Source: Author's estimates using Quarterly Census of Employment and Wages from the Bureau of Labor Statistics.

manufacturing plants were affected, the scale of the effect is much smaller than that of the healthcare establishments. Employment decreased by less than half a percent and the number of plants decreased by 2 percent.

However, the total failure of Puerto Rico's power grid had lasting effects on pharmaceutical manufacturing as all the manufacturing plants became idle. In the months that followed, many companies had to rely on generators to keep their plants partially operating. These delays led to shortages for many common medicines. Hospitals faced shortages of intravenous (IV) saline and dextrose bags primarily produced in Puerto Rico and used to administer medicines and rehydrate patients. They are the foundation of basic IV compounding for hundreds of drugs that need further dilution, such as antibiotics, chemotherapy drugs, and electrolytes. The shortage of IV bags created a domino effect as drugs normally administered through an IV now needed to be injected, which led to a shortage of syringes, vials, and sterile water.

As this chapter was finalized, the disruption of the supply chain for drugs and medical devices produced in Puerto Rico was creating much concern on the U.S. mainland as well as the island. Decisions on how to move forward will surely have strong ramifications for the economic and health well-being of Puerto Rico and the general health of the entire United States.

DISCUSSION AND CONCLUDING REMARKS

To improve the health status of Puerto Ricans, there are three major changes that need to be accomplished. First, economic recovery is a necessary and priority goal not just for the health sector, but for the general economic well-being of the inhabitants of Puerto Rico. A major step to improve economic growth in Puerto Rico is a roll back of Section 936, which would allow the manufacturing sector of Puerto Rico to blossom again. Not only would this policy change increase employment, but it would also decrease reliance on publicly funded health insurance such as Medicare and Medicaid, and it would increase the tax base to help pay outstanding debts.

Second, the federal government needs to treat Puerto Rico equally to the U.S. states with respect to Medicaid. Medicaid reimbursement rates should not be capped; if anything, they should be the equivalent of those given to Mississippi, the poorest state in the union. Failure to do so not only reduces access to healthcare locally in Puerto Rico, but it also provides incentives for Puerto Rican healthcare workers and Puerto Rican working-class workers to leave the island. The healthcare workers can leave for greater pay and benefits in the states while the working poor in Puerto Rico can leave to receive Medicaid benefits denied to them in Puerto Rico.

Finally, the federal government should consider funding additional medical residency slots in Puerto Rico. Young physicians tend to practice relatively close to where they completed their residency training. Increasing the number of residency slots in Puerto Rico could aid in the recovery of longer-term healthcare shortages.

Chapter 7

The Health Profile of Puerto Ricans before and after Hurricane Maria

Fernando I. Rivera, Rebecca Sanchez Santiago, Valeria Quiñones Rodríguez, Veronica Arroyo Rodríguez, and Adriana Solla

ABSTRACT

This chapter discusses the health issues experienced by Puerto Ricans, both on the island and mainland, before and after Hurricane Maria. It also provides a comprehensive review of the literature on the health profile of Puerto Ricans. For years, Puerto Ricans have displayed unfavorable health conditions, conditions that were exacerbated by Hurricane Maria. This chapter argues it is imperative to improve the socioeconomic and health conditions for Puerto Ricans on the island and mainland, and to increase their access to quality and culturally sensitive healthcare.

The delineation point for the history of Puerto Rico for years to come will be September 20, 2017. Significant attention (including by other authors in this volume) has been put on the conditions of the island after the hurricane and the fortunes of those who were displaced by the storm. However, much of the perceived misfortunes for Puerto Ricans after the storm were the results of years of economic struggles that fueled extensive out-migration to the continental United States (Mora, Dávila and Rodríguez 2017a). One particular outcome that has been impacted by these struggles is the health of the Puerto Rican community, which is the emphasis of this chapter and complements the previous chapter by Jose M. Fernandez. Specifically, this chapter discusses the health issues experienced by Puerto Ricans, both stateside and on the island, before Hurricane Maria, for the period 2014–2017, and post-Maria through 2018. The chapter concludes with a discussion of the key health implications facing Puerto Ricans.

BACKGROUND ON PUERTO RICAN HEALTH

There is extensive evidence that Puerto Rican health is characterized by high levels of chronic disease, disability, and other unfavorable physical and mental health outcomes, particularly when compared to other Latinx subgroups in the United States (Rivera and Burgos 2010). Similarly, island Puerto Rican health outcomes are unfavorable with high rates of cardiovascular disease risk factors (Daviglus et al. 2012), obesity (Isasi et al. 2015), asthma (Szentpetery et al. 2016), and other mental health outcomes (Rivera, Molina and Nicado 2019).

Latinx groups, primarily recent Mexican immigrants to the United States, benefit from strong protective familial and social support, a term coined as the Latino (or Hispanic) Health Paradox. However, ample evidence suggests that Puerto Ricans do not benefit from these protective mechanisms when moving or living in the continental United States (Acevedo-Garcia and Bates 2007; Rivera and Burgos 2010). Nonetheless, a recent comparative review of psychiatric disorders among mainland and island Puerto Ricans found that social support was an important factor in reducing rate differences between the two groups (Canino et al. 2019).

Several explanations have been put forward to understand these phenomena, including cultural practices (Rivera et al. 2008), perceived discrimination (Rivera et al. 2011), and prejudice (Aranda and Rivera, 2016). The strongest empirical evidence suggests that the main driver of these health disadvantages is the less than favorable socioeconomic conditions that Puerto Ricans experience both on the mainland and island (Rivera et al. 2008; Alarcon et al. 2016). These past results provide the backdrop for the health review of this chapter. We begin by summarizing research findings from studies before Hurricane Maria, between 2014 and 2017.

PRE-HURRICANE MARIA HEALTH OUTCOMES (2014–2017)

Physical Health

In a 2017 article, Burgos, Rivera, and Garcia reviewed the research literature from 1999 to 2017 with regards to physical health outcomes among Puerto Ricans living on the U.S. mainland in comparison to other groups. Their review found that Puerto Ricans reported higher rates of poor health across various health outcomes compared to other groups, including a higher prevalence of diabetes, hypertension, self-reported bronchitis, higher body mass index (BMI) levels, and higher prevalence of asthma.

According to health statistics published by the Kaiser Family Foundation, 34 percent of Puerto Ricans on the island reported having poor general health in comparison with 13 percent of participants from the continental United States (Kaiser Family Foundation, 2016). Some of the health issues experienced in Puerto Rico could be a result of several factors including, but not limited to, climate, environmental conditions, diet, and social status. As noted in the previous chapter by Fernandez, one of the major health problems that most residents of Puerto Rico face are chronic diseases, such as diabetes, hypertension, respiratory, and cardiovascular conditions. Moreover, there was an increase of 2.2 percent of adults diagnosed with diabetes mellitus between 2011 and 2014, primarily among women (Centers for Disease Control and Prevention [CDC], 2017).

Another important chronic disease seen in all ages is the chronic obstructive pulmonary disease. In 2014, it was reported that 3.8 percent of the island population confirmed being diagnosed with this condition, with the majority being women (CDC, 2017). This condition along with several other respiratory and pulmonary diseases is expected to be prevalent on the island due to the high level of environmental contamination as well as the yearly Saharan Air Layer that hits Puerto Rico due to its extremely high temperatures and humid weather during certain times of the year.

It is also worth highlighting that in 2015, the CDC along with the Puerto Rico Department of Health confirmed the first case of Zika virus infection on the island. By the end of 2016, around 34,060 cases and five deaths were reported as a result of this endemic disease (Pan-American Health Organization). However, less publicized was that a year before Puerto Rico's confirmation of being affected by the Zika, approximately 26,000 residents had already gone through similar circumstances with the appearance of a new mosquito bite infection called the Chikungunya (Department of Health. Statistics, registry and publications).

Mental Health

The 2016 report by the Administration of Mental Health and Anti-Addiction Services (ASSMCA) on serious mental illnesses in Puerto Rico estimated that approximately 7.3 percent or 165,497 Puerto Ricans between the ages 18 and 64 had a serious mental illness (ASSMCA 2016). The report also found that the most common disorders in Puerto Rico were anxiety disorders and mood disorders, and women were more likely than men to be diagnosed with general anxiety disorder, major depression, and dysthymia (ASSMCA 2016). Another study on Puerto Rican elders revealed a 19.7 percent rate of depression (Serra-Taylor and Irizarry-Robles, 2015).

Mental illnesses, such as depression, are associated with certain elements and stressors. Many Puerto Ricans on the island are exposed to poverty and unemployment (Caetano et al. 2016). Other factors that might influence mental health are the decrease in population, abuse, inaccessible healthcare, economic crisis, and high crime rates (Canino et al. 2019).

Nonetheless, prevalence rates for mental illness in Puerto Rico are similar to those in the U.S. mainland (Canino et al. 2019). Glorisa Canino and her colleagues (2019) found that island Puerto Ricans have more social support than the general population in the United States as well as Puerto Ricans living in the continental United States. This could relate to the higher incidence of mainland Puerto Ricans having a higher risk of anxiety and mood disorders due to increased risk of facing stressors, such as discrimination and the loss of social support.

THE IMPACT OF HURRICANE MARIA ON HEALTH ACCESS AND OUTCOMES

Hurricane Maria struck Puerto Rico on September 20, 2017. As noted throughout this volume, as a Category 4 hurricane with winds up to 155 miles per hour, Hurricane Maria devastated the island, leaving its then 3.3 million residents without electricity and means of communication. It lasted approximately 17 hours and featured rivers overflowing and flooding in multiple areas. As Puerto Ricans on the island endured the storm, family members and friends living across the continental United States watched in horror as images of the destruction provided by news outlets came on an hourly basis. As a result, the subsequent Puerto Rican diaspora had higher levels of post-traumatic stress disorder (PTSD) symptoms than those of island Puerto Ricans (Scaramutti, Vos, Salas-Wright, and Schwartz 2018).

Furthermore, comparisons indicate that those living in rural areas in Puerto Rico had greater levels of PTSD (66.7% vs 48.8%) and anxiety (41.4% vs 23.5%) than those living in the urban metropolitan areas (Scaramutti et al., 2019). Conditions in rural areas were characterized by the feeling of being farther away from help as well as experiencing poor living conditions, such as weak wooden houses. Moreover, the rural areas were among those without electricity, running water, and telecommunications for the longest amounts of time, including waiting for up to nearly a year to have electricity restored. We also know from Fernandez in the previous chapter that the areas along Hurricane Maria's path across the island were among the hardest hit in terms of the closure of healthcare establishments. The economic damage was estimated at more than $94 billion, with a recovery marked by inefficiency and confusion (e.g., Rivera and Rivera 2019).

The health consequences were devastating, particularly the death toll associated with the lack of electricity and medical care. An initial official death toll of 64 that stood for several months was later refuted by a public health study which estimated the death toll close to 4,000 deaths (Kishore et al. 2018). Subsequently, based on a study commissioned by the Government of Puerto Rico, the government put the official estimated death toll at 2,975 deaths (Santos-Burgoa et al. 2018). Both estimates attest to the significant pressure that Hurricane Maria put on the island's fragile healthcare system.

The situation was described by Jesse Roman as follows:

> Emergency rooms were rendered inoperative and hospitals were forced to close surgical suites. Patients incapable of fending for themselves were transferred to other locations when possible. Clinics remained closed, while patients waiting for dialysis, chemotherapy, and transfusions became impatient. For those with chronic respiratory disorders, the lack of electricity to power mechanical ventilators, oxygen concentrators, and nebulizers further exacerbated their anxiety and their conditions. (Roman 2018, p. 293)

In these pressing circumstances, health providers had to adapt, and the documentation of their experiences varied. For instance, the Auxilio Mutuo Hospital in San Juan was able to remain open with the use of generators and a water well to take care of transplant patients. To communicate with patients, they relied on the work of a FEMA employee that happened to be a former transplant nurse. She had access to central operations and was able to identify transplant patients with the most critical needs and coordinated transportation to the hospital (Pullen 2018).

With the lack of electricity and communication, access to medication became problematic. In an article detailing the response of pharmacists in Puerto Rico after Hurricane Maria, Melin, Maldonado, and Lopez-Candales (2018) described the conditions experienced by community pharmacies, which included a loss of energy, supply of medicines, and access to patient medication records. They also detailed the response of pharmacists to continue to provide medication under extraordinary circumstances. For instance, a pharmacy in the mountain town of Lares dispensed medications for almost a month without receiving any payments from patients or insurance companies. To provide services without access to electricity (hence no electronic records), the pharmacist created handwritten notices of payment to clients to pay later when electricity was restored. The authors recommended establishing a system where nonnarcotic prescriptions can be dispensed when prescribing physicians are not available as well as emergency protocols for medication reimbursement during a crisis.

Internal medicine residents at the University Hospital of Adults at the Puerto Rico Medical Center found themselves improvising their response with limited disaster medicine instruction in their internal medicine training curriculum (Hernandez-Suárez et al. 2018). They were able to put together a response plan that was successful in meeting the circumstances they faced, including property loss; lack of communication; and difficult access to fuel, transportation, and food.

Radiation oncology centers suffered the same challenges caused by a lack of electricity, communication, and transportation of resources for patients (Lopez-Araujo and Burnett, 2017). Some lessons learned for radiation oncology providers include establishing a preparation plan to deal with the conditions faced after a major hurricane, such as the inability to obtain and store fuel, lack of communication, transportation challenges, and the emotional fatigue experienced by providers (Gay et al. 2019). On this last aspect, a personal narrative captures the scope of the circumstances faced by providers:

> It was very difficult to balance the crisis in our homes: without water and without power, in my case for 40 days, the long lines at the very few gas stations open, lack of groceries in supermarkets, rationing of bottled water, and many other things that I do not even want to remember. Because of the crisis, one did things automatically. If you thought about it a lot, you would fall into depression. In addition, we spent a lot of time without receiving payment from medical plans and the little money we had was used for major repairs and payroll. As of today, the insurance has not paid us a penny for the substantial material losses and damages to the equipment. (Gay et al. 2019, p. e15)

It should also be noted that a consequence of the use of generators as sources of electricity in the aftermath of Hurricane Maria was an increase in air pollution. A group of researchers (Subramanian et al. 2018) deployed air quality monitors in San Juan and found significant air pollution well beyond Environmental Protection Agency safety thresholds.

Suicides Post-Hurricane Maria

Two months after Hurricane Maria, 32 suicides were reported (Dickerson 2017). From September 2017 to December 2017, there was a 55 percent increase in the suicide rate for that time of year as well as a 29 percent increase in the annual suicide rate (Aponte 2018). The majority of the suicide victims were in their late 50s. Puerto Rico already had preexisting issues with poor disease management, with some of the leading causes being type II diabetes and Alzheimer's, which might have been contributing factors to why these victims decided to make such a decision (Downer et al.

2019). Moreover, calls to Puerto Rico's main suicide hotline, Línea PAS, more than doubled within six months after the hurricane, and one of Puerto Rico's biggest mental health centers, located at the Ponce Health Sciences University, treated several thousand patients per month (Jervis 2018). It seems that Hurricane Maria was the spark that exacerbated these symptoms, even among those who had not previously reported feeling anxious or depressed (Michaud 2017).

Restoration and Status of Healthcare Services Post-Maria

A month after Hurricane Maria, 89 percent of health centers were operating; however, they were working under unfavorable conditions as demonstrated by the examples provided earlier in this chapter (see also Shin et al. 2017). Furthermore, only 13 percent of 70 centers visited by Peter Shin and his colleagues had their power restored by mid-October (Shin et al. 2017). On top of the evident lack of electricity, health centers were in urgent need of vaccines and drugs, and many saw an elevated risk of infectious disease (including but not limited to Zika, influenza, dengue, asthma, and acute infections). These problems were present well before the hurricane, and the storm accelerated the process. As Fernandez discussed in the previous chapter, Puerto Rico is medically underserved, suffering from a lack of doctors and medical resources.

One year after Hurricane Maria, community health centers had increased the number of patients they treated, and a majority of their illnesses were chronic diseases that had regressed because of a lack of "treatment management" (most likely caused by the lack of medical aid immediately after the hurricane). However, health centers had increased their staff numbers and were better suited to meet patient needs pertaining to basic primary care. Still, many patients who needed more complex forms of treatment are at a loss as private healthcare providers have fled to the U.S. mainland (as noted in the previous chapter). Because health centers do not have the necessary resources to treat such patients, they must rely on referrals to specialized provider services. These referrals were already limited before the hurricane and increasingly depleted afterward. The referrals then (and up through at the time this chapter was finalized) prove rather meaningless as specialized doctors and caretakers reside in the U.S. mainland, with the neediest of patients not being able to reach them (Shin et al. 2017).

In the months following Hurricane Maria, the exodus of private healthcare providers from Puerto Rico to the mainland increased, resulting in a greater lack of individualized healthcare and treatment for complex conditions such as diabetes and dialysis. Community health centers simply do not have the necessary resources to accommodate patients with these conditions.

As the Medicaid "fiscal cliff" was approaching in September 2019, the progress that had been made on the island was expected to deteriorate and a more deteriorated healthcare system would be exposed (Hall et al. 2019). As discussed in the previous chapter, federal Medicaid funding goes uncapped and a 100 percent match is guaranteed in the states; however, as a commonwealth, Puerto Rico is not able to reap the same benefits. Medicaid only matches 55 percent of medical bills and has a cap of how much money can be given in Puerto Rico (Hall et al. 2019). After Hurricane Maria, the federal government made an exception for both Puerto Rico and the U.S. Virgin Islands, allowing them to receive the same Medicaid plan as the states, but this exception ended in 2019. This is especially important considering that a large segment of the island population relies on Medicaid for their health insurance (49 percent of island residents are more likely to rely on Medicaid compared to 20 percent in the U.S. mainland) (Hall et al. 2019).

LIFESTYLE FACTORS AFFECTING THE HEALTH STATUS OF PUERTO RICANS

Many believe that the true testament to defining the struggles of a country after a natural disaster is the change in the physical health of its citizens. Unfortunately, there was no baseline of data in regards to the physical health of Puerto Ricans before Hurricane Maria. Certain health disparities and results have been published since the hurricane made landfall in late 2017. As many medical researchers expected, Puerto Ricans living on the island suffered a considerably higher death rate than those living in the U.S. mainland, with most deaths resulting in complications from chronic diseases (including but not limited to diabetes, kidney disease, pneumonia, influenza, and cancer). These findings can be attributed to the diminishing number of healthcare providers on the island. Health centers do not have the necessary resources to treat patients with individualized care for their complex conditions. Puerto Ricans both on the island and mainland (in contrast to the Latino Health Paradox) rank among having the highest health risks for racial and ethnic groups in the United States (especially for diabetes).

A 2018 study published by Taylor et al. in the *Journal of Health Disparities Research and Practice* analyzed four lifestyle factors that were part of the Healthy People 2010 goals: tobacco use, BMI, physical activity, and fruit/vegetable consumption. Lifestyle factors and behaviors are important indicators for the physical health trends of a population. The authors found that not a single country met the Healthy People 2010 goals for all lifestyle factors; however, Puerto Rico had the worst results in terms of meeting the goals.

With a continual lack of federal government funding for Puerto Rican healthcare, these results are expected to deteriorate.

Most recently, a cross-sectional study was conducted by Mattei and her colleagues in 2018 to better understand the health and lifestyle risk factors of Puerto Ricans living on the island. The authors surveyed 380 individuals, the majority of were women and middle-aged individuals. The results showed that Puerto Ricans have an increased chance of having chronic disease because of their lifestyle choices (sedentary lifestyle, ignoring medical advice for better diet and exercise, etc.). Perhaps a more important factor toward understanding the causes of the results produced by the study is the lack of economic stability among those surveyed. Almost half of the participants reported receiving government food assistance and had a low annual household income even though many had earned a college education or higher.

It is evident that Puerto Ricans have suffered from less than favorable physical health outcomes, even before Hurricane Maria. Sadly, in its aftermath, these trends are expected to worsen.

HEALTH TRENDS AND CONTEXTUAL FACTORS AFFECTING THE HEALTH OF PUERTO RICANS

For years, Puerto Ricans have displayed unfavorable health conditions and recent evidence suggests that Hurricane Maria exacerbated those conditions. Based on the review of the evidence presented in this chapter, there are some overarching conclusions regarding the health of Puerto Ricans.

Alarming Health Trends

This chapter demonstrates the unfavorable health that Puerto Ricans continue to experience. These alarming trends, which Hurricane Maria exacerbated and brought to the forefront, are longer-term results, including from Puerto Rico's severe economic recession that started in 2006, impacting several social determinants of health such as low income, unsafe neighborhoods, and substandard education (Center for Disease Control and Prevention, 2018). Unfavorable socioeconomic conditions often translate into poor health conditions such as the ones experienced by Puerto Ricans. According to the U.S. Census Bureau's American Community Survey, in 2017, 43.1 percent of persons in Puerto Rico lived in poverty with a median household income of $19,775 (U.S. Census, 2019a). A 2019 report by Brian Glassman indicates that Puerto Rico's poverty rate remained higher than the U.S. national rate of 13.1 percent and was almost double the highest state poverty rate (Mississippi) at 19.7 percent. The poverty rate for stateside Puerto Ricans in

2017, while lower than on the island, stood at 22.5 percent, a significantly higher percentage than the overall U.S. population.

Contextual issues are also important. While socioeconomic conditions tend to be higher for stateside Puerto Ricans with a median household income of $44,731 in 2017 (U.S. Census Bureau 2019b), there is no discernable health advantage as discussed earlier in this chapter, which sometimes comes at the expense of losing important protective factors, such as extended family social support, and social capital networks. In addition, exposure to discriminatory experiences impacts health outcomes as well. For instance, disability rates in the 2017 American Community Survey (U.S. Census Bureau 2019c) were 12.7 percent for the U.S. population and 14.8 percent for stateside Puerto Ricans. In Puerto Rico, the disability rate was 15.2 percent (U.S. Census Bureau 2019a).[1]

Inequality is an important predictor of health outcomes that might be the result of the alarming health trends that Puerto Ricans continue to experience. In his seminal work, Michael Marmot (2004) suggested that higher socioeconomic status allowed individuals to have better living conditions and greater access to social and human capital resources, which in turn lead to better health. This theory, better known as the social gradient, posits a social class gradient to health in which those at the top of the hierarchy experience better health, while those below and each subsequent social class gradient experience less favorable health. Previous research has found a strong association between low socioeconomic status and health outcomes among Puerto Ricans (Alegría et al. 2007; Rivera et al. 2008). This association is also indicative of the effect of the overrepresentation of Puerto Ricans in unfavorable socioeconomic conditions, such as poverty and low levels of education, among others (Acosta-Belén and Santiago 2006).

Unfortunately, inequality continues to expand in the United States and Puerto Rico. A recent report by the U.S. Census Bureau states that income inequality, as measured by the Gini Index, increased from 2017 to 2018. Puerto Rico and the District of Columbia had the highest Gini indexes, and Florida (which as noted in chapter 1 by Mora, Rodríguez, and Dávila, now has more Puerto Ricans than any other state) had higher Gini indexes than the index for the United States overall (Guzman, 2019).

DISCUSSION AND CONCLUDING REMARKS

At all levels, Hurricane Maria inflicted a devastating blow to the health of Puerto Ricans, from the elevated death count, the healthcare complications resulting from lack of electricity and communication, to the collective trauma experienced during and after the hurricane. This was in addition to the increase in the number of suicides and the massive net out-migration leaving a shrinking and rapidly aging population behind. In all, the hurricane exposed the frail conditions of the infrastructure of the island, including the power grid, roads, healthcare facilities, and communication systems. This failure contributed to lingering health issues beyond the immediate impact of the storm. They were the result of a long economic recession surging for more than a decade before Hurricane Maria, previous fiscal management, and a less than favorable health profile.

Hurricane Maria also affected those displaced to the continental United States, particularly in Florida. For instance, Ariana Valle (2018) analyzed data from 17 in-depth interviews with Puerto Ricans displaced by Hurricane Maria in the Orlando, Florida, metropolitan area (the largest receiving area of Puerto Rican migrants from the island, as noted in chapter 1). She found that some respondents were dealing with the trauma of experiencing the hurricane itself in addition to experiencing trying living conditions after the storm and moving to the mainland with health conditions that could not be treated in Puerto Rico. Another study by Scaramutti and colleagues (2019), with a sample of participants of Puerto Ricans in Florida and Puerto Rico six months after Hurricane Maria, found that those who migrated to Florida reported higher severity of PTSD symptoms and were more likely to meet the corresponding clinical criteria than those who stayed in Puerto Rico.

Rosaura Orengo-Aguayo and colleagues (2019) also found high levels of reported PTSD and depression symptoms among a sample of public school students in Puerto Rico. More insights into how Hurricane Maria affected mental health conditions of Puerto Ricans are discussed by Amy Nitza and Shao Lin as well as by María Rolón-Martínez and her colleagues in the next two chapters. Three years after the hurricane struck, Puerto Rico remained too early to assess its long-term impacts on the health of Puerto Ricans. Based on the evidence reviewed and past health trends, it is more than likely that Puerto Ricans will continue to have unfavorable health outcomes for the foreseeable future.

Implications

Puerto Ricans continue to experience a less than favorable health profile. The evidence discussed in this chapter suggests the profound impact that the hurricane had and will continue to have in the future on the Puerto Rican community on the island and the mainland. Attention must be paid to the socioeconomic conditions that Puerto Ricans experience stateside and on the island. As suggested, these conditions are important determinants of health, and policies that emphasize access to healthcare are warranted and welcomed. Perhaps it is time to emphasize health reforms that consider the improvement of living conditions and access to healthier lifestyles that higher socioeconomic conditions tend to facilitate.

On the surface, it seems that Puerto Ricans are entrapped in a never-ending circle of unfavorable health outcomes. Further, there is no discernible evidence that moving to the continental United States will improve health outcomes, perhaps because they may lose the social support when they move that has served as a protector for mental health on the island. There is also evidence of the resilience of Puerto Ricans in coping with the aftermath of Hurricane Maria.

Much work needs to be done to reverse the unfavorable health outcomes that Puerto Ricans continue to experience. These include reforms to improve the socioeconomic conditions of both island and stateside Puerto Ricans. Access to quality and culturally sensitive care for those already experiencing health and mental health conditions could be provided. Finally, there must be a realization that reducing inequality is likely to improve the health profile of Puerto Ricans.

NOTE

1. In addition, some studies suggest that mainland Puerto Ricans are chronic over-utilizers of health services, and at the same time, the uninsured health rate remains low in Puerto Rico (Perreira et al., 2017). This low rate is due to a healthcare reform that provides access to healthcare for island Puerto Ricans. This reform continues to add to the increased public debt but there is no clear indication that it has helped improve the health profile of Puerto Rico.

Chapter 8

Expected Impacts and Consequences of Hurricane Maria and Power Outages on Mental Health and Other Morbidity in Puerto Rico

Current Status and Lessons Learned from the Past

Amy Nitza and Shao Lin

ABSTRACT

This chapter reviews the mental health and health risks associated with Hurricane Maria on the Puerto Rican population and describes ongoing mental health recovery efforts in Puerto Rico. The unique factors of this particular disaster along with the response that followed are also discussed, taking into account family and school environments along with social support. Moreover, based on studies of the health impacts of Hurricane Sandy, this chapter discusses how the lessons learned from that event might apply to the impact and recovery from Hurricane Maria in Puerto Rico.

The mental health and health impacts of natural disasters such as hurricanes are increasingly recognized as a key consideration throughout all phases of disaster response and recovery. The factors that affect mental health outcomes postdisaster allow for targeted interventions to those most in need. The size and scope of Hurricane Maria contributed to a sustained risk for mental health problems for survivors and created a need for ongoing systems of mental health support as a component of the overall recovery efforts.

The extreme level of devastation of Hurricane Maria (outlined in previous chapters), sustained over such a long period, suggests that almost everyone in Puerto Rico has been affected in some way. As this chapter was finalized, the island continued to be recovering more than three years after Hurricane Maria, in the midst of other ongoing complex economic and political circumstances as well as the 2020 earthquakes and the emergence of the COVID-19 pandemic. The combination of these stressors has culminated in what Puerto Rican psychologist Eduardo Lugo has referred to as a mental health pandemic (Garofalo, 2020). As such, it is essential that mental health recovery be included in all aspects of the long-term recovery effort (including for Puerto Ricans on the mainland whom were also affected by Hurricane Maria, as discussed by Fernando I. Rivera and colleagues in the previous chapter).

This chapter describes how the unique factors of this particular disaster in the context of Puerto Rico, and of the response that followed, played a role in the mental health impact on Puerto Ricans. As part of this discussion, we consider the role of family and school environments along with other forms of social support. We also review studies on the health impacts of Hurricane Sandy that struck the U.S. northeast coast in October 2012, and consider how the resulting power outages and environmental changes might apply to the impact and recovery from Hurricane Maria in Puerto Rico. We conclude with considerations for the ongoing psychosocial recovery efforts across the island.

CONTEXTUAL CONSIDERATIONS: PUERTO RICO BEFORE THE STORM

As with any disaster, the mental health impacts of Hurricane Maria in Puerto Rico can only be fully understood by considering the context in which it occurred. As noted by Amy Nitza (2019):

> Community reactions to tragedy reflect and are shaped by the social and political forces around them. Pre-existing social inequities continue to play out in the aftermath of a disaster. Because traumatic experiences induce a sense of powerlessness and loss of control (both real and perceived), an individual's understanding of a traumatic event will be shaped by their experiences of privilege, oppression, colonization, and other social factors. (p. 133)

In this way, the sociopolitical and economic situation in Puerto Rico prior to Hurricane Maria heavily influenced the recovery climate and the experiences of individuals, families, and communities. It is worth noting that the political protests and governmental transitions on the island in 2019 and the related chaos surrounding the 2020 primary election, which was unfolding when finalizing this chapter, will also likely shape the recovery context in as-yet undocumented ways.

As described by Marie Mora, Alberto Dávila, and Havidán Rodríguez (2017a)—and noted throughout this volume—Hurricane Maria made landfall on an island that was already experiencing:

> . . . massive outmigration on a scale not seen for 60 years; a shrinking and rapidly aging population; a shutdown of high-tech industries; a significant loss in public and private sector jobs; a deteriorating infrastructure, including education, health care, and public utilities; higher sales taxes than any of the states; $74 billion in public debt plus another $49 billion in pension obligations; and defaults on payments to bondholders. (p. xvii)

The storm devastated an island in the midst of a humanitarian crisis unfolding for over a decade, exacerbating the crisis and creating what can be referred to as an "acute-on-chronic" stress situation. The extent of this crisis heightened the vulnerability of already socioeconomically vulnerable groups, and put many others at risk leaving the island, both the people and the infrastructure, with diminished capacity for resilience in the face of such a massive disaster.

The sociopolitical relationship of Puerto Rico to the United States has also shaped response and recovery efforts. For example, as described by Mora, Dávila, and Rodríguez (2017a), the delay in temporarily waiving the Jones Act restrictions that were hindering relief efforts "exemplified the complicated relationship Puerto Rico has with the United States" (p. xxiv). Comparisons by the media of the federal government responses to Hurricanes Maria in Puerto Rico and Harvey in Texas, which occurred less than 30 days apart, revealed troubling disparities that furthered popular perceptions that the people of Puerto Rico were receiving a substandard response from the federal government as compared to those in Texas. A report published in 2018 by *Politico* concluded:

> No two hurricanes are alike, and Harvey and Maria were vastly different storms that struck areas with vastly different financial, geographic and political situations. But a comparison of government statistics relating to the two recovery efforts strongly supports the views of disaster-recovery experts that FEMA and the Trump administration exerted a faster, and initially greater, effort in Texas, even though the damage in Puerto Rico exceeded that in Houston. (Vinik, 2018)

This seemingly disparate treatment only served to further the view of injustice on an island that some have noted experienced colonization, formally or informally, from the arrival of Christopher Columbus in 1493 through to the present day. Consider also the establishment in 2016 of the federal oversight board appointed under the Puerto Rico Oversight, Management, and Economic Stability Act (recall chapter 1) stripped the elected government of much of its financial authority that created an additional layer of complexity and confusion in the response to Hurricane Maria.

MENTAL HEALTH RISKS

While most people who live through a natural disaster experience some type of post-traumatic reactions, for most survivors these symptoms will dissipate over time. Only a percentage will go on to develop psychopathology that meets criteria for a psychiatric disorder. What is more, rates of postdisaster psychopathology generally decrease over time (Norris, Friedman, and Watson, 2002). Nevertheless, for those who develop a psychiatric illness, the symptoms can be long lasting and debilitating, resulting in impairments in their ability to work, maintain relationships, and otherwise function in life (Halpern and Vermeulen, 2017). Post-traumatic stress disorder, major depressive disorder, complicated/traumatic grief, and increased substance use (particularly among those with a previous history of substance abuse) are among the severe reactions that can be debilitating to survivors if not properly identified and treated.

The severity of the mental health impact of a disaster on any individual is the result of a combination of factors of both the individual and the environment. Environmental factors contribute to an individual's level of distress in a dose-response relationship, with dose being composed of scope, intensity, and duration, or "how big, how bad, and how long" the disaster was for any individual (Halpern and Vermeulen, 2017). The larger the dose of the disaster an individual experiences, the greater the psychological impact is likely to be. From this perspective, prolonged challenges in the recovery environment result in exposure to a greater dose of the event and thus to more prolonged mental health symptoms.

Hobfoll and colleagues (2007) further explicated the aspects of disasters that increase the intensity of their impact on the mental health of individuals and communities. In addition to the circumstances of the disaster itself (experiencing or witnessing physical and psychological pain, loss, and destruction), the loss of resources in the recovery environment inhibits recovery capacity, particularly in settings that were already suffering from depleted resources (both economic and psychosocial). What is more "the loss, or threatened loss, of attachment bonds that occurs in disaster and instances of mass casualty comes close in its intensity and effect to the previous elements of witnessing horrors and direct personal threats" (Hobfoll et al., 2007, p. 285). A loss of territory or physical space through destruction, relocation, or ongoing threats is an additional risk factor. Finally, many survivors also struggle with issues of meaning and justice following disasters. The intensity and duration of the impact of Hurricane Maria in Puerto Rico, the complexity of the ongoing recovery environment, and the extent of both physical and relational losses mean that much of the island is facing many of these risk factors for negative mental health outcomes.

Direct Impact of the Disaster and Subsequent Resource Loss

As noted previously, the physical devastation of Hurricane Maria was experienced to some degree by almost everyone on the island. Recent research has documented the extent to which children across Puerto Rico experienced direct exposure. A survey of over 96,000 public school students in grades 3–12 completed 5–9 months after the hurricane (Orengo-Aguayo et al., 2019), which will be further discussed by María Rolón-Martínez, Joy Lynn Suárez-Kindy, and Rosaura Orengo-Aguayo in the following chapter, found that 29.9 percent of respondents perceived their lives to be at risk, 45.7 percent reported damage to their own homes, and 83.9 percent saw homes damaged. Sixteen percent reported having a family member, friend, or neighbor injured, while 6.6 percent had a family member, friend, or neighbor who died as a result of the storm.

A large number of children also experienced subsequent resource loss related to the devastation. In the survey of public school students cited above, 32.3 percent experienced shortages of food or water after the storm, and 16.7 percent still had no electricity five to nine months posthurricane (Orengo-Aguayo et al., 2019). A survey of families with children under the age of 18 published by the Instituto Desarrollo Juventud (Estudios Técnicos, Inc. and University of Puerto Rico, Río Piedras, 2019) found that families were without electricity for an average of 103 days (nearly 3.5 months) and were without water service for an average of 55 days (just under two months). A large number of survivors struggled with access to shelter for an extended time as well. For example, Pietri et al. (2018) reported that seven months after the storm, over 2,500 families remained in temporary housing across Puerto Rico and 34 states.

Negative post-trauma reactions tend to persist under conditions of ongoing threat; these reactions are gradually reduced once safety is restored (Hobfoll et al., 2007). As these statistics suggest, the extensive damage caused by Hurricane Maria and the slow rebuilding and recovery created an environment of prolonged instability and insecurity which included not only extensive damage to homes and communities but also lengthy periods of time without access to basic needs conducive to psychosocial recovery. The severity of distress experienced by Puerto Ricans is reflected in an escalation in suicide rates on the island five to seven months after the storm (recall Fernando I. Rivera and colleagues also discussed this escalation in the previous chapter). Cases of suicide nearly doubled, from 16 to 30, between August 2017 (the month before the storm) and April 2018 (Pietri et al., 2018; Departamento de Salud, 2018). A related measure is the number of calls taken by Linea Pas, the suicide prevention hotline in Puerto Rico, which more than doubled, from 1,264 to 2,996, between August 2017 and November 2017. The number of calls peaked at 3,473 calls in January 2018, tripling the August 2017 number (Departamento de Salud, 2018).[1]

Social Support

There is a substantial body of research documenting the importance of social support and sustained attachments in buffering the effects of disaster exposure and trauma (Norris et al., 2002). Numerous studies from around the world have demonstrated that increased social support is related to better recovery following mass trauma (Hobfoll et al., 2007). The high levels of net out-migration before the hurricane, which as discussed by Mora, Rodríguez, and Dávila (chapter 1), further intensified in the year after the storm, combined with other social disruptions such as the extent of school closures described below, have likely affected many Puerto Ricans' perceptions of their social support. These changes have important implications for the mental health of those who remained in Puerto Rico as well as those who migrated to the mainland.

Reduced levels of social support and disruptions in attachment relationships may have particularly affected Puerto Rican children (a topic also discussed in the following chapter). For example, recent studies have found that nearly one-third of families reported their intent to migrate as a result of the hurricane, and nearly 6 in 10 (57.8%) of children indicated having a friend or family member leave the island (Estudios Técnicos, Inc. and University of Puerto Rico, Río Piedras, 2019; Orengo-Aguayo et al., 2019). Children are also affected by the impact of the event on their support systems, including their families and schools (Bonanno et al., 2010).

The Family Environment

There is a well-established positive relationship between parental stress levels and children's levels of psychosocial distress symptoms post-disaster. This stems from not only to shared exposure to trauma but also to parental levels of stress in dealing with the demands of the recovery environment. While no published studies have been identified to date that explore the impact of Hurricane Maria on family relationships in Puerto Rico, evidence from studies conducted after Hurricane Georges moved across Puerto Rico (from east to west) on September 21, 1998, as a Category 3 hurricane, offer some evidence. The impact of Hurricane Georges in Puerto Rico on children's risk for internalizing disorders was mediated by the impact of the disaster on family relationships, a finding that was evident 18 months after the disaster (Felix, You, Vernberg and Canino, 2013). This timeframe highlights the need for ongoing support of youth and families over an extended period following a disaster.

The School Environment

Schools also provide an important context for restoring connections as well as familiar roles, routines, and a sense of securing following disasters (Felix, You and Canino, 2013), and the temporary closure of schools island-wide following the hurricane disrupted students' support networks and sense of security. At the same time, many of these schools were used as community centers to provide basic resources and services to families which, although not without controversy, was experienced by some teachers and families as providing an important source of connection and support (Guth, Surinon, Puig, Nitza, Georgiana, and Freytes, 2020). (Some of these resources and services will be further discussed in the next chapter.)

Even as many schools began to reopen in the weeks and months following the storm, a significant number did not. Jennifer Hinojosa, Edwin Meléndez, and Kathya Severino Pietri (2019) reported that a total of 265 schools (24%) have been permanently closed, resulting in approximately 47,000 students and 4,000 teachers being displaced. The closures disproportionately impacted rural areas, from where 65 percent of the closures came, resulting in children from these areas having to travel longer distances to get to schools, thus increasing the likelihood of absenteeism and decreasing opportunities for parental involvement (Hinojosa, Meléndez and Pietri, 2019). As with other results of Hurricane Maria, these school closures served to exacerbate a trend that existed prior to the hurricane. The total number of schools operating on the island declined from a high of 1,515 in 2006 to 855 in 2018.

At the same time, there were a number of disruptions in the schools that remained open following the hurricane. Large increases in enrollment and/or changes in the school population shift the existing climate in those schools, potentially disrupting students' experiences of schools being a safe and secure base as well. Changes in students' attitudes and behaviors as a result of their direct exposure to traumatic events resulted in additional strain on teachers, administrators, and staff.

A survey of 6,375 K-12 teachers in public schools in Puerto Rico two years after Maria (Nitza and Surinon, 2019) explored their perceptions of the impact of the storm on students' functioning. Results indicated that teachers perceived an overall negative impact on children across all grade levels and regions of the island. A majority of teachers reported a decrease in academic performance (72%) as well as cognitive (69%), emotional (65%), and behavioral (56%) functioning. Notably, the length of time that schools were closed predicted teachers' perceptions of changes in academic performance and cognitive functioning. Teachers whose schools reopened after more than one month perceived a greater decrease in academic performance and cognitive functioning than teachers whose schools reopened within a month following the storm.

These educators were personally affected as well, leaving them to balance the need to manage their personal lives as well as their classroom and school communities. Two years after the storm, more than 30 percent of teachers reported feeling ongoing profession stress and decreased job satisfaction. What is more, 25 percent of teachers reported feeling ill-equipped to deal with the challenges faced by their students (Nitza and Surinon, 2019).

The strain on educators trying to balance their personal and professional roles was exemplified by comments such as:

- "It was a very difficult time for most of us, since we had to deal with our students and our own situations, both personal and professional."
- "Teachers should never be pressured to return to their workplace soon after a serious hurricane event. Teachers have homes and families and personal problems to deal with first before being forced to deal with their students' issues."

Perhaps not surprisingly, teachers in this survey also identified a need for mental health resources and interventions and training on classroom strategies for supporting students' psychosocial needs. At the same time, they expressed a strong need for better working conditions in general and for greater support from the government and from parents (Nitza and Surinon, 2019). These results suggest that, as with most other aspects of life in Puerto Rico, the impact of the hurricane on teachers and students served to exacerbate preexisting challenges.

The strain on teachers identified in this study has the potential to have a further impact on students, setting up a negative cycle. Such strain may influence students' perceptions of their teachers' attitudes toward them, which are in turn related to students' motivation and attitudes toward school (Eccles et al., 1993). As described by Felix and colleagues, "Even the most motivated, compassionate, supportive and efficacious teacher who was also disaster-affected may have less to give students than usual during the first few years of post-disaster recovery" (2013, p. 1022).

MENTAL HEALTH AND HEALTH IMPACTS OF HURRICANE SANDY: IMPLICATIONS FOR PUERTO RICO

Other risks to both health impacts and mental health created by Hurricane Maria are the result of the extended power outages and the environmental hazards it left in its wake. While few epidemiologic studies have been conducted following Hurricane Maria, multiple studies have measured the public health impacts of Hurricane Sandy in 2012. Because Hurricane Sandy and its related power outage were of similar scale as Hurricane Maria, lessons learned about the mental health and health impacts of the power outages and environmental hazards created by Hurricane Sandy offer valuable information for understanding the ongoing risks and responses in Puerto Rico.

Power Outages

On Monday October 29, 2012, Hurricane Sandy hit the Northeastern United States, causing extensive damage and devastation. The loss of power after Hurricane Sandy probably posed the greatest and most direct threat to the public, and had large geographic variations, especially in communities with low socioeconomic status (SES), such as in Bronx County. Emergency department (ED) visits for mental health problems significantly increased after power outages in New York following Hurricane Sandy. Substance abuse accounted for most mental health ED visits after Sandy, as described by Shao Lin and colleagues (2016). In a dose-response relationship, with every 1 percent increase of blackout coverage, the Bronx had almost an eightfold increased risk of mental health ED visits, and Queens had a 1.5-fold increased risk (Lin et al. 2016). Further, the mental health effects started to climb two to three days after the massive power outage coverage and reached its peak four days after the power outage, suggesting that the longer the blackout, the more mental health-related visits to the ED were reported.

There are several mechanisms through which power outages impact mental health. Darkness has been found to induce stress, confusion, and aggregation among people with preexisting psychological conditions (Klinger et al. 2014). Previous studies have also found that the loss of electrical service is directly associated with post-disaster symptoms, worry, and depression, especially among residents in rural areas (Gros, 2012). Loss of electricity can lead to loss of essential services to communities, such as access to clean water (due to water tower shut down), food (lack of supply or no refrigeration), and transportation (subway, etc.). After Hurricane Sandy, many elderly residents and people with access needs living in urban high-rise apartments were unable to descend stairways and became trapped for days and even weeks due to nonfunctioning elevators during periods of prolonged blackout, keeping them separated from crucial basic needs.

Power outages also cause the closure of cellular towers and reduce electronic communication, during a time when information is increasingly accessed via web-based sources, apps, and social media. Since many of these services were down or individuals could not charge their cell phones, their access to critical information, including evacuation information, health information, distribution points for food and water, and so on, after the storm was limited. The loss of communication technology not only reduces access to information but also reduces access to social support as well. As previously noted, social isolation itself can serve as a stressor, particularly for vulnerable groups like the elderly and people with chronic conditions as it limits access to social support, which is essential to recovery as described above (Bourque, 2006).

The island-wide power outage caused by Hurricane Maria was the largest in U.S. history, with 45 percent of the island's then-3.3 million residents remaining without power at the end of January 2018 (four months after Maria); full power was reportedly not restored until August 2018, nearly a year after Maria. (Additional details on the failure of Puerto Rico's electrical grid are discussed by Marla D. Pérez-Lugo, Cecilio Ortiz-Garcia, and Didier Valdés in chapter 5). Given the scale and longevity of Puerto Rico's power outage following Hurricane Maria, evidence from Hurricane Sandy demonstrates the severe mental health stressors endured by the millions of American citizens on the island.

Environmental Hazards

An often-overlooked variable following a hurricane that may result in negative impacts on health and mental health is the many environmental hazards that occur as coexposures. The hazards that occurred after Hurricane Sandy in New York and New Jersey offer an example of the environmental impacts that Puerto Rico was likely to experience. Multiple coenvironmental hazards occurred during Sandy, which intensified or multiplied this disaster's impacts. These include impacts on air quality, fire, and water contamination, all of which can affect survivors' experience of loss of physical space, one of the factors identified by Hobfoll et al. (2007) as contributing to the intensity of the impact on survivors.

After hurricanes, air quality can become a problem as a result of demolition and building activity and increased reliance on gas-fueled generators and tools due to the previously mentioned electrical outages. Burning and demolishing of damaged homes can introduce dangerous pollutants that contribute to respiratory symptoms or cancer (Manuel, 2013). Immediately after Hurricane Sandy, there were significantly lower levels of fine particulate matter ($PM_{2.5}$), likely as a result of less traffic on the road and the blackouts that resulted in the shutdown of many power plants and industrial facilities (Lin et al., 2016). However, additional monitors set up by New York State Department of Environmental Conservation (EPA, 2015) in different locations recorded $PM_{2.5}$ levels exceeding the EPA's 24-hour standard for two days (Manuel, 2013). The temporary increases of $PM_{2.5}$ could reflect emissions from widely used temporary generators and the building of support equipment. These findings suggest that monitoring outdoor air quality after hurricanes should occur in multiple locations over time, with an emphasis on areas with high demolition or building activity. Recall from the previous chapter that, following Hurricane Maria, researchers found significant air pollution in the San Juan metropolitan area that was well beyond Environmental Protection Agency safety thresholds.

Carbon monoxide poisoning is another risk associated with hurricanes and the resulting loss of power. Hurricane Sandy was accompanied by a cold front, and it is not uncommon for people to heat their homes using gas stoves or ranges without other options. Additionally, increased use of generators increases the risk of carbon monoxide poisoning. After Hurricane Sandy, one study found a 299 percent increase in carbon monoxide exposure during the period of outages, as compared to the year before (Schnall, 2017).

Fire poses another hazard to affected communities following hurricanes. The community of Breezy Point in Queens County, New York, had a well-known fire that destroyed over 100 homes as Hurricane Sandy struck the area. The cause of that fire was elevated seawater coming into contact with a home's electrical system (Manuel, 2013). Local ED visits peaked with 113 cases due to mental health problems the next day and increased numbers of mental health cases (but not statistically significant) for several days after this fire (Lin et al., 2016).

Water contamination was another major health concern after Hurricane Sandy. Although there were few changes in levels of physiochemical properties and microbacterial contamination in drinking water in the eight affected counties during Sandy and the associated aftermath, this superstorm knocked out power and damaged approximately 80 sewage treatment systems in New Jersey, leading to approximately 2.75 billion gallons of untreated waste flowing from the plant into the nearby bay (Byme, 2013).

Other Health Outcomes

Numerous additional health outcomes after Hurricane Sandy warrant attention as a means of gaining insight into potential health outcomes among Puerto Ricans after Hurricane Maria. For instance, ED visits, outpatient visits, and hospital admissions for cardiovascular diseases (CVDs), respiratory diseases, and injury among the elderly were more than twice as high immediately, four months, and 12 months after Hurricane Sandy, compared to the identical time window pre-/post-Sandy in affected areas and nonaffected areas (Lawrence et al., 2019). In another study evaluating the immediate and lasting impact of Hurricane Sandy on pregnancy complications in eight affected counties of New York State, Xiao and colleagues (2019) found that ED visits for overall pregnancy complications increased 6.3 percent during the months after Sandy, especially for threatened abortion, threatened labor, early onset of delivery, renal diseases, and diabetes. Gestational hypertension and renal diseases were elevated 7–8 months after Hurricane Sandy.

The increase in health and mental health needs following Hurricane Sandy was intensified by a healthcare system that experienced its own infrastructure damage. More than 6,300 patients had to be evacuated from New York City hospitals, nursing homes, and assisted living facilities (Adalja et al., 2014). With many smaller community healthcare facilities closed due to storm damage and power outages, people with nonemergency ailments visited EDs, exacerbating an already stressed system (Adalja et al., 2014). Survivors with preexisting conditions had difficulty getting medications filled; lost records, closed offices and pharmacies made it difficult for pharmacies to verify crucial information (Manuel, 2013). In chapter 6, Jose M. Fernandez provides new evidence on the closures of healthcare establishments in Puerto Rico following Hurricane Maria, demonstrating the severity of unmet healthcare needs on the island.

Population Vulnerability and Geographic Variations

The health implications of hurricanes may not affect all communities equally. Low SES communities are often most vulnerable to the negative impacts of natural disasters compared to high SES communities. Differences may reflect community vulnerability due to healthcare access and other demographics such as hospital density, population density, and sociodemographic composition. For instance, although Nassau County was affected the most by blackouts during Hurricane Sandy in terms of power outage coverage and duration, Bronx County had the highest rates of overall and multiple subtypes of mental health ED visits, where there are the highest proportions of Hispanic, African American, and low-income households, as well as low educational levels.

Some evidence suggests that lower SES communities may not always have the greatest vulnerability. In a study examining the impacts of power outages, individual sociodemographic characteristics were observed to play a significant role on adverse mental health susceptibility. That study found that females and the elderly had higher risks for mental health compared to males and those of a younger age during a disaster, which is consistent with previous findings (Lin et al. 2011). Surprisingly, the study found that whites and high SES individuals had significantly higher rates of ED visits during Hurricane Sandy than Black and Hispanic individuals (Lawrence et al. 2019). This is consistent with findings from the Northeast Blackout of 2003 (Lin et al. 2011) and our research findings on other health endpoints after Hurricane Sandy, although the previous study indicates that lower SES groups are more susceptible to impacts during extremely hot days in New York City (Lin et al. 2009). A possible explanation is that higher SES individuals are more likely to use nebulizers or other electric home aids and air conditioners/heaters than low SES groups. This could be the result of their dependence on electric equipment to manage disease and adaptation to living in optimal home conditions, making them more susceptible to a hurricane's effect during a power outage.

In the context of Puerto Rico, these results highlight the importance of recognizing and planning for the effects of power outage on mental health, and considering potentially large geographic variations by sociodemographics. Rebuilding the power transmission and distribution network is an enormous task; public health officials need to monitor consequent adverse health impacts, and focus on susceptible populations and vulnerable geographic areas across the island.

ONGOING RECOVERY EFFORTS FROM HURRICANE MARIA

The consequences of the storm continued to affect the island and recovery efforts were ongoing at the three-year anniversary of Maria's landfall in Puerto Rico. At that time, the continued emergence of new community groups and the development of new institutional partnerships represent community-outreach consequences of the delayed and insufficient response of the federal government.

The mobilization of community groups, both formally and informally for people to assist and support each other, has resulted in a new or increased sense of empowerment and connectedness among many Puerto Ricans (Guth et al. 2020). One example is the emergence of *centros de apoyo mutuo* (CAMS; mutual support centers) across the island. Velez-Velez and Villarubia-Mendoza (2018) explored the development and work of these CAMs which, while operating independently of each other, all have in common a commitment to *autogestion* and community empowerment. The CAMs focus on different areas, including education and mental health, and these areas have evolved beyond the emergency period immediately following the hurricane.

Velez-Velez and Villarubia-Mendoza (2018) noted that CAMs recognized that the community problems they were addressing predated Hurricane Maria, and that the hurricane highlighted and exacerbated these problems.

Other recovery efforts are the result of collaborations between Puerto Rican institutions and mainland institutions to address identified needs. For example, the survey results described above (Nitza and Surinon, 2019) reveal a need to provide teachers with the support, training, and resources they need in order to effectively do their jobs in the face of ongoing adversity. A partnership among the Puerto Rico Department of Education, the University of Puerto Rico, UNICEF USA, and the Institute for Disaster Mental Health at the State University of New York at New Paltz is developing programming to address this need island-wide. Beginning with the start of the 2019–2020 school year, a two-tiered program was developed that included both universal and targeted interventions. The first tier focuses on the infusion of trauma-informed classroom training in schools throughout the island. Using a train-the-trainer model, over 24,000 professionals including school psychologists, counselors, social workers, and teachers have received this training to date. The second tier of the intervention provides a psychoeducational group intervention for children in need of additional mental health support beyond what can be provided in the classroom. These groups are being facilitated by graduate students in Rehabilitation Counseling from the University of Puerto Rico—Río Piedras in selected schools in the east of the island, which was particularly hard hit by Hurricane Maria.

This partnership has grown out of the larger *New York Stands with Puerto Rico* initiative described in chapter 12 by Havidán Rodríguez and colleagues that, while directly focused on home repair on the island, appears to indirectly be having a positive mental health impact by offering homeowners a sense of hope, connectedness, and support. Additional initiatives involving the Puerto Rico Department of Education are discussed in the following chapter.

LONG-TERM MENTAL HEALTH AND RELATED CONSEQUENCES

Follow-up studies from Hurricane Sandy offer some additional information regarding long-term risks from Hurricane Maria. For example, the analysis from a mental health follow-up study (Lawrence et al. 2019) found that the negative effects persisted for three years following Hurricane Sandy, with increased rates of ED visits due to mood disorders during the three years following the event. However, data from Hurricane Sandy also reveal that potential health impacts of hurricanes may be significantly reduced by effective preparedness and timely response efforts. New York County had the fastest power recovery among the affected counties in the state, which may demonstrate the local government's rapid and effective response to Hurricane Sandy. Similarly, although Queens and Kings are located next to Nassau County, they suffered far less severe blackouts, which may also indicate the effectiveness of disaster response efforts by New York City's government.

Further, evidence of multiple diseases, such as hospital admissions due to CVDs, respiratory diseases, and even food-/water-borne diseases, was significantly reduced during and after Sandy, when compared to pre-Sandy multiyear data (Sharp et al. 2016; Bloom et al. 2016). This could be explained by the joint and timely efforts from multiple state and federal agencies in the immediate aftermath of Hurricane Sandy, including providing more than 170 shelters for medical care, establishing 68 Disaster Recovery Centers, and supplying more than one million liters of water and one million meals to those in need within 24 hours (Lin et al. 2016).

As Puerto Rico continues to rebuild and recover, it is essential to understand and respond effectively to the long-term mental health and related health consequences. Trajectories of impairment for individuals following traumatic events vary significantly (Bonnano 2004). While some people remain healthy and others recover over time, a third category of survivors who show symptoms at the outset will continue to struggle over months and years, developing chronic problems. A fourth category of survivors will have delayed onset of impairment; that is, they will initially function well but will develop increased symptoms and decreased functioning over time.

DISCUSSION AND CONCLUDING REMARKS

Moving forward, monitoring and surveillance programs to assess risks and inform response efforts to both mental health and health consequences are essential. This should include regular mental health and public health screening, as well as devoting attention to the environmental consequences of the storm that put people at ongoing risk. Rapid and effective response efforts coordinated by different levels of governmental agencies are crucial to reducing health burdens associated with a disaster. Therefore, it is crucial to understand and report how the effects of lacking clean water and food intensified and exacerbated Puerto Rican's health impacts. A medical monitoring or surveillance program to follow-up with the long-term health impacts would also be beneficial to Puerto Rico's residents as well as those living on the mainland after being displaced by Hurricane Maria. In doing so, it is important not to assume that lower SES groups always have higher vulnerability than high SES groups, as higher SES groups may have elevated vulnerability to adverse health problems in some situations.

Programs and services supporting youth and families in Puerto Rico should “assess, monitor, and address the quality of family relationships and parenting, and provide needed therapeutic supports to parents who are struggling” (Felix et al. 2013, p. 122). Programs to monitor and address the school climate and the well-being of teachers and students are equally essential. Support for CAMs and other locally developed systems of social support and connectedness is also crucial to ensuring ongoing resilience and sustainability of progress made. Finally, as in all long-term disaster recovery settings, support for professional responders across disciplines and others who are caring for survivors is also essential in order to reduce the risks and consequences of compassion fatigue and vicarious trauma.

NOTE

1. We do not have corresponding suicide statistics for Puerto Ricans living on the mainland, but this would serve as a worthy topic to explore in future research, especially among the Puerto Rican diaspora displaced by Hurricane Maria in light of the potential loss of social support (described elsewhere in this chapter).

Chapter 9

Facing Disaster in a Complex System

Mental Health Initiatives within the Puerto Rico Department of Education Post-Hurricane Maria

María Rolón-Martínez, Joy Lynn Suárez-Kindy, and Rosaura Orengo-Aguayo

ABSTRACT

This chapter focuses on Hurricane Maria's impact on the mental health and educational outcomes of children and youth in Puerto Rico. The discussion highlights socioemotional initiatives that the Puerto Rico Department of Education undertook post-Maria to better serve students' mental healthcare needs. It also highlights the challenges and opportunities for strengthening socioemotional health after a natural disaster within a complex public educational system, which can inform policies and the enactment of plans to address children's socioemotional needs before, during, and after a natural disaster.

Hurricane Maria critically impacted mental health in Puerto Rico. This once-Category 5 hurricane resulted in fear and anxiety among Puerto Ricans before, during, and after the storm. With approximately one-third (based on preliminary estimates) of the 2,975 deaths attributed to delayed or lack of access to medical attention, Maria left vulnerable populations (e.g., children, the elderly, the sick) at great risk (Kishore et al., 2018). A study conducted by the Youth Development Institute (2018) revealed that the most impacted and vulnerable areas were community and educational housing and infrastructure, disruption of the educational process, loss of household income, and impacts on mental health.

The experience of Hurricane Maria should guide Puerto Rico and the United States overall, as well as other countries, in the development of public policy related to post-disaster health, education, and socioeconomic development. We highlight Hurricane Maria's impact on child and youth mental health and educational outcomes, complementing the previous two chapters by Fernando I. Rivera and colleagues and Amy Nitza and Shao Lin. The chapter also discusses socioemotional initiatives that the Puerto Rico Department of Education (PR-DE) undertook post-Hurricane Maria to better serve students' mental health needs as well as the challenges and opportunities for strengthening socioemotional health after a natural disaster within a complex public educational system. This information can inform policies and the enactment of plans to address students' socioemotional needs before, during, and after a natural disaster.

SOCIOECONOMIC REALITIES OF PUERTO RICO BEFORE AND AFTER HURRICANE MARIA

To provide context, it is important to discuss the socioeconomic realities of Puerto Rico before and after Hurricane Maria from the perspective of children and youth on the island. Consistent with information on the pre-Maria socioeconomic outcomes of Puerto Ricans discussed in other chapters in this volume, the Youth Development Institute's report of 2017 shows that prior to Hurricane Maria, 57 percent of children and youth in Puerto Rico lived below the federal poverty threshold. The island, compared to the U.S. mainland, had the highest percentage of:

- Children living in single-parent households (56.5%);
- Families with children in which at least one parent is unemployed (43.3%);
- Youth who do not engage in daily physical activity (32.2%);
- Students between grades 9 and 12 who did not attend school because they felt unsafe (12%);
- Infants with low birth weight (10.6%); youth between the ages of 16 and 19 who do not attend school and are unemployed (2.4%); and
- The lowest median income in families with children younger than 18 ($20,292 per year).

Moreover, in Puerto Rico, 44.7 percent of households with children under 18 years receive food stamps and 34.8 percent of grandparents are responsible for their grandchildren under the age of 18. Furthermore, 17.1 percent of students between 9th and 12th grades reported that they had seriously considered attempting suicide during the 12 months before the survey (Youth Development Institute, 2017).

Another study commissioned by the Youth Development Institute in 2018 found that several months after Hurricane Maria impacted the island, one-third of households had a reduction in monthly income resulting from loss of employment and fewer hours worked. This loss of income disproportionately impacted low-income families who reported difficulty accessing the most basic needs post-disaster, including paying utilities (40%), purchasing food (38%), buying clothing (24%), and securing school materials for their children's education (21%).

The Youth Development Institute (2018) states that poverty, combined with a rapidly shrinking population of children (Puerto Rico's child population fell by 35 percent between 2007 and 2017) poses a threat to Puerto Rico's economic development. Taken together, the socioeconomic context of Puerto Rican families and children prior to Hurricane Maria was one of the significant poverty and socioeconomic disparities. Hurricane Maria further exacerbated these grim socioeconomic realities and disproportionately affected an already vulnerable population of children and their families.

Psychological research has demonstrated that living in poverty has a wide range of negative effects on the physical and mental health and well-being of children (American Psychological Association [APA] 2018). Poverty impacts children within their various contexts such as at home, in school, and in their neighborhoods and communities. It is linked with negative conditions such as substandard housing, homelessness, inadequate nutrition and food insecurity, lack of access to healthcare, unsafe neighborhoods, among others. Poorer children and youth are at greater risk for experiencing negative outcomes such as poor academic achievement, school dropout, abuse and neglect, behavioral and socioemotional problems, physical health problems, and developmental delays. These effects are compounded by the barriers children and their families encounter when trying to access physical and mental healthcare (APA 2018).

Natural disasters can further aggravate the impact of poverty and barriers in access to medical and mental healthcare for vulnerable families. For example, prior to Hurricane Maria, given the healthcare undercoverage described in previous chapters, approximately 50 percent of children with medical conditions who required medication had access to their medications. Of these, around 30 percent had trouble accessing their medications after Maria and those families that had access struggled to purchase them because of a reduction or lack of income posthurricane (Youth Development Institute 2017).

Natural disasters can also exacerbate already existing societal problems such as community violence and domestic violence (Bonanno, Brewin, Kaniasty, and La Grec 2010). Community violence was another serious public health problem in Puerto Rico already impacting the physical and mental integrity of its citizens prior to the hurricane (Pérez-Pedrogo et al.,

2016). This type of violence is among the most damaging experiences that children and young people can experience, affecting their thinking, feelings, and behaviors (Guerra and Dierkhising 2011). Community, domestic, and sexual violence increased in Puerto Rico after Hurricane Maria, with several studies underway assessing the financial, structural, psychological, and social impacts (e.g., Morris et al., 2018) which may have been exacerbated by the decline in law enforcement services (e.g., Levantesi 2018; Pacheco 2018).

Natural disasters can further impact children's and youth's mental health by exposing them to adverse events such as lack of access to basic needs, loss of caregivers, disruption in daily routines, or by aggravating already existing mental health conditions as a result of new adversities related to the storm (Bonanno et al. 2010). Puerto Rico's children and youth were already affected by health disparities in general, and mental and behavioral health disparities in particular, prior to Hurricane Maria. For example, as noted by Rivera and colleagues in chapter 7, inadequate access to mental health services existed in Puerto Rico even before Hurricane Maria, particularly for underserved regions of the island—the rural and mountain regions.

The lack of coverage by medical insurance companies for mental and behavioral health represented one of the main barriers post-disaster. Another barrier was the long waitlists and time between referrals when the children could be seen, mostly due to a shortage in mental health providers. Families with lack of transportation, ability to take time off from work, and limited income also encounter barriers in access to healthcare.

Owing to these numerous structural, socioeconomic, and logistical barriers, behavioral and mental health services in Puerto Rico tend to be offered in fragmented and inconsistent ways. For example, for children and youth, most of these services are provided by schools, communities, and nonprofit organizations as opposed to established healthcare providers; evidence-based mental and behavioral health interventions exist on the island, yet access to these services within an integrated care framework was already lacking prior to Hurricane Maria (Rolón and Moreno, 2018).

The lack of preventive and intervention services before Maria placed children and families at greater risk by not having effective tools and strategies to manage stressful events and not receiving care for predisposing conditions. After Hurricane Maria, as discussed by Jose M. Fernandez in chapter 6, many healthcare providers either left the island or had to close their businesses temporarily or permanently given the lack of power, water, and clients who could afford services (see also Michaud and Kates, 2017), resulting in an even greater gap of mental and behavioral health professionals who could offer services to Puerto Rican children and youth. The need for immediate crisis intervention and for the long-term trauma interventions was not met, which affected mental health in children and their families.

DISASTER EXPOSURE AND MENTAL HEALTH IMPACT OF HURRICANE MARIA ON PUERTO RICAN CHILDREN

Research studies show that up to one-third of children will develop chronic symptoms such as post-traumatic stress disorder (PTSD), depression, anxiety, substance abuse, suicidal ideation, and aggressive behaviors within one year of a natural disaster (e.g., Bonanno et al., 2010). The majority of children and youth manifest resilience in the aftermath of traumatic experiences, specifically after a single-incident exposure. Youth who have been exposed to multiple traumas, have a past history of mental health problems, or have experienced family adversity are likely to be at a higher risk of showing symptoms of post-traumatic stress (APA, 2008). Research also shows that the recovery process for trauma can be impacted by internal factors, like psychiatric diagnosis and by external factors such as family stressors and poverty. Individual, family, cultural, and community strengths and supports can facilitate recovery and promote resilience (APA, 2008). These symptoms were studied by Orengo-Aguayo et al. (2019) and the results are similar to what we report here: even though Puerto Rican children were at a higher risk of developing PTSD symptoms, they followed the behavioral patterns predicted by extant research. Future research should explore how these observations are associated with resiliency factors in the Puerto Rican culture that highlights community attachment and family support.

POST-MARIA SURVEYS OF FACTORS AFFECTING THE SOCIOEMOTIONAL HEALTH OF PUBLIC SCHOOL CHILDREN

Shortly after Hurricane Maria impacted Puerto Rico, the PR-DE conducted an island-wide needs assessment of all public school students to better understand the impact of this natural disaster on Puerto Rican children and youth's socioemotional health, with the ultimate goal of using the data to direct the limited available psychological resources on the island to schools with the most need. The PR-DE partnered with trauma experts at the Medical University of South Carolina (MUSC) who recommended the use of the National Child Traumatic Stress Network Hurricane Assessment and Referral Tool (Kronenberg et al., 2010) to assess common psychological outcomes after a natural disaster such as post-traumatic stress and depression, as well as predictors of postdisaster recovery such as disaster exposure, loss, and access to social support.

The fully bilingual MUSC team translated the survey into Spanish with the permission of the developers, and Puerto Rican psychologists on the island provided feedback to ensure its readiness for use on the island. The survey results (described below) have been published in the *JAMA Network Open* (Orengo-Aguayo, Stewart, de Arellano, Suárez-Kindy, and Young 2019) and represent one of the largest post-disaster screening efforts in U.S. history and the largest to be conducted with a sample of Hispanic youth affected by a natural disaster. (Nitza and Lin in the previous chapter also discussed some of these results.)

PR-DE and MUSC Survey Results

A total of 96,108 students in grades 3–12 in public schools across Puerto Rico completed the voluntary survey between February 1, 2018, and June 29, 2018 (5–9 months post-Hurricane Maria). This was a 42.4 percent response rate, with an even split between female (50.3%) and male (49.7%) respondents. The results revealed the following.

- 83.9 percent youth saw houses damaged or destroyed;
- Nearly half (45.7%) had their own houses damaged;
- One-sixth (16%) saw or heard of a friend, family, or neighbor get injured during the hurricane;
- One-quarter (24.1%) helped rescue someone during or after the hurricane;
- 57.8% had a friend or family member leave the island after post-Maria;
- One-third (32.3%) experienced shortages of food or water;
- One-sixth (16.7%) had no electricity 5–9 months post-Maria;
- Nearly one-third (29.9%) thought they might die during the hurricane; and
- 6.6 percent lost a family, friend, or neighbor as a result of Hurricane Maria.

Furthermore, after the hurricane, 17.7 percent reported thefts in their neighborhoods, 12.5 percent reported community violence, 5.7 percent had to relocate to a new school, and 11.4 percent reported their parents lost their jobs. Overall, 7.2 percent (6,900) of youth who responded to the survey reported clinically significant symptoms of PTSD, with girls reporting higher levels of PTSD (8.2%) compared to boys (6.1%). Interestingly, these devastating effects were experienced by youth regardless of socioeconomic status or location on the island, suggesting that all children and youth were significantly impacted by Hurricane Maria (Orengo-Aguayo et al. 2019).

Results from the Youth Development Institute Household Survey

The Youth Development Institute (2018) also conducted a representative survey of 705 homes with children under 18 years of age in Puerto Rico between July and September 2018 (10–12 months post-Hurricane Maria).

The comprehensive report found that children under five years of age were not able to return to preschool or daycare an average of three months (92 days) after the hurricane. Moreover, 7.2 percent of children surveyed in this age group were already showing socioemotional effects at the time of the survey such as fear of being separated from caregivers, difficulties concentrating, and lack of interest in activities. Children and youth ages 5–17 were unable to return to school an average of 78 days post-hurricane. Of the 27.7 percent of children on the island receiving special educational services, 85 percent had their services disrupted an average of 97 days.

The study also found that nearly one-quarter (23%) of the students ages 5–17 surveyed showed a marked change in their behavior according to caregivers. Specifically, 12 percent of these students were having trouble concentrating, almost 10 percent showed declines in academic achievement, 8.3 percent showed a lack of interest in school, 5.8 percent showed conduct-related problems, and 3.1 percent showed difficulties socializing with their peers. Also reported in the survey, having a preexisting history of mental health problems and suffering a personal or material loss as a result of the hurricane correlated with a significant increase in maladaptive changes in student behavior post-hurricane.

Contextualizing the Survey Results

It is important to highlight that prior to Hurricane Maria, Puerto Rican youth were also experiencing significant stressful and adverse conditions such as poverty, community violence, and declining socioeconomic conditions.[1] As mentioned in the previous section, children and youth in need of mental health services were faced with limited access to providers, lack of evidence-based services available, particularly in underserved areas of the island, and multiple barriers in accessing care whenever services were available. Consequently, schools—places where children and youth spend a significant amount of their time—stepped up to fill this gap.

SOCIOEMOTIONAL RECOVERY EFFORTS WITHIN THE DEPARTMENT OF EDUCATION POST-HURRICANE MARIA

Social, community, and governmental support networks are critical for recovery particularly when an entire community or island, in this case, is affected after a natural disaster (e.g., APA 2012; Bonanno et al. 2010). Post-disaster socioemotional recovery efforts are typically grouped into three phases: (1) immediate aftermath of the event (starting the day of the event to a few weeks), (2) short-term recovery and rebuilding phase (one month up to a year), and (3) long-term recovery phase (one year up to a few years). The goals of the socioemotional interventions implemented within each timeframe depend on the unique needs of the affected population and context in which the disaster occurred (La Greca and Silverman 2009).

In the immediate aftermath of a disaster, restoring access to basic needs (e.g., food, water, clothing, medical attention, shelter), promoting a sense of safety and security, and reconnecting loved ones should be the primary priority of any intervention. Interventions can be offered to reduce or prevent long-term distress and dysfunction in children and families by providing practical assistance with basic needs and promoting a sense of safety, security, calm, connectedness, hope, and self and community efficacy (e.g., Psychological First Aid [PFA]; Brymer et al. 2006; Hobfoll et al. 2007).

With devastating disasters such as Hurricane Maria, children and youth will likely need additional support to aid in their socioemotional recovery after the initial days and weeks of the storm. Therefore, in the short-term recovery phase it is important to continue with Level/Tier I interventions that target all children and families, such as PFA, as well as introducing Level/Tier II interventions focused on building coping and resiliency skills for those who have developed moderate-to-severe distress. As communities and families transition into long-term recovery efforts, Level/Tier III interventions, such as evidence-based mental health treatments for those who develop clinically significant and persistent emotional and behavioral problems, will also be important (e.g., Trauma-Focused Cognitive Behavioral Therapy [TF-CBT]; Cohen, Mannarino, and Deblinger 2017).

A level/tiered socioemotional model of intervention after a disaster allows for the often-limited available mental health specialists to treat the most severely impacted youth, while also offering basic coping and resiliency building skills to all children, youth, and the adults with whom they come in contact (e.g., parents, caregivers, teachers, and school staff). Schools provide an ideal setting in which to implement these socioemotional tiered-level supports given the amount of daily time children spend in this setting, which eliminates the most common logistical barriers to accessing mental health services (e.g., lack of transportation, caregiver work schedules, insurance). Schools can also help restore a sense of routine and normalcy in children, and be a safe place where they can access food and shelter as well as where families can receive resources, information, and services post-disaster. Schools also already have a built-in workforce (e.g., teachers, social workers, psychologists, nurses, and counselors) that can be trained to lead the above-mentioned socioemotional activities, which in turn can facilitate post-disaster recovery of students (Orengo-Aguayo, Stewart, de Arellano, et al. 2019).

Immediate Response Phase to Hurricane Maria

Days after Hurricane Maria, the PR-DE made efforts to supply basic needs to families as well as emotional support in accordance with the aforementioned three-tiered model of support. The first step in this process crucial to promoting recovery was to open schools as community centers, providing a "safe space" with hot meals, teachers, and social workers where the children and their families could go in the midst of the post-disaster chaos. School-based community centers opened not only to that specific school community but also to anyone who arrived through the doors. Evidence-based resources (e.g., National Child Traumatic Stress Network) were handed out to teachers and social workers so they could do different socioemotional activities with the children and their families. At the same time, multiple national and local experts in natural disaster management, recovery, and trauma/mental health volunteered to help the PR-DE create to coordinate a short- and long-term recovery plan that was subsequently implemented and continued with the initial goal of providing these programs at least two years post-Hurricane Maria. Indeed, these experts provided workshops and self-care spaces for teachers, social workers, and other school personnel across the island days after Maria and continued these efforts months after the storm.

Short-Term Recovery Phase from Hurricane Maria

Once the immediate response phase was underway (starting with Hurricane Maria and lasting about three months), the short-term phase of the recovery began (approximately three months to a year after Hurricane Maria's landfall). School personnel across the island were trained in best practices on socioemotional recovery after a disaster. All these efforts were possible due to collaborations and partnerships with local and national nonprofit organizations and universities that offered their services either through their own grants or free of charge. The Puerto Rican diaspora (i.e., Puerto Ricans in the U.S. mainland or abroad) particularly offered their unconditional help, resources, time, expertise, and most of all, emotional support to those who faced the challenge of assisting in the socioemotional recovery of students and staff post-Hurricane Maria.[2]

The U.S. Department of Education also awarded funds to the PR-DE to provide a yearlong wellness program to help school personnel recover from their own trauma and socioemotional adversities as a result of Hurricane Maria. During this phase, school social workers and nurses also received evidence-based trainings such as Skills for Psychological Recovery (SPR; Berkowitz et al. 2010) and best practices for post-disaster mental health screening to further support students' socioemotional recovery and access to socioemotional supports.

Long-Term Recovery Phase from Hurricane Maria

During the long-term recovery phase (one to two years after Hurricane Maria), a selected group of PR-DE psychologists underwent a nine-month intensive training along with consultation support to implement TF-CBT, considered to be the gold standard evidence-based mental health treatment to treat post-traumatic stress and associated symptoms in children and youth. Other schools were "adopted" by local nonprofit and academic sectors to promote socioemotional recovery, wellness, and mental health services to students and staff. It is worth noting that approximately two years after Hurricane Maria, the PR-DE had gone from minimal training and local capacity for trauma and mental-health-informed practices in the classroom, to being trauma informed and offering evidence-based mental health services to students within their schools.

ADDITIONAL INITIATIVES TO ADDRESS MENTAL HEALTH IN SCHOOLS

Hurricane Maria highlighted the significant gap in availability of dedicated mental health services for children and youth within schools in Puerto Rico. To provide context, the PR-DE serves as both the state education agency and the sole local education agency in Puerto Rico, serving approximately 300,000 students in 856 schools. For decades, the PR-DE had fallen short in providing appropriate mental health services to children. Most psychologists that work with the PR-DE students are tasked with conducting eligibility assessments for special education services, with minimal to nonexistent time to dedicate toward offering mental health services.

One-third (33%) of students in Puerto Rico receive special education services, much higher than the U.S. national average of 13 percent, possibly due to the lack of preventive mental and behavioral health services offered in schools and communities. In some cases, special education services are the only mechanism that parents and teachers have to obtain socioemotional and behavioral support for children or youth in Puerto Rico. Besides the professionals subcontracted through special education funding, a range of 15–30 psychologists are contracted yearly with state funds to address other issues not related to special education, such as identifying gifted students and addressing behavioral problems among children and youth.

Since Hurricane Maria, the PR-DE began focusing on (1) increasing services for prevention, interventions, assessment, consulting, and monitoring of students; (2) the sustainability of these services to provide a safe and supportive learning environment; and (3) collecting data and use evidence-based monitoring tools to measure progress toward these goals. To address the socioemotional needs of children, the PR-DE structured the Student Services Program to include more mental health professionals at the regional and central level and hired, for the first time in PR-DE history, a school psychologist to lead these socioemotional efforts. Also, a Parent Engagement office was established, as well as a Restorative Practices and At-Risk Youth office, directed by clinical psychologists.

A Multi-Tiered Systems of Support framework for prevention and intervention was designed in order to structure the services to be provided by the PR-DE to the students, faculty, and families served. Tier 1 involved establishing support systems for the entire school community, including programs focused on social-emotional development. Tier 2 focused on targeted programs and interventions for managing high-risk behaviors in a subset of schools. Finally, Tier 3 focused on specialized and individualized psychological intervention for students identified based on need. In particular, in the first year and a half after Maria, the PR-DE invested in establishing structures and recruiting staff to implement these tiered supports, as shown in table 9.1.

CHALLENGES AND OPPORTUNITIES FOR IMPROVING MENTAL HEALTH SERVICES WITHIN SCHOOLS

The PR-DE focused on hiring staff and setting up structures to support students' mental health needs post-Maria to further integrate them into systemic structures in Puerto Rico and to promote resiliency measures that address and prevent the risk of trauma. PR-DE staff needed professional development and coaching on how to deepen these initiatives and truly integrate efforts across

Table 9.1 Puerto Rico Department of Education's Investments and Established Structures after Hurricane Maria

Position	*Role*	*Investment*
Social workers in schools	Counseling and guidance regarding socioemotional needs and promotion of healthy school climate.	1 per 250 students
Professional counselors in schools	Counseling and guidance services to promote school retention, support students in transitioning grades, and support students in meeting graduation requirements.	1 per 500 students in secondary school
Nurses in schools	Evaluate and refer students based on their health needs.	435 nurses (1 per 2 schools)
Psychologists in schools	Specialized treatment of trauma and other mental health needs.	107 psychologists

Source: Puerto Rico Department of Education.

the department to maximize the impact on students. The PR-DE also realized the importance of bringing in local and national partners—agencies, nonprofits, academic sectors—to amplify this work. The success of this post-disaster response was largely dependent on these multidisciplinary, cross-agency, and local as well as national collaborations.

Unfortunately, there are limited resources and still limited access to services. The public education budget in Puerto Rico is $2.3 billion for 307,000 students, or approximately $7,500 per student compared to an average of over $11,000 across the United States. In the 2018–2019 school year, for the first time in history, as part of its investment strategy, the PR-DE hired school-level nurses and psychologists to provide services for students. However, when finalizing this chapter, the PR-DE still needed to identify sustainable funding sources for these initiatives to continue. Another significant challenge in moving forward is the political structure and culture of the Puerto Rican government. Enhanced communication with the Financial Oversight and Management Board (created by PROMESA) for Puerto Rico could ensure these types of budgets are approved and sustained over a longer period of time to ensure the mental health services coverage of children and youth. Given that appointments to lead government agencies are made in Puerto Rico by the governor or designee, changes in political party, administration, or leadership might lead to interruptions that can hinder achieving consistent, evidenced-based initiatives.

That said, mental health initiatives are now integrated into educational public policy in Puerto Rico. The 2018 Education Reform Act, or Law 85, recognizes the role of the PR-DE in ensuring the social and emotional development of students.[3] Guidelines were established for developing restorative practice initiatives focusing on school climate and socioemotional learning, conducting Positive Behavioral Intervention Supports training for support personnel in all schools, and integration of families through sustained engagement efforts.

The PR-DE also established a number of local and national partnerships and networks to launch this work which will hopefully continue. These partnerships and networks include the following.

Local Partnerships

- Pan-American Hospital and Capestrano Hospital have led workshops for teachers on issues related to mental health and student interventions.
- Carlos Albizu University/Instituto Tercera Misión provides professional development for PR-DE psychologists, trauma intervention with students as well as collaboration in different grants.

National Partnerships

- The MUSC helped the PR-DE conduct a comprehensive island-wide needs assessment of disaster exposure and trauma symptoms among public school students post-Hurricane Maria. They also provided numerous trainings to PR-DE social workers, teachers, administrators, and psychologists around the island, including PFA-Tier 1 level intervention, SPR-Tier II level intervention, and TF-CBT-Tier III level intervention. These efforts began the day after Hurricane Maria impacted the island and continued almost two years later with funding from the Substance Abuse and Mental Health Services Administration awarded to MUSC.
- Stanford University and Pure Edge have provided ongoing professional development to teachers regarding mindfulness.
- Sanford Harmony provided a Social Emotional Learning program, as well as professional development to teachers regarding students' social and emotional development in grades K–8.
- Overcoming Obstacles provided a Social Emotional Learning program for counselors, as well as professional development from grades 8 to 12.
- The PR-DE is part of the Northeast and Caribbean Mental Health Technology Transfer Center (MHTTC) from Rutgers University.
- NYC Department of Health and Mental Hygiene offered workshops around the island to teachers, school counselors, and social workers.
- Save the Children adopted 12 schools on the island and provided socioemotional support, teacher training, solar panels for schools, and other resources.

PR-DE Participation in Networks for Capacity Building

Examples of networks in which the PR-DE participates for the purpose of capacity building include the following.

- The National Child Traumatic Stress Network, to develop trauma-informed protocols and structures;
- Collaborative for Academic and Social Emotional Learning Collaborative States Initiative, to develop strategies for teaching social-emotional skills in schools; and
- The MHTTC National School Mental Health Learning Collaborative.

DISCUSSION AND CONCLUDING REMARKS

The PR-DE encountered a significant challenging task of aiding in the socioemotional and mental health recovery of its students and staff after the catastrophic devastation of Hurricane Maria in September 2017. Conditions of severe poverty, physical and health disparities, and lack of access to evidence-based mental and behavioral healthcare plagued the island long before Hurricane Maria, exacerbated by the effects of Puerto Rico's severe economic crisis that started surging in 2006 (discussed by Marie T. Mora, Havidán Rodríguez, and Alberto Dávila in chapter 1).

Subsequently, studies discussed in this chapter and others in this book (including the three previous chapters by Fernandez, Rivera and colleagues, and Nitza and Lin) have shown the significant mental health impact of the storm on Puerto Rican children and youth, and identified significant deficits of systems and structures in place to address these needs. In collaboration with local and national partners, most of whom donated their time and resources, the PR-DE established an immediate, short-term, and long-term socioemotional recovery plan aimed at helping students and staff recover from Hurricane Maria.

From our perspective, these efforts have led to an impressive transformation (that can be used by other policymakers and scholars as a benchmark) of an entire educational system striving to be trauma-informed, focusing on the socioemotional well-being of its students and on increasing access to school-based mental health services to address systemic and long-standing barriers in access to care. This chapter (which captures our own journey)[4] shows the importance of establishing educational and public policy to support children and youth post-disasters, and move toward prevention rather than addressing mental health in schools after disasters occur. Finally, the experiences discussed here point to how significant changes within complex public systems take vision, determination, collaborations with outside agencies and partners, and a clear commitment to using evidence-based approaches.

NOTES

1. Comparing the results from these surveys with those from surveys including students affected by other natural disasters, such as Hurricane Sandy (the effects of which are discussed in the previous chapter by Nitza and Lin) and Hurricane Katrina that devastated parts of the U.S. Gulf Coast in 2005, goes beyond the scope of this chapter. However, it serves as a worthy topic for future research.

2. Writing from the perspective of those involved firsthand, it was particularly humbling to see the outpouring of support, including emotional support, of the Puerto Rican diaspora.

3. In March 2018, Puerto Rico's then-governor signed Law 85, known as the Education Reform Law, which recognizes the need of supporting students'

socioemotional learning to serve the whole child and improve academic outcomes. This law highlights the need for socioemotional supports for children and amplifies the role of mental health professionals within schools.

4. It has been a great pleasure being part of this journey and we hope our successors continue these initiatives.

Chapter 10

Puerto Rican Visual Art as Social Catharsis

What Post-Hurricane Maria Art Is Saying through the Frame of Disaster

Carlos Rivera Santana and
Bettina Pérez Martínez

ABSTRACT

This chapter presents a critical analysis of the Puerto Rican aesthetics crafted to "make sense" and (therefore) "purge" the post-hurricane trauma through Puerto Rican visual arts produced in the aftermath of Hurricane Maria. The versatility in visual arts to show the complex story of Puerto Rico after Maria likely explains the significantly greater expressive surge. This chapter also provides brief contextualization of Puerto Rican visual arts and their relationship with hurricanes as well as a description of the aesthetic expressions, illustrative exhibitions, and art pieces post-Hurricane Maria.

> "*Si no pudiera hacer arte, me iba.*" [If I could not do art, I would leave (Puerto Rico).]—Artist in Puerto Rico two weeks after Hurricane Maria

When a traumatic event occurs, neuroscience tells us that its recollection cannot be fully encoded at a rational register because the brain tries to protect itself and, as a result, it mainly relegates its codification to the sensory register (Pinel 2018, pp. 211–270). For most psychological approaches in individual therapy, the task is to bring the affective codification to the rational register through a narrativization of the event. Art can be an affective language that tells the story of a traumatic event (Carey 2006). While this neuroscientific knowledge is often used from a psychopathological framework and associated with post-traumatic stress disorder (which, as discussed in the previous set of chapters, was a significant outcome of Hurricane Maria in Puerto Rico), it can also be the foreground of what happens at the collective level when communities face disaster.

From a cultural studies perspective, we argue that when examining art as social catharsis encoded in the narrative frame of disaster, Puerto Rican visual arts are telling a story of post-Hurricane Maria imbued with the environmental catastrophe of climate change and the sociohistorical context of colonization. To arrive at this point we explain how art functions as a means of social catharsis. After this, we present illustrative post-hurricane artistic practices to showcase the diverse breadth of aesthetic responses to the storm. Lastly, we discuss four illustrative artists' responses to Hurricane Maria's aftermath.

BACKGROUND

Unlike studies using art solely as an intervention, this chapter reviews Puerto Rican visual art in the way it was produced as a reaction to Hurricane Maria (at least within the first two years of its landfall) and what it is saying. Aesthetics and art certainly play an important role in community interventions, particularly in community-owned organizations on the island. However, the premise of this piece is that art naturally emerges as a reaction to disastrous situations, and more than appreciating this art, it is also important to seriously consider the messages it communicates.

At the same time, art here is not examined from an art historical perspective; it is viewed as a form to encode a story and ultimately a history, as art can become history. Furthermore, art is not considered here as solely a product of an artist—art pieces are a product of a social discourse: art is produced by the artist but the art piece gains meaning through the viewers and the people who have informed them (Carey 2006; Rivera Santana, 2019). This is particularly the case with Puerto Rican art (Carragol-Barreto 2005).[1] While linear ways of communicating "what happened" in a disaster such as Hurricane Maria are important to consider, art's versatility to convey many messages at once, being able to include an affective component, and also serve as a healing activity, are important to consider in the story of Hurricane Maria.

PUERTO RICAN VISUAL ART AS SOCIAL CATHARSIS

Past hurricanes (and other natural disasters) called forth representation in the arts in Puerto Rico, although not in the proportion that we have seen with Hurricane Maria's disaster. For instance, Rafael Tufiño echoed the song

Temporal—a plena song inspired by the anxieties of Hurricane San Felipe (1928)—in a piece entitled *Plena No. 11* (n.d.) around the time of Hurricane Santa Clara (1956). Also, Carlos Raquel Rivera created *Huracan del Norte* (1955), a widely acclaimed piece commenting on a destructive force haunting Puerto Rico from the "north" (the United States) in the form of death, perhaps of cultural death.

Yet no hurricane until Hurricane Maria has called for an aesthetic reaction from Puerto Rican art that is similar to the aesthetic reaction of events like the persecution of nationalist independence movements from the state and the United States, and the Vieques controversy caused by the U.S. Navy.[2] As this brief and incomplete Puerto Rican art history description states, modern Puerto Rican visual art from its beginnings has displayed political content and messages. Hurricane Maria's disaster is beyond the natural, as many scholars and writers have stated; thus the Puerto Rican visual arts react to its sociopolitical dimension.

When facing disasters, it can be easier for communities to represent their understandings of the events through imagery (Carey 2006). There is considerable evidence that in the face of a traumatic event, the arts can facilitate the narrativization of the understanding of the event in order to signify what happened. This enables a community to understand the event at large, and in many cases including Puerto Rico post-Hurricane Maria, the context in which an event takes place and how the community can react more realistically. An article published by Huss and colleagues in *Disasters* addressing post-tsunami Sri Lanka states:

> The arts enabled the retrieval and reprocessing of traumatic memories that are often encoded in images rather than words. They are a natural way of creating resilience in that they recreate a connection between cognition, emotion and the senses that enables new perspectives and effective problem solving. On the community level, traumatic experiences gain coherence and meaning when described or reflected back through symbolic productions that enable the reconstruction of a culturally contextualised narrative of disaster. (Huss et al. 2015, p. 284)

These same authors, as a result of their examination of art as a form to build community understanding and action, also restate a recommendation for disaster policy calling for recovery funds to include artistic activities and policy framed from a humanities perspective. Furthermore, art can serve as a vehicle of (social) catharsis that in and of itself can be a healing activity. Creative crafts, such as imagery production, indeed can communicate more than "a thousand words" can say, especially in the face of disaster.

Post-hurricane Puerto Rican aesthetics is (still) functioning as a way to purge or as a form of catharsis that aims to make sense of the societal issues that surrounds the disaster of Hurricane Maria. The affective process of (social) catharsis through art does not refer here to using art to overcome psychological disorders in individual therapy for psychological trauma (which is an important topic in light of the mental health issues brought upon by Hurricane Maria discussed in the previous four chapters). Here, using art for social catharsis refers to an aesthetic process in which people can collectively express the complex or contradictory social, cultural, and political situations that confront them (Constantino and White, 2010; Vygotsky 1972, p. 564) such as the sociopolitical factors that made Hurricane Maria's disaster even more disastrous.

In aesthetics, catharsis is a common form that serves as a purge for both artists and art consumers. Vygotsky, in a classical essay about aesthetics and catharsis, and from a sociocultural perspective, explains:

> Though little is known at present about the process of catharsis, we do know, however, that the discharge of nervous energy (which is the essence of any emotion) takes place in a direction which opposes the conventional one, and that art therefore becomes a most powerful means for important and appropriate discharges of nervous energy. (1972, p. 580)

Similar to other aesthetic types or genres in novels, plays, and visual arts, such as tragedy, comedy, conceptualism, and others, we find that in the aesthetic form that characterizes post-hurricane Puerto Rican artistic expression, an aesthetic of disaster, which generates a relationship of antagonism between the human and the natural in its depiction of visual artistic expression (Constantino and White, 2010; Vygotsky 1972). This means that post-hurricane visual expression uses the narrative of disaster to depict the entanglements between naturally produced disasters and sociopolitical disasters. These tensions produce a vacuum that calls for sense-making storytelling. In the case of post-hurricane aesthetic expressions, the contradictions between natural and human disasters ignite that charged vacuum demanding that we reexamine the Puerto Rican colonial and ecological sociopolitical context and produce some worthwhile political action (this will be elaborated on further).

Social catharsis produced by visual art serves as a means to manifest sociopolitical discontent and not solely an individual's expression. More specifically, this Puerto Rican post-hurricane aesthetics of disaster processes sociopolitical realities by expressing the clashing realities of a history of colonization dramatically thrown into reprieve by the natural and subsequent tragic human disaster in Puerto Rico.

AESTHETIC REACTIONS POST-HURRICANE MARIA: AN INCOMPLETE INVENTORY

What follows is an inventory of aesthetic reactions of Puerto Rican arts to the traumatic experience of Hurricane Maria. We briefly address community art projects, art exhibitions, and residencies, and mention some comedy performance arts as well. In this section we do not aim to present a representation of the totality of all aesthetic reactions, not even specifically in the visual arts because it is not the aim nor in concordance with the cultural studies framework of this piece; however given the currency of the ongoing post-hurricane period we can claim that in fact we have examined most of the Puerto Rican visual art pieces for this chapter when this book went to press. The aim of this section is to present illustrative samples of post-hurricane aesthetic reactions that can showcase the prevalence of a post-hurricane aesthetics in various artistic media.

Puerto Rican arts have directly engaged with the post-hurricane emergency and its recovery through community interventions. Many researchers starting to examine the community organizations that were the first responders to the emergency (given that the government, especially at the federal and commonwealth levels, was arguably not ready for the magnitude of the devastation as discussed in previous chapters) have stated that most had an aesthetic or artistic element that featured in their services. For instance, *Casa Pueblo* (The People's House), a historic ecological community-led organization in the heart of the mountains in Puerto Rico, often arranged for art-led workshops and community theater performances for intervention and entertainment purposes given that many communities did not have power for several months, and at times, for close to a year.

Other community art projects directly addressed the devastation within communities such as *Defend Puerto Rico* in Comerio, *Yauchromatic 2*, *Amanecer Borincano* (Puerto Rican Dawn) in Aguadilla, and others. Two specific community mural art projects in Yauco and Aguadilla were designed by artist Samuel Gonzalez on impoverished houses, and community members and volunteers painted their houses in a collective approach. *Yauchromatic 2* (in Yauco, seen in figure 10.1) and *Amanecer Borincano* (the larger of these two macro-murals, in Aguadilla) not only aesthetically revitalized the structures of the communities and their collective sense of community, but they also serve as a tourist landmark because of their chromatic splendor economic impact.

Theater and Performing Arts

Furthermore, there exists a plethora of important forms of creation that emerged after Hurricane Maria and its aftermath and exist outside the visual arts cannon. In theater, there were a few collectives that traveled around the

Figure 10.1 Yauchromatic 2 Project, 2018. *Source*: Author' Personal Photograph. To view this illustration in color, please locate this book on the publisher's website at www.rowman.com and click on the book's Features tab.

island, reaching marginalized and remote communities in efforts to provide a sense of joy and laughter through comedy, or a sense of solidarity, through narratives surrounding loss and deprivation, in the immediate aftermath.

The theater collective Agua, Sol y Sereno, which had been focusing on community driven and multidisciplinary theater and workshops for over 25 years when Hurricane Maria made landfall, organized by actor and director Pedro Adorno, toured around Puerto Rico following the immediate and most difficult months after the hurricane.[3] Their shows consisted of directly engaging with the community through means of storytelling and puppetry, bringing different narratives surrounding post-hurricane reconstruction. Other notable theater collectives that focused on reaching removed communities are the activist theater and puppet collective Papel Machete, Teatro Rodante with their show *Ay Maria*[4] and *Y No Había Luz.*

Using humor as a coping mechanism[5] to provide a cathartic form of comedy, such as stand-up and improv, served as a way to address the collective grief that struck Puerto Rican communities following Hurricane Maria. For example, comedian Chente Ydrach did an island-wide comedy tour telling stories and providing humor through the devastation. Also, theater collective and improv comedy troupe Teatro Breve produced a sold-out show called *Después de Maria* (After Maria). Teatro Breve comedian Lucienne Hernández, in an interview (Cassanova-Burgess 2017) with WNYC podcast *On the Media*, mentioned how both performers and audience members used this show as a form of therapy, following the effects and adverse living conditions brought by Hurricane Maria and the government's inefficient recovery process.

Loss of Studio Space

Following the effects of Hurricane Maria, various visual artists, artist-run spaces, and exhibitions suffered damage, loss, and a halt in their production and careers. Examples such as Richard Santiago (TIAGO) and Cuban artist, based in Puerto Rico for nearly 40 years, Zilia Sánchez, were just two of many who lost their studio space and various artworks to the damage caused by the hurricane. Sánchez's prolific yet little known, work and career, characterized by sculptural forms of painting with erotic undertones, is now receiving international credit following a 70-year retrospective of Zilia Sánchez's work, *Soy Isla*, presented in the Phillips Collection in Washington, DC, from February until April 2019 and later in El Museo del Barrio from November 2019 until March 2020.

As stated by curator Laura Roulet in "Aglutinación: The Collective Spirit of Puerto Rican Art": "Desperate times call for collective means. Building on a long tradition of workshops, collectives, collaborative art, DIY artist-run initiatives, and social practice, Puerto Rican artists have resurged" (Roulet 2017, 235). The importance of the diverse forms of opportunities and artworks that emerged following Hurricane Maria attests to the communal spirit behind visual art creation on the island that existed before the hurricane, largely in part due to lack of funding and opportunities from governmental and private museum sectors.

The effects and negligence following Hurricane Maria resulted in the stagnation or cancellation of all exhibitions and programming set to take place in the following months. In December 2017, two exhibition openings took place despite various immediate recovery challenges and obstacles (such as the lack of electricity), *Catársis: Reconstruyendo después de Maria* in the Museum of the Americas in San Juan and *Aa-Zz*—a solo show of visual artist Manuel Mendoza Sánchez in Hidrante, located in Santurce. *Catársis*, which emerged from an open call by museum executive director Maria Ángela López Vilella and visual artist Nick Quijano, for artists spanning from various creative disciplines, was held primarily as a way to unify the artistic community in Puerto Rico and bring a sense of catharsis to those severely affected by the hurricane.

PM Exhibition

One of the most in-depth exhibitions to successfully and exclusively engage with post-Maria themes, as well as provide a critical examination of Puerto Rican sociopolitical structures, was *PM*, curated by Christopher Rivera and Manuela Paz and held from January 27 to March 17, 2018, in Embajada—an art gallery located in Santurce (located in the San Juan *municipio*). The list included almost 100 phrases using the acronym "PM," and among the artists were Rebecca Adorno, Amara Abdal Figueroa, Radames Juni Figueroa, Frances Gallardo, Daniel Lind Ramos, Natalia Martínez, Manuel Mendoza, Joel Yoyo Rodriguez, Lorraine Rodriguez, Chemi Rosado-Seíjo, Gabriella Torres Ferrer, Yiyo Tirado. *PM* caused a great public impact by being one of the first exhibitions to tackle complex themes of loss and devastation, while in contrast with the space, providing visceral experience for viewers. As one of the authors of this piece stated in *Cultural Studies*:

> *PM*'s curation also focused on a clear curation of space that produced an immersive experience into the chaotic, and at the same time, a calm and comforting post-hurricane experience considering the gallery was a controlled experience within a still post-destruction Puerto Rico with the majority of its people without basic needs such as electricity. (Rivera-Santana 2019, p. 10)

Diasporic Post-Hurricane Maria Interventions to Assist Puerto Rican Artists

Following Hurricane Maria, some diasporic interventions aimed to assist artists rebuild and reconstruct after suffering physical and economic losses. A notable example is the artist residency, The Studios, that opened in MASS MoCA—specifically aimed to transport and give studio spaces to visual artists affected by Hurricane Maria and to give them the opportunity to continue their production. As the residency's description and artist profile section states, "The devastation to the island has disrupted the careers of many artists in Puerto Rico, and we created this residency opportunity to provide much needed time, space, and financial and professional support to help artists rebuild their art practices and pursue new opportunities" (Assets for Artists 2018). Visual artists who participated in this exhibition included Gamaliel Rodríguez, Ada Bobonis, Ivelisse Jiménez, Lilliam Nieves, Natalie Falero, and Rogelio Baez-Vega.

Another notable example of a residency geared toward Puerto Rican artists includes the *Focus on Puerto Rico* residency, developed by Mana Contemporary in partnership with Clocktower Productions and MECA International Art Fair, which took place in December 2017 in Downtown Miami. *Focus on Puerto Rico* aimed to "celebrate Puerto Rican artists and provide a platform to garner broader access to, and understanding of, Puerto Rico's contemporary social-political landscape—addressing issues facing the territory in relation to the U.S. policy and the Caribbean at-large" (Mass MoCA, n.d.). Puerto Rican visual and sound artists that partook in this residency included Roberto "Yiyo" Tirado, Rafael Vargas Bernard, Andria Morales, Matotumba, Elizabeth Robles, Daniel Bejar, Poncili Creation, and Ulrik López.

> Surviving the phenomenon and becoming active agents of solidarity and selflessness has led us [artists] toward an ideological shift, in which audiences can internalize social issues and revalue educational alternatives. Culture and the arts are tools for human beings to reconstruct themselves (Melendes 2018, p. 2).

Defying Darkness Exhibition

In October 2018 *Defying Darkness*, an exhibition curated by Dr. Josie López in 516 Arts, located in Albuquerque, New Mexico, presented the work of prominent contemporary Puerto Rican artists both from Puerto Rico and the diaspora who approach themes of the impacts of colonialism, economic crisis, and climate change. *Defying Darkness* included a vast range of emerging, midcareer and established Puerto Rican artists, providing a variety of voices and mediums. The artists presented were Adal Maldonado, Jo Cosme, Hector Arce-Espasas, Ramón Bonilla, Nathan Budoff, Myritza Castillo, crashlovedog, Frances Gallardo, Kai Margarida-Ramírez, Antonio Martorell, Elsa Maria Meléndez, Patrick McGrath Muñiz, Chemi Rosado-Seijo, Aby Ruiz, Juan Sánchez, and Rafael Trelles. In the exhibition's main text "El Arte de Bregar," López highlighted the resilience that has characterized Puerto Rico's visual arts production since before Hurricane Maria: "Though the destruction of hurricane Maria has heightened the urgency to act for the artists participating in this exhibition, their resilience and resourcefulness is anything but new" (Pérez 2018, p. 2).

Defying Darkness took its name from the post-Maria energy crisis that left millions without electricity for months, largely in part to an already faulted electrical system and the post-hurricane governmental negligence (as discussed in other chapters). However, others have seen the blackout as a cathartic revelation, one of coming from darkness to light (of making sense of what happened), to become illuminated and clearly see Puerto Rico's lack of sovereignty and its collapsing economy as disastrous as any other natural disaster that might hit Puerto Rico to make the situation even worse. As filmmaker and writer Frances Negrón-Muntaner stated in "Blackout: What Darkness Illuminated in Puerto Rico" in 2019, "The darkness, however, not only revealed; it clarified."

Summary of the Illustrative Collection

This incomplete inventory serves as an illustrative collection that demonstrates the diversity of the aesthetic reactions to the aftermath of the hurricane. Each artistic practice showcased messages that in general suggested that the hurricane's disaster was not completely the outcome of natural devastation—a theme echoed in other chapters in this book. In the following section we focus on two prevalent messages that post-hurricane visual art is conveying aesthetically—that climate change and colonization are important issues that exacerbated the natural disaster and they required urgent attention in the aftermath of Hurricane Maria in Puerto Rico.

AESTHETIC MESSAGE: HOW ART IS TELLING THE POST-HURRICANE STORY

> Colonization and climate justice exist in the same historical frame, as colonialism's primary manifestations began with the exploitation of natural and mineral resources, cultural and natural objects. From this point, the decolonization efforts in Puerto Rico and the movements towards climate justice are inextricably linked and must be studied within the same historical framework. (Atiles-Osoria 2013, 11)

To examine the effects of Hurricane Maria, we must engage with climate change and the colonial political structures of the Caribbean. To exemplify this analysis that Puerto Rican visual art is communicating, we focus on the post-hurricane aesthetic reactions of four artists: Gabriella Torres Ferrer, Patrick McGrath Muñiz, Frances Gallardo, and Daniel Lind-Ramos. We do not claim that these artists and their post-hurricane pieces are necessarily representative of the overarching themes that dozens of artists have engaged with in their art. We used these artists' works because they are *illustrative* to two themes that we have found heavily repeated in post-hurricane art, the relationships between disaster, colonization, and climate change. To this end, we interpret these illustrative art works as a form of thinking: art as a form of thinking through the complexities of the aftermath of Hurricane Maria.

Patrick McGrath Muñiz's *Diasporamus*

Patrick McGrath Muñiz is a conceptual contemporary artist who discusses the historical continuity between the initial colonization in the Caribbean and the capitalist-driven neocolonial processes entwined with climate change and migration. McGrath Muñiz adopts Spanish classical art techniques, in his paintings, to present colonial imageries in content and in form that narrates the story of colonization, consumerism, and climate change through satire, melancholia, and the depiction of the Puerto Rican quotidian imagery. *Diasporamus* (2018), presented in figure 10.2, is an example of a piece that invites the viewer to contemplate the web of an aesthetic of disaster weaved by the themes of post-hurricane disaster, colonization (by referring to Spanish renaissance art), climate change, capitalism, and forced displacement.

Figure 10.2 Diasporamus, Patrick McGrath Muñiz, 2018. *Source*: Reprinted courtesy of the artist. *Note*: Oil on canvas. To view this illustration in color, please locate this book on the publisher's website at www.rowman.com and click on the book's Features tab.

When contemplating McGrath Muñiz's work, what immediately jumps to the eye is the image of the shirtless, anguish-stricken man in the center of the painting holding a roll of paper towels—a direct reference to the controversial incident involving U.S. president Donald Trump when he visited Puerto Rico, and threw a roll of paper towels to Puerto Ricans in October 2017 to display his intent of contributing in disaster relief—over a visibly saddened woman in an almost fetal position, presumably protecting herself from the surrounding disaster situation suggested in the painting as a whole. This allegorical work functions as a conceptualist loop of gyrating local and global narratives of disaster that yarn themes of climate change, consumerism, and colonization through: (1) comments on Spanish colonization seen in the multiple references to Renaissance art such as *The Birth of Venus* (1484–1486) by Botticelli and *The Dog* (1823) by Goya; (2) the explicit comments on the effects of climate change seen in the depiction of vicious floods and the familiar image of Puerto Ricans trying to get cell phone signal after Hurricane Maria, and ecological displacement and migration; and (3) consumerism seen in the iconic symbols of global capitalism (namely Starbucks, Shell and Yamaha), rephrased as *Yamejo-di.*[6]

Furthermore, one can see other connecting narratives of these themes in the Puerto Rican cultural iconic representations that range from the mundane to the satirical (for instance, the pig that travels in the small vessel with the *jíbaro*, the manatee swimming in the floods waters, and more), among other (sometimes hidden) narratives and symbols.

Diasporamus capitalizes twice on the (European) renaissance artistic forms from the past and the previous Puerto Rican histories of migration to the United States, suggesting a comment on the two histories of colonization—Spain and the United States—simultaneously. Yet what places the piece into the present, and even launches it to a not-too-distant future, is the overarching frame of disaster because it is able to weld together the themes of colonialism, capitalism, climate change, post-Hurricane Maria disaster, and more. McGrath Muñiz uses an aesthetics of disaster in this piece to tell the complex story of how post-hurricane effects can be tied to colonization, displacement, capitalism, and Puerto Rican culture.

Gabriella Torres's *Valora Tu Mentira Americana*

Another example is Gabriella Torres's *Valora tu mentira americana* (Value Your American Lie, 2018), seen in figure 10.3, which displaces the room with an unembellished piece of the Puerto Rican Power Authority's failed infrastructure—a utility pole—that expresses one of the main problems in post-Hurricane Maria Puerto Rico discussed in nearly all of the chapters in

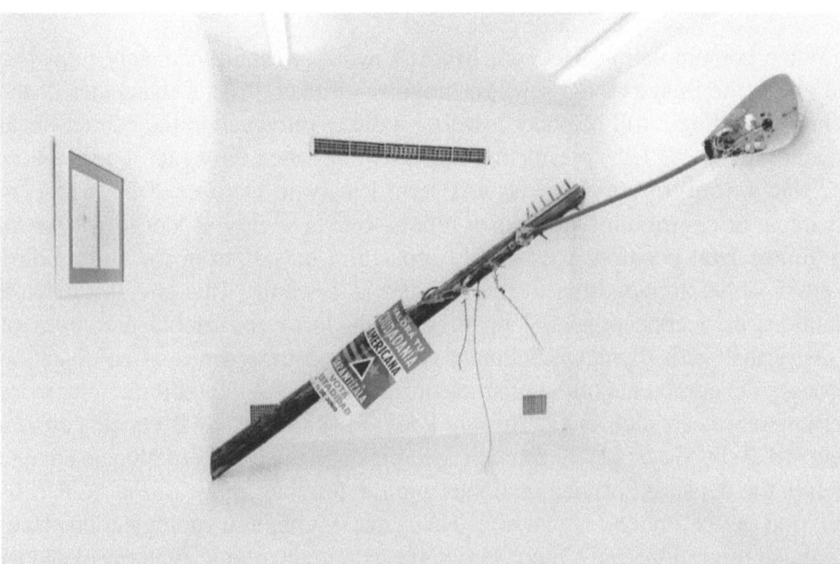

Figure 10.3 Valora Tu Mentira Americana, Gabriella Torres Ferrer, 2018. *Source*: Reprinted courtesy of the artist. *Note*: Mixed media, installation. To view this illustration in color, please locate this book on the publisher's website at www.rowman.com and click on the book's Features tab.

this book: the lack of electricity. The surreal experience of devastation is contained in the gallery, reproducing the experience of disarray and the danger of torn hanging electrical cables, and it allows (almost calls) the viewer to closely examine the story that this object is telling.

Utility poles in Puerto Rico are often used for political propaganda, and this is reflected in Torres's piece, which features a flyer attached to the middle of the utility pole. The flyer reads "Valora tu ciudadanía americana" (Value your American citizenship), and it continues below with "Garatízala, vota estadidad, 11 de junio" (Guarantee it, vote for statehood on June 11), which alludes to a highly questionable plebiscite on Puerto Rico's relationship with the United States that occurred two months before Hurricane Maria. The June 11, 2017, plebiscite was highly controversial because the options available to voters did not include an "evolved" version of the current commonwealth status, an option put forward by one of the major political parties. Moreover, the plebiscite suffered from massive voter abstention (Robles 2017).

The irony of the piece's title, *Value Your American Lie* (as translated into English), also provokes the viewer to remember the political event of the plebiscite in the context of a post-hurricane disaster that showcased, through the shattered utility pole, the futility of Puerto Rican politics in the face of its infrastructure's fragility. Given how the piece contains disaster, the message in the political propaganda displays the contradiction between the perceived protection of U.S. citizenship in Puerto Rico and the post-hurricane destruction and ongoing infrastructural disaster—focusing on electrical infrastructure—that the artist links with the futility of Puerto Rican politics, which she extends to the political (colonial) relationship with the United States. In the face of bare destruction, Torres's piece leads the viewer to question the apparent safety net of Puerto Rican political status, its U.S. citizenship, and therefore its (presumed) preferential relationship with the federal government—causing the rude awakening that Puerto Ricans are colonial subjects—while also inviting the viewer to question the lie or ask, How did we arrive at this "lie"?

Frances Gallardo's *Hurricane Series*

Hurricane Maria, itself a result of climate change that manifests itself in the augmentation of superstorms in the Caribbean, should also be examined from a similar eco-critical perspective. Even before Hurricane Maria, Puerto Rican contemporary artists were examining sociopolitical and ecological matters that created their own metaphorical storm on the island. Contemporary Puerto Rican visual artist Frances Gallardo engages with an eco-critical framework[7] exploring themes of colonial environmentalism and political ecology by focusing on the rise of extreme weather patterns and ecological alterations in the Caribbean.

Through her elaborately cut paper sculptural work (examples shown in figures 10.4 and 10.5), Gallardo has been commenting on the formation of

Figure 10.4 Carmela (from the Hurricane Series), Frances Gallardo, 2011. *Source*: Reprinted courtesy of the artist. *Note*: 27.5 in. × 39.5 in., cut paper, collage. To view this illustration in color, please locate this book on the publisher's website at www.rowman.com and click on the book's Features tab.

meteorological impacts upon the Caribbean region, and its subsequent migrations, since 2011 by using satellite-generated imagery posted on the U.S. National Oceanic and Atmospheric Administration archives and website to reference for her *Hurricane Series* (2011–ongoing), creating work by engaging with a culturally recognizable symbol. She approaches meteorological formations and their effects on the region as a way to create a dialogue with historical, political, and ecological epistemologies specific to the Caribbean and Puerto Rico. In an interview with the artist, Gallardo states that the hurricane is not the agent of destruction, as they have existed in the region for thousands of years, but rather the human component behind climate is the true cataclysmic and destructive force.

Frances Gallardo's *Murmuration*

In the previously mentioned exhibition, *Defying Darkness*, Frances Gallardo presents *Murmuration (Mosquito Cloud)* (2017), a 6-feet diameter visual representation of a satellite image of a hurricane, composed of small paper-cut sculptures of mosquitos and hung using dressmaker pins (see figure 10.6). In her article "Aglutinación: The Collective Spirit of Puerto Rican Art," written for the exhibition catalogue for *Relational Undercurrents:*

Figure 10.5 Gabriel (from the Hurricane Series), Frances Gallardo, 2013. *Source*: Reprinted courtesy of the artist. *Note*: 27.5 in. × 39.5 in., cut paper, collage. To view this illustration in color, please locate this book on the publisher's website at www.rowman.com and click on the book's Features tab.

Contemporary Art of the Caribbean Archipelago, curator Laura Roulet describes these patterns as being "the micro fingerprint whorls to the macro meteorological patterns, personalizing human vulnerability when confronted by the catastrophic effects of climate change" (Roulet 2017, p. 237). The artist creates intricate patterns depicting the winds of the hurricane, providing a measured chaos and a calculated execution to the otherwise disordered cluster of winds of the hurricane. Her use of paper highlights the fragility of human livelihoods when confronted with natural and not-so-natural disasters, creating an ontological paradox.

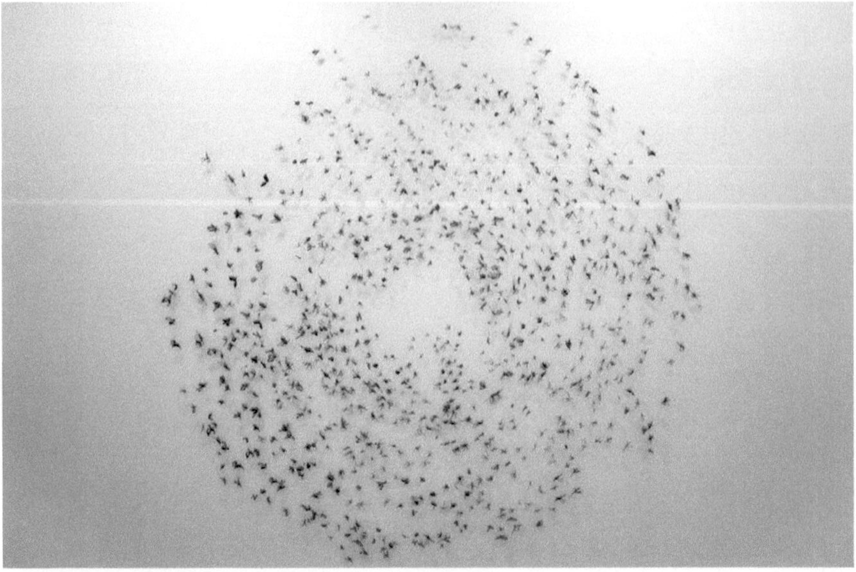

Figure 10.6 Murmuration (Mosquito Cloud), Frances Gallardo, 2017. *Source*: Reprinted courtesy of the artist. *Note*: 6 ft diameter, installation of laser cut paper pinned on wall. To view this illustration in color, please locate this book on the publisher's website at www.rowman.com and click on the book's Features tab.

Daniel Lind-Ramos's *Maria-Maria*

Similarly, *Maria-Maria* (2019) by Daniel Lind-Ramos (shown in figure 10.7) evokes the dual nature of hurricanes, its sacredness and its disastrous power where the piece adopts a syncretic yet colonial form of a shrine of a Virgin Mary or Chango (a syncretism inspired by the Orisha-African deity) while using objects found and used in the aftermath of the hurricane. Lind-Ramos, a mixed media contemporary artist who draws from the Afro-Puerto Rican aesthetic and historical traditions particularly from his community of Loíza, was selected to exhibit in the prestigious 2019 Whitney Biennial. His works in the biennial have been exceptionally reviewed by art critics and his sculpture *Maria-Maria* was featured on the cover of the cultural section of the *New York Times* (Cotter 2019).

The piece was created from wood, beads, coconuts, and a blue FEMA (the U.S. Federal Emergency and Management Administration) tarp, an unharmonious mix between natural and human-made materials that in the arrangement of the piece acquires a meticulous order to form the Virgin Mary (Maria). *Maria-Maria* reminds us of the value of intricate design in the way it can allow seemingly contradictory elements—such as the chaos of natural disaster (the hurricane), colonially imposed imagery (the Virgin Mary), colonial politics (U.S. FEMA), post-hurricane trauma (represented in the objects

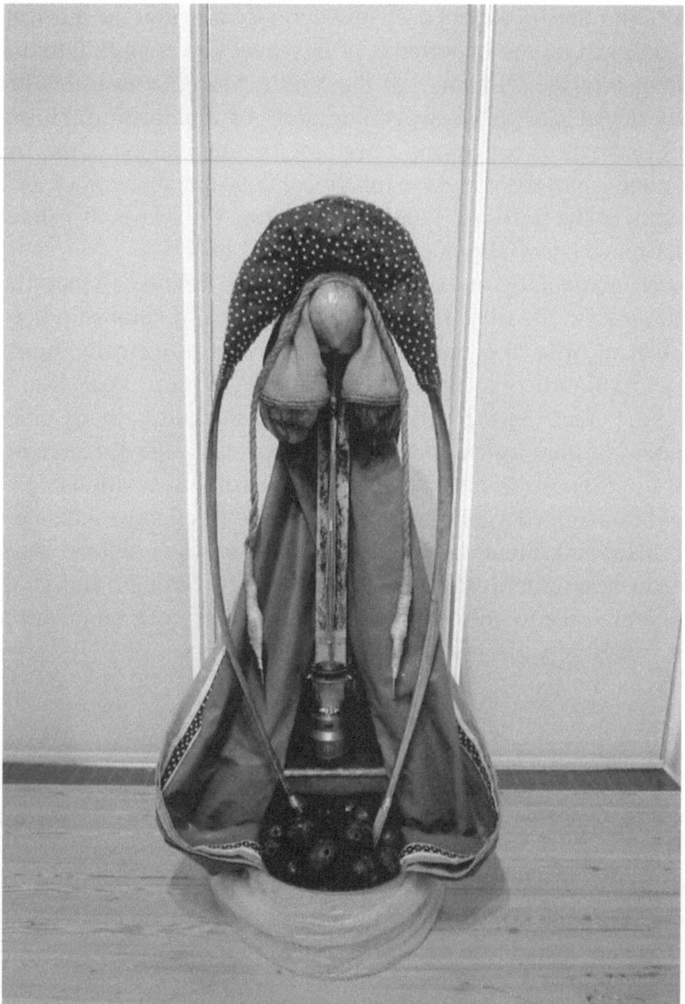

Figure 10.7 Maria-Maria, Daniel Lind-Ramos, 2019. *Source*: Reprinted courtesy of the artist. *Note*: Mixed media from wood, beads, coconuts, and a blue FEMA tarp. To view this illustration in color, please locate this book on the publisher's website at www.rowman.com and click on the book's Features tab.

used), personal and social order (represented in the meticulous assemblage of the materials)—to complexly coexist.

This piece makes a comment in the form of the divinity or beyond human character of Hurricane Maria, yet its content is formed by mostly human artifacts which comments on the precariat of the aftermath of the disaster yet also the capacity for these materials to be assembled in a useful order that constitutes a "chaos that is not chaotic" (Glissant 1997, 201). The battery-fueled lamp in the center of the piece—widely used by Puerto Ricans after the hurricane—also makes a comment on the importance of electrical power and illumination, and the importance of the "divinity" of the Virgin Mary because this imagery is historically depicted with a surrounding glow or illumination. However, this lamp is off in the piece suggesting a need for the illumination of this imagery to be "on" or activated, the recursive functional conceptualization of a chaos that is not chaotic in the ancestral relationship among the forces of nature, natural and human-made materials, culture, politics, and history.

The piece perpetually starts and begins with "Maria" (hence the repetition of the name in the title) suggesting the cyclical relationship between the natural objects from the environment, and the historically human-made material and cultural objects, such as the FEMA tarp, skull-like coconuts (one being the "face" of the Virgin Mary), and the culturally assembled conceptualization of the virgin and Maria the hurricane. The message here is the importance of (ancestral) history when considering the relationships between natural and human order, and how there can be a reflexive balance between natural disaster and human governance. Lind-Ramos is making a decolonial comment on how colonization can be addressed through ancestral knowledges that were able to consider both, natural order with human order, even when they seemingly clash with each other.

CONCLUDING REMARKS

Climate change and its effects upon the Caribbean are no longer imminent, but a present reality. The long-standing history of colonization frames this current scenario, of which Puerto Rican visual art is making sense and communicating. Through our incomplete inventory of artistic production following the effects of Hurricane Maria, we juxtapose different forms of creative interventions that rose from Puerto Rico's post-Maria recovery and subsequently the need for societal catharsis. As showcased prominently by visual artists, Puerto Rico's colonial and political history amplified the disastrous effects of Hurricane Maria and exposed the already fraught infrastructure that Puerto Rico held long before the storm, but it also surfaced the interconnected nature of political ecology and colonization.

As American art critic and scholar TJ Demos defined the politics of ecology: "The term 'political ecology' . . . acknowledges approaches to the environment that, although potentially divergent, nevertheless insist on environmental matters of concern as inextricable from social, political, and economic forces" (Demos 2016, p. 7). The artistic expressions not only tap into how societal catharsis exists in directly confronting traumatic events through an artistic medium, but it also illustrates the closely tied relations between a decolonial and eco-critical examination of extreme weather conditions through the disaster of sociopolitical components following Hurricane Maria in Puerto Rico.

NOTES

1. Puerto Rican arts have historically addressed urgent political situations affecting Puerto Rico and Puerto Ricans. However, we must state that historically, Puerto Rican visual arts have been marginalized under the notions of not being a reflection of the U.S. (and thus European) art production, because of the cultural differences, or part of Latin American and Caribbean art production because of its sociopolitical and economic relation to the United States. In other words, Puerto Rican visual arts as an industry and canon of art history occupy an undervalued position similar to the unequal relationship that Puerto Ricans have in many other realms, such as in economics, politics, and racial relations, among others (Ramírez 2005, 150–178).

2. One of the most important political events to which Puerto Rican artists reacted in the past two decades was the political struggle against the disaster caused by the U.S. Navy's use of Puerto Rico for war-like exercises, weapons testing, and other military purposes. On April 19, 1999, civilian employee David Sanes Rodríguez was accidentally struck and killed during a U.S. Navy bomb testing in Vieques. This incident activated already growing resentment and concern about the social and ecological damage of the presence of military occupation in Puerto Rico, which led to years of political and ecological activism calling for the Navy to abandon their operations. "La Marina" (short for "La Marina de Guerra de Estados Unidos") in Vieques played an important role in shaping politically and ecologically engaged narratives in Puerto Rican art that sought to contest the island's colonial relationship and ecological concerns, including artist collective Allora and Calzadilla and filmmaker and artist Beatriz Santiago Muñoz, whose works became associated with the protests that caused for the evacuation of the Navy in Vieques.

3. Following this island-wide tour, Adorno and his collaborators collected various stories of loss and death in each part of the island they toured, and as a way to provide visibility to the unaccounted for deaths of those in the communities they visited, they wrote and directed the play *Corazón de Papel*, which toured on the east coast of the United States.

4. Intersecting both theatre and comedy, the acting troupe Teatro Rodante created *Ay Maria!*, a play produced by Mariana Carbonell and directed by Maritza Pérez Otero, that recounted stories of solidarity through a humorous lens, while also providing social and political critical engagement.

5. In December 2017, WNYC Studio podcast, *On the Media* interviewed anthropologist Yarimar Bonilla for "Dark Humor after Maria" where she states Puerto Ricans are using their "strong tradition of humor to make sense of their plight."

6. This means "Now I am fucked," yet in Spanish it works as a provocative play in words that is similar to "Yamaha."

7. When studying the Caribbean and Puerto Rico's ecosystem, one must think about it from the perspective of the study of political ecology. Coming from a specifically Caribbean perspective, in *Introduction: Towards an Aesthetic of the Earth*, authors Elizabeth DeLoughrey and George B. Handley engage with an eco-critical theory that, quoting Guyanese writer Wilson Harris, seeks to create a "profound dialogue with the landscape" (2011). DeLoughrey and Handley follow Harris's idea by creating a historical narrative that takes into consideration the epistemology of space and time in relation to the specific locations' ecology. The authors expand on the idea that "the decoupling of nature and history has helped to mystify colonialism's histories of forced migration, suffering, and human violence" (2011). This separation between nature and history has allowed for the continuation of extractive views over landscape and populations being seen as commodities under a capitalist system, a view that helped create the colonial machine in the Caribbean.

Chapter 11

Voter Registration and Turnout among Island-Born and Mainland-Born Puerto Ricans in the 2018 U.S. Congressional Elections

Mark Hugo Lopez, Antonio Flores, and Jens Manuel Krogstad

ABSTRACT

This chapter explores voter turnout trends among Puerto Ricans living in the 50 U.S. states and D.C. It discusses changes in the number of eligible voters (adult U.S. citizens), voter registrations, and turnout rates among island-born and mainland-born Puerto Ricans in congressional and presidential elections between 1998 and 2018. The chapter concludes with a discussion of preliminary results from the 2020 presidential election in the battleground states of Florida and Pennsylvania, major receiving areas of migrants from the island.

Hurricanes Maria and Irma accelerated a long and ongoing out-migration from the island of Puerto Rico to the U.S. mainland. Since 2004, when the island's population peaked at 3.8 million people, the number of people living there has fallen by about half a million, with the largest one-year change happening in the year after the hurricanes hit Puerto Rico (Flores and Krogstad 2019).

Out-migration—and its potential effects on U.S. elections—has been an emerging element in the story of Puerto Rican voters and, more broadly, Latino voters (Malo and Brasileiro 2018). This is especially true in the state of Florida, a place where Latino voters have grown in number and proportion as well as in importance in midterm and presidential election years, including 2020. Latino voters in Florida are a larger group and more diverse in their origins than Latino voters in most other places around the country. For example, no origin group makes up a majority of Latino voters in the state and most are Cubans, Puerto Ricans, Colombians, Dominicans, and Mexicans, a sharp contrast to other states like California or Texas where Mexicans make up the majority of Latino voters (Flores, Lopez and Krogstad, 2018). And as discussed by Marie T. Mora, Havidán Rodríguez, and Alberto Dávila (chapter 1), a larger number of Puerto Ricans lived in Florida than the state of New York shortly before Hurricane Maria. Moreover, those born in Puerto Rico are U.S. citizens by birth and can be eligible to vote once they move to any of the 50 U.S. states or the District of Columbia (see also Venator-Santiago 2017). This chapter explores voter turnout trends among Puerto Ricans living in the 50 U.S. states and D.C.

PUERTO RICO OUT-MIGRATION AND PUERTO RICAN ELIGIBLE VOTERS

In 2018, 3.6 million Puerto Ricans, both island born and stateside born, were eligible to vote (adult U.S. citizens), according to the U.S. Census Bureau's November 2018 Current Population Survey, Voting and Registration Supplement (see table 11.1). Just over half (1.9 million, or 54%) of Puerto Rican eligible voters were born in the U.S. mainland and 1.6 million (46%) were born in Puerto Rico. They are the second-largest origin group among Hispanic eligible voters in the United States.

Nationally, the number of eligible voters of Puerto Rican origin has been rising. In the 50 U.S. states and the District of Columbia, this number grew by 1.6 million between 1998 and 2018, or 83 percent. This growth has come from both the island's net out-migration (discussed in chapter 1 by Mora, Rodríguez, and Dávila) and the coming of age of mainland-born Puerto Ricans. The number of island-born Puerto Rican eligible voters in the United States was up 73 percent during this time, rising from 945,000 in 1998 to 1.6 million in 2018. And the number of mainland-born Puerto Rican eligible voters grew 92 percent over the same period, from 1 million to 1.9 million. Overall, about two million Puerto Ricans were eligible to vote in 1998, according to the U.S. Census Bureau's November 1998 Current Population Survey's Voter and Registration Supplement, with 945,000 or about half (48%) island-born Puerto Rican eligible voters.

More recently, the number of Puerto Rican eligible voters born in Puerto Rico and living in the mainland has grown while the number of Puerto Rican eligible voters born stateside has remained flat. But while the number of island-born eligible voters nationally has grown on the mainland, it is unclear how much of an impact Hurricanes Maria and Irma had on growth in the number of Puerto Rican eligible voters, the number of registered voters, or in the number of voters. In 2014, 1.4 million Puerto Rican eligible voters were island born and lived stateside (see table 11.1). By 2016, the number had risen

Table 11.1 Puerto Rican Eligible Voters, Registered Voters, and Voter Turnout: 1998, 2014, 2016, and 2018

	Eligible Voters (in Thousands)	*Registered Voters (in Thousands)*	*Registration Rate among Eligible Voters*	*Voters (in Thousands)*	*Voter Turnout Rate among Eligible Voters*
2018					
All Puerto Ricans	3,578	1,994	56%	1,396	39%
Island born	1,637	832	51%	574	35%
Stateside born	1,941	1,162	60%	822	42%
2016					
All Puerto Ricans	3,670	2,050	56%	1,685	46%
Island born	1,507	757	50%	615	41%
Stateside born	2,163	1,294	60%	1,070	49%
2014					
All Puerto Ricans	3,519	1,883	54%	892	25%
Island born	1,389	808	58%	410	30%
Stateside born	2,130	1,075	50%	483	23%
1998					
All Puerto Ricans	1,958	1,127	58%	643	33%
Island born	945	552	58%	336	36%
Stateside born	1,013	575	57%	307	30%

Note: Eligible voters are adult U.S. citizens living in the 50 U.S. states and the District of Columbia. Estimates of the number of registered voters and number of voters are based on self-reports. Population estimates are rounded to the nearest 1,000. All results are weighted.
Source: Authors' tabulations of data from the U.S. Census Bureau's November Current Population Survey, Voter and Registration Supplement, 1998, 2014, 2016 and 2018.

to 1.5 million, an increase of 118,000 voters or 8.5 percent between elections. As noted in previous chapters, Hurricanes Irma and Maria hit Puerto Rico a few weeks apart in September 2017. By 2018, U.S. Census Bureau data sources showed some 1.6 million island-born Puerto Ricans eligible to vote living stateside. This 8.6 percent increase of 130,000 eligible voters between 2016 and 2018 was similar to the increase seen between 2014 and 2016.

Despite this steady growth, Puerto Rican eligible voters made up a smaller share of all Hispanic eligible voters in 2018 than two decades prior. Between

1998 and 2018, the number of Hispanics eligible to vote more than doubled, from 12.4 million to 29 million (Krogstad, Noe-Bustamante and Flores 2019). At the same time, the number of Puerto Rican eligible voters grew—from 2.0 million to 3.6 million—but did not double in size. As a result, Hispanic eligible voters of Puerto Rican origin (both island born and stateside born) accounted for about 12 percent of Hispanic eligible voters nationally in 2018, down from about 16 percent in 1998.

VOTER REGISTRATION AMONG STATESIDE-BORN PUERTO RICANS ROSE SHARPLY AFTER 2014

About two million Puerto Ricans said they were registered to vote in 2018, up from 1.9 million in 2014. Puerto Ricans born stateside accounted for 78 percent of this rise, as their numbers increased from 1.1 million in 2014 to 1.2 million in 2018.

The number of island-born Puerto Ricans who said they were registered to vote slightly increased, from 808,000 in 2014 to 832,000 in 2018. By comparison, the number of island-born Puerto Rican eligible voters increased by a larger amount during this time, from 1.4 million in 2014 to 1.6 million in 2018. This suggests while more Puerto Ricans arrived from the island in recent years, many did not register to vote.[1] As a result, voter registration rates among the island born *decreased* between 2014 and 2018. At the same time, registration rates increased among the stateside born. In 2018, 60 percent of stateside-born Puerto Ricans on the mainland said they were registered to vote, unchanged from 2016 and up from 50 percent in 2014. By contrast, the voter registration rate among island-born Puerto Ricans on the mainland was 51 percent in 2018, unchanged from 2016, but below their 58 percent voter registration rate of 2014.

Mainland voter registration rates among the island born had been higher than those among the stateside born, but the pattern reversed in 2016. For example, the island-born voter registration rate was eight percentage points larger than the rate among mainland-born Puerto Rican eligible voters in 2014 (58% vs 50%), this flipped by 2018 to a nine-percentage-point deficit for island-born eligible voters (51% vs 60%).

HURRICANES MARIA'S AND IRMA'S IMPACT ON FLORIDA VOTER REGISTRATIONS IS UNCLEAR

As out-migration from Puerto Rico increased in the run up to and the aftermath of Hurricanes Maria and Irma, some political analysts expected a large impact in voter registration and voter turnout among Puerto Ricans in Florida and elsewhere (Barfield Barry 2018). But as the November election drew closer in 2018, political and news analysts began to note many Puerto Ricans who had left the island for Florida after Hurricanes Maria and Irma were still getting settled (Daugherty, Ostroff and Vassolo 2018). Voter registration data showed uneven growth in the state's Puerto Rican population centers. It is likely that voting in the 2018 midterm election was not necessarily a top priority for these recent island-born migrants.

Ahead of the 2018 midterm elections, the number of Hispanics registered to vote, according to the Florida Division of Elections, reached 2.2 million people, up 8.4 percent over 2016 (Krogstad, Flores and Lopez 2018). This was nearly double the 4.6 percent growth rate in Hispanic voter registrations in Florida between 2012 and 2014. But much of this growth happened statewide, not just in counties with significant Puerto Rican populations, suggesting Puerto Ricans who had moved to Florida after the hurricanes had a modest impact on overall Hispanic voter registration (Hohmann 2018). In the four counties with the largest Puerto Rican populations, Hispanic voter registration growth between 2016 and 2018 was about the same as the increase seen statewide. For example, Orange County saw a 9.0 percent increase in the number of Hispanics registered to vote between 2016 and 2018, only slightly higher than the growth rate statewide. By comparison, Hillsborough county, also in Central Florida, was up 5.7 percent while Miami-Dade was up just 4.5 percent (Krogstad, Flores and Lopez 2018).

Yet the influx of Puerto Ricans both before and after the hurricanes has changed the demographics of the state's Hispanic population, and it remains to be seen what impact they will have on future elections. As discussed in chapter 1, Florida has been a new destination for Puerto Ricans moving from the island in the current out-migration flows (see also Mora, Dávila and Rodríguez 2017, 5–6), capturing about a third of the pre-Hurricane Maria out-migration wave (Cohn, Patten and Lopez 2014) and an even greater share after Hurricane Maria. In addition, as Florida became more of a destination for island-born Puerto Ricans, it also became a destination for stateside-born Puerto Ricans. Recall from chapter 1 the number of Puerto Ricans living in Florida surpassed the number in New York State sometime in the mid-2010s. By 2018, 1.19 million Puerto Ricans lived in Florida, compared with 1.07 million in New York.

Within Florida, Puerto Rican population growth has shifted the origins of the state's Hispanic electorate. In the 1990s, Cubans made up nearly half (46%) of all Hispanic eligible voters in the state (Flores, Lopez and Krogstad 2018). By 2018, according to the American Community Survey (ACS), the sizes of the Puerto Rican and Cuban eligible voter populations were about the same, accounting for about 29 and 27 percent, respectively, of the state's Hispanic eligible voters (Noe-Bustamante 2020).

MAINLAND BORN DRIVE NATIONAL VOTER TURNOUT GAINS AMONG PUERTO RICANS IN 2018

Interest in the 2018 midterm elections was high among many groups of Americans (Geiger 2018) and resulted in a sharp increase in voter turnout rates over 2014 (Misra 2019). This was also true nationally for Hispanics. Their voter turnout rate was almost double the rate of 2014, the previous congressional election, and rivaled Hispanic voter turnout in recent presidential elections. Among Puerto Rican eligible voters in the 50 U.S. states and D.C., voter turnout was up sharply too, mirroring broader national trends. In total, 1.4 million Puerto Ricans said they voted in 2018, up from 892,000 who said the same in 2014. Their voter turnout rate increased to 39 percent, up from 25 percent in 2014. Among all Hispanic eligible voters, the voter turnout rate increased to 40.4 percent, up from 27 percent in 2014 (Krogstad, Noe-Bustamante and Flores, 2019).

The sharpest increase in voter turnout was among those born stateside. In 2018, 822,000 mainland-born Puerto Rican eligible voters said they cast a vote, up 339,000 voters from 2014's turnout of 483,000 voters—a 70 percent increase. By contrast, the number of island-born voters grew as well, though more modestly. In 2018, 574,000 island-born eligible voters cast a vote, up 164,000 votes from 2014 when island-born turnout reached 410,000. This increase of 40 percent is impressive but is smaller than increases seen among other Hispanic eligible voters between 2014 and 2018. It also matches reports from after the midterm election, suggesting Puerto Rican voter turnout lagged other groups of voters (Padró Ocasio and Chen 2018). Nonetheless, this increase in the number of voters outpaced growth in the number of Puerto Ricans eligible to vote nationally, which was up 1.6 percent between 2014 and 2018 from 3.52 million to 3.58 million.

In terms of voter turnout rates, the island born have historically voted at higher rates than the mainland born among Puerto Rican eligible voters. But 2018 reversed the pattern. Some 42 percent of mainland-born Puerto Rican eligible voters cast a vote, compared with 35 percent of island-born Puerto Rican eligible voters. By comparison, in 2014, just 23 percent of mainland-born Puerto Ricans voted while 30 percent of the island born did. And in 1998, 36 percent of island-born eligible voters cast a vote, compared with 30 percent among the stateside born.

Even so, voter turnout rates for both island-born Puerto Rican voters and stateside-born Puerto Rican voters increased between 2014 and 2018, reflecting a broad national trend in higher voter turnout rates among Hispanics and all U.S. voters (Krogstad, Noe-Bustamante and Flores 2019).

DISCUSSION AND PRELIMINARY RESULTS FROM THE 2020 PRESIDENTIAL ELECTION

Journalists, political commentators, and Hispanic activists for years have highlighted the growing potential of Hispanic voters in state and national elections, and that is no surprise. The potential of Hispanic voters grows each election cycle as the number of Hispanic eligible voters reaches new highs and Hispanics grow as a share of all voters. For 2020, the Pew Research Center projected the number of Hispanic eligible voters reached 32 million—a new high—and, for the first time, exceeded the size of the Black eligible voter population (Cilluffo and Fry 2019).

This rapid growth in the Hispanic eligible voter population has largely been driven by the coming of age of young, U.S.-born Hispanics who together account for about three-quarters of the additional four million Hispanics who become eligible to vote between presidential election cycles (Krogstad et al. 2016). The second largest source of new voters for Hispanics are naturalizations of immigrants. The third largest source is the arrival of Puerto Ricans from Puerto Rico to the mainland. While an important source, on a national scale, this increase is small compared with the other two sources of growth.

Even so, the potential impact of island-born Puerto Ricans on national elections could be larger than first expected since so many island-born Puerto Ricans have been moving to states often important in national elections, such as Florida. Yet, evidence from 2018 shows a mixed story on the impact of the island born on voter registrations, despite accelerating out-migration from the island.

Heading into 2020, the growing Puerto Rican electorate in battleground states like Florida and Pennsylvania was poised to play an important role in the outcome of the presidential election. While detailed data were not available as this book went to press to conduct a thorough analysis of the turnout and voting patterns of Puerto Ricans in the 2020 presidential election, preliminary data suggest Puerto Rican turnout increased just as it did for all Americans. About 160 million Americans (United States Elections Project 2020) cast a ballot in 2020—a new record. And 2020 saw the highest voter turnout rate—about 66 percent—among all U.S. eligible voters in more than a century (Schaul, Rabinowitz and Mellnik 2020). This happened in places with many Puerto Rican voters just as it did elsewhere. For example, according to data from the Orange County Florida Supervisor of Elections Office (2020), voter turnout was up 19 percent compared with 2016. Among all eligible voters in Orange County, which is where Orlando is located, 16 percent are Puerto Rican.[2]

In the two battleground states, Puerto Rican voters may have played important roles in determining outcomes. According to the 2019 ACS, Puerto Ricans made up 27 percent of Florida's Latino eligible voters or 6 percent of all eligible voters in the state. Exit poll data for Florida, as reported by CNN (2020), shows they supported Democrats Joseph Biden and Kamala Harris over Republicans Donald Trump and Michael Pence 69 to 31 percent.[3] Yet Trump won Florida in part because of a better result among Latino voters in the state in 2020 compared with 2016, including (possibly) among Puerto Ricans (Sesin 2020). A *New York Times* analysis of precinct-level data from Puerto Rican areas around Orlando shows Trump won a greater share of votes in 2020 than in 2016 in them even as Biden won each by big margins (Cai and Fessenden 2020).

In Pennsylvania, Puerto Ricans accounted for 56 percent of Latino eligible voters and 3 percent of all eligible voters in the state, according to the 2019 ACS. Exit poll results as reported by CNN show Biden and Harris won Latino voters by a wide margin, 69 to 27 percent, helping the Democrats win the state and the presidency in 2020. But in Pennsylvania too, the *New York Times* analysis shows that in Philadelphia's majority Latino precincts (largely Puerto Rican areas), Trump did better in 2020 than in 2016. The *New York Times* analysis shows similar shifts in the Bronx in New York City.

CONCLUDING REMARKS

With a growing presence in states like Florida, New York, New Jersey, Pennsylvania, and elsewhere, Puerto Rican voters could shape primary and general election results in coming years. Historically, Puerto Rican voters have shown strong support for Democratic presidential candidates. The 2020 election is no exception, even if Trump may have done better among Puerto Ricans than expected in some places.[4] But 2020 also shows Puerto Rican voters can shift their support for candidates from either party (Boryga, Valdez and Ariza 2020). If voter turnout remains high in future elections as it did in 2020 and 2018, the Puerto Rican vote could become more important in close elections across Florida, Pennsylvania, and nationally, perhaps in unexpected ways.

NOTES

1. The U.S. Census Bureau's Voter and Registration Supplement to the Current Population Survey asks respondents why they had not registered to vote. However, sample sizes for the overall island-born Puerto Rican population are not large enough to report reliable findings for the group (fewer than 100 island-born Puerto Ricans

were asked why they had not registered to vote in 2018, for example). Even so, the reasons they gave for not registering to vote were no different from those given by stateside-born Puerto Rican voters, with the top reason for each group "not interested in the election" or "not involved in politics." For both groups, at least 3-in-10 eligible voters who did not register to vote reported these two reasons.

2. When more data are available from the U.S. Census Bureau, a better picture of Puerto Rican turnout, nationally and across some states and demographics, will be possible.

3. The COVID-19 pandemic upended how elections were conducted in the United States in 2020. Because most voters cast their ballot early (27%), by absentee ballot or by mail (46%) rather than in person (27%) in 2020 (Pew Research Center 2020), there is concern about how well exit polls captured the demographics of voters and how they voted (Bronner and Tabb 2020). As a result, findings from the exit polls should be interpreted cautiously. There were two major exit poll efforts in 2020 by Edison Research and by the Associated Press.

4. The Associated Press' VoteCast exit poll shows Puerto Rican voters nationally supported Democrats Biden and Harris with 66 percent, and Republicans Trump and Pence with 32 percent (Campo-Flores and Findell 2020). As noted earlier in this chapter, however, 2020 exit poll findings should be interpreted cautiously.

Chapter 12

New York Stands with Puerto Rico

A Case Study of the State University of New York (SUNY) Response to Hurricane Maria

Havidán Rodríguez, Mark Lichtenstein,
Sally Crimmins Villela, and Michael A. Alfultis

ABSTRACT

This chapter takes the form of a case study that focuses on the engagement of the SUNY with disaster response in Puerto Rico post-Hurricane Maria. It also discusses the unique and extensive partnerships, including with Puerto Rican organizations, that developed and the stakeholders that were engaged, all of which helped make the initiative a success. Further, we review the mobilization of SUNY's network of individual campuses and the deployment of hundreds of college students over a period of two years, which resulted in a large and complex response process focused on providing support and assistance in the disaster relief and recovery efforts aimed at communities impacted by Hurricane Maria in Puerto Rico. Finally, nine important lessons learned are discussed, framed around the themes of leadership, community engagement, and collective action.[1]

The impact of Hurricane Maria on the island of Puerto Rico and the resulting outcomes were catastrophic for an island population of (then) roughly 3.3 million American citizens. As highlighted throughout this book, Hurricane Maria became the most devastating hurricane to impact Puerto Rico in nearly a century, and it exacerbated a number of preexisting social, economic, demographic, and health-related issues that had severely impacted the island's population for decades (see Mora, Rodríguez, and Dávila, 2017a).

It is also important to highlight that the local, commonwealth, and federal response to Hurricane Maria—especially the latter—generated a surge of controversies regarding their timeliness, speed, and impact on the overall disaster relief process and the subsequent recovery and rebuilding efforts. Consensus exists that the response and recovery efforts at the commonwealth and federal levels failed to provide severely impacted communities the help and resources they desperately needed in a timely manner.

The Federal Emergency Management Agency (FEMA) recognized that they did not enter the 2017 hurricane season with optimal force strength to deal with the devastating events that impacted Puerto Rico, the U.S. Virgin Islands, and the continental United States. FEMA's own after-action report (2018:25) notes that their logistical efforts "featured notable and persistent coordination challenges," which significantly impacted their response and ability to meet the emerging community needs following this devastating event. The report also acknowledges that the agency was neither prepared nor adequately resourced to respond effectively to such a catastrophic event. As the *New York Times* (July 12, 2018) reported, "FEMA was sorely unprepared" for Puerto Rico's hurricane and they "vastly underestimated how much food and fresh water it would need, and how hard it would be to get additional supplies to the island."

However, despite the adverse and negative impacts and consequences of the storm discussed throughout this book, positive and encouraging stories must also be told. For example, the resiliency of the Puerto Rican people in the most desperate of circumstances has been key to response and recovery efforts on the island. Further, the coming together of the Puerto Rican diaspora in the continental United States, such as in Florida, New York, and in other communities, demonstrates how communities can work together to provide critically needed support and assistance during disaster response and recovery processes in the absence of adequate local or federal response. Also, the significant and positive impact of initiatives under the leadership of state governments, university systems, and other public entities/organizations has been essential in helping these communities begin to recover and rebuild from the devastating consequences of Hurricane Maria.

Soon after the storm, the state of New York, the State University of New York (SUNY), and the City University of New York (CUNY) activated substantial resources to assist the island of Puerto Rico and its inhabitants. Spanning the next two and a half years, the result was the deployment of numerous New York State employees and resources; members of building trades; and hundreds of SUNY and CUNY faculty, staff, and students, all who worked hand-in-hand with local Puerto Rican agencies, citizens, and organizations. The nature of this engagement, the lessons learned, and the outcomes make this an important case study to review and share with wider audiences. This case study focuses on one component of the overall effort—the SUNY Stands with Puerto Rico initiative.

A COORDINATED AND IMPACTFUL RESPONSE: SUNY STANDS WITH PUERTO RICO

In the immediate aftermath of the hurricane, New York State Governor Andrew M. Cuomo mobilized and directed numerous New York assets and resources to Puerto Rico, many of which remained into 2020. For example, during this span of time, Governor Cuomo ordered the deployment of over 1,000 personnel and distributed about 4,400 pallets of supplies collected from donation sites across the state (New York State 2019). In addition, the governor and members of his staff, along with the New York State Legislature, made several trips to Puerto Rico after Hurricane Maria's landfall in direct support of the island's recovery and rebuilding efforts. Further, according to a news release by the Governor's Office (June 9, 2019), "Under the Governor's leadership, New York State (NYS) has dedicated approximately $13 million to support the more than 11,000 displaced Hurricane Maria victims living in New York." NYS responded in a strategic and coordinated fashion, deploying technicians and specialists of different trades, equipment, and emergency supplies focusing on the immediate aftermath of the hurricane.

SUNY STANDS WITH PUERTO RICO: A SYSTEM-WIDE INITIATIVE FOCUSED ON RESPONSE, RESILIENCY, AND SUSTAINABILITY

In October 2017, in direct response to the impacts of Hurricane Maria in Puerto Rico, and in collaboration with the aforementioned NYS initiative, then-SUNY chancellor Kristina Johnson established a system-wide Task Force to focus on disaster response and recovery as part of the SUNY Stands with Puerto Rico initiative. SUNY—the largest comprehensive system of public higher education in the United States—consists of 64 colleges and universities distributed throughout the state and serves more than 1.3 million students annually. As a public system of higher education, in addition to its broad academic and research portfolio, SUNY's mission includes a commitment to community engagement and service.

The SUNY Stands with Puerto Rico initiative, through its participating colleges and universities, focused on disaster relief aid, including distribution of food, water, and other supplies to island residents, as well as medical care; neighborhood relief efforts; restoration of residential houses; agricultural work; debris management technical assistance and direct cleanup in communities, beaches, and other areas; the establishment of a temporary recovery assistance legal clinic; and examining the mental health impacts of this devastating event, among other projects. In addition to these disaster response and recovery efforts, SUNY focused on building long-term, multifaceted partnerships with institutions of higher education on the island, emphasizing disaster preparedness, resiliency, and sustainability.

Given the significant historical, cultural, and family ties between New York and the Caribbean, especially Puerto Rico, New Yorkers were motivated to assist in the recovery of Puerto Rico. This response effort aligned well with SUNY's priorities in the areas of individualized education, service learning, intercultural learning, and community engagement, as well as with SUNY's regional outreach priorities in the Caribbean (State University of New York, n.d.). The SUNY Puerto Rico Task Force, co-chaired by Havidán Rodríguez, president of the University at Albany (UAlbany) and a native of Puerto Rico, and Rear Admiral Michael Alfultis,[2] president of SUNY's Maritime College, was one of the first systematic post-Hurricane Maria disaster response and recovery initiatives led by a U.S. public university system to work in Puerto Rico.

Then-chancellor Johnson charged the Task Force to focus on medium- and long-term engagements in Puerto Rico. Its mission has been to channel the significant expertise, service, and generosity of the broad SUNY community to meet the needs of the Puerto Rican community, informed by, and in partnership with Puerto Rican education, governmental, and nongovernmental entities. The goals of the Task Force were as follows.

- Develop an action plan that enhances the long-term sustainability and vibrancy of Puerto Rican society as defined by residents of Puerto Rico through extensive and ongoing consultation with local partners and constituent groups.
- Create reciprocal long-term and sustainable partnerships with selected Puerto Rican institutions and other entities on the island that provide opportunities for SUNY students, faculty, and staff to support recovery, rebuilding, and resiliency efforts in Puerto Rico while contributing to the revitalization of local communities.
- Leverage appropriate expertise and community service capacity of SUNY campuses, faculty, staff, and students to support disaster relief and recovery efforts in Puerto Rico in consultation with local partners and constituent groups, while encouraging local community engagement.
- Develop a model for higher education crisis response using a service-learning framework that can be applied to other disasters, nationally and internationally.
- Foster academic and research collaborations with institutions of higher education in Puerto Rico.[3]

AN EXTENSIVE SUMMER COMMUNITY SERVICE PROGRAM

As a core component of the New York Stands with Puerto Rico initiative, in April 2018, Governor Cuomo announced his intention to send 500 SUNY and CUNY students to Puerto Rico for relief work during the summer of 2018. In roughly six weeks, the SUNY System, working closely with its campuses, selected about 250 participants from more than 1,700 applications for placement in the summer internship program. CUNY followed a similar process. Students were involved in two-week-long service deployments; they received a stipend and were offered up to three academic credits. This program was replicated for the summer of 2019, and in some cases extended to three-week-long deployments.

Among the partnering organizations of the New York Stands with Puerto Rico initiative were three major disaster response nongovernmental organizations (NGOs): All Hands and Hearts, which formed after the 2004 Tsunami in Southeast Asia; Heart 9/11, which grew out of a team of 9/11 first responders from New York City, including building trades and fire, police, and port-authority departments; and NECHAMA, a Jewish disaster response organization established in 1993 in the wake of significant flooding in the Midwest region of the United States. Importantly, local organizations in Puerto Rico, such as the Boys and Girls Club of Puerto Rico, ViequesLove, and others, evolved as strong partners. The three primary hosting NGOs took the responsibility of managing the all-volunteer effort, and integrated faculty, staff, and student volunteers into their own disaster response work. SUNY and CUNY students worked side-by-side with other volunteers from Puerto Rico, and across the United States and the globe.

Another unique aspect of this program was that some students also worked alongside and under the mentorship of building tradespeople and union members from the New York City area. The building trade organizations actively participated, sending volunteers to lend specialized knowledge and devote countless work hours to the rebuilding efforts in Puerto Rico. These tradespeople set an example for the students by going above and beyond the call of duty, such as the member of the International Brotherhood of Electrical Workers Local #3 who extended his stay to volunteer to install electrical wiring in the home of an elderly man of limited means. SUNY asked students who volunteered during the summer of 2018 to share anonymous reflections about their experience. One student indicated, "Working with the union people was a great way of guiding the students." Another added, "The tradesmen we worked with were always helpful, patient, and understanding with the students. The best part about working under our NGO was working with the tradesmen."

UNICEF USA was also a founding partner of the New York and SUNY initiatives, and provided important funding during the first year to support the work of SUNY, CUNY, and the NGO partners. In addition, they stationed a representative in Puerto Rico for several months in preparation for the collaborative projects, as well as during the extended period of student service. Moreover, UNICEF USA provided critical coordination on the ground, ensuring a well-informed, high-quality humanitarian response focused on the needs of Puerto Rico's children and families.

Over the nearly two-year period of service, 35 SUNY campuses[4] participated in disaster recovery and relief projects and initiatives in Arecibo, Barranquitas, Loíza, Mayagüez, Orocovis, Patillas, Santa Isabel, Toa Baja, Utuado, Vieques, Yabucoa, and other communities across Puerto Rico. From May 2018 through July 2019, nearly 1,000 SUNY and CUNY students engaged in volunteer work, mostly through the partnerships with locally based NGOs. Students were involved in restoring and waterproofing concrete roofs, rebuilding houses and schools, debris removal in communities, cleanup of beaches, assistance to farmers, and rebuilding a pedestrian bridge connecting two neighborhoods. As a result, in 2018 alone, 178 homes were restored by SUNY, CUNY, and New York tradespeople, representing approximately 41,000 volunteer hours valued at more than one million dollars.

EXPANDING SUNY'S ENGAGEMENT EFFORTS: CAMPUSES MOBILIZE AND RESPOND

Cornerstone events epitomizing the scope of New York State's response involved the presence of the *Empire State VI* (a 700-passenger vessel owned by the U.S. Government and operated by SUNY's Maritime College) in San Juan on two separate occasions. On its first trip, the ship arrived within weeks of Hurricane Maria, as it had been activated earlier that month by the federal government to assist with relief efforts following Hurricanes Harvey and Irma. Immediately following Hurricane Maria, as the ship was preparing to depart the Florida coast where its services were no longer required, it was retasked by the federal government to Puerto Rico, becoming one of the first vessels leading the response effort. While docked in the San Juan harbor, the *Empire State VI* and SUNY Maritime provided housing, food, and water to emergency relief workers for seven weeks. In addition, the vessel also carried 46 pallets of bottled water, food, and other items for the residents of Puerto Rico.

In May 2018, the *Empire State VI* returned to San Juan for the first stop on its summer sea term academic program. While there, SUNY Maritime and its cadets coordinated a volunteer response effort that included not only the nearly 500 cadets onboard, but an additional cohort of approximately 60 students, faculty, and staff from UAlbany and the College of Environmental Science and Forestry (ESF) who performed service in communities throughout the island. UAlbany's College of Emergency Preparedness, Homeland Security and Cybersecurity (CEHC) organized the initial deployment of 30 students (selected from a pool of more than 280) to Puerto Rico through an application process and predeployment procedures. These students traveled to Puerto Rico for a four-day deployment along with 15 ESF students and the Maritime cadet corps.

Moreover, in July 2018, then-Chancellor Johnson, along with representatives from SUNY System Administration, SUNY's Alfred State College, and ESF, participated in a solar energy solution project with We Share Solar, a company that creates portable solar energy solutions. One noteworthy installation was undertaken in partnership with the University of Puerto Rico (UPR)-Cayey on the roof of an important affiliated community center in Cayey. The SUNY and UPR-Cayey chancellors hoisted tools for the installation of a photovoltaic panel that will provide reliable solar power during future power outages in that community.

Other SUNY institutions offered essential services as well. Stony Brook University sent 23 staff members for a two-week mission in Puerto Rico offering relief to healthcare professionals who had been working around the clock with patients since Hurricane Maria made landfall. The School of Law at the University at Buffalo established the Puerto Rico Recovery Assistance Legal Clinic to provide practical legal research and pro bono services to island residents. Students from SUNY's campuses at Geneseo and Alfred State worked with local partners assisting with neighborhood relief efforts during spring break. SUNY New Paltz and its Institute for Disaster Mental Health focused on trauma suffered by residents on the island (this particular initiative is described in more detail later in this chapter).

ESF was also active within weeks of the storm by sending Mark Lichtenstein, its chief of staff and chief sustainability officer and a waste management expert, to Puerto Rico and the U.S. Virgin Islands to assist with recovery efforts. Lichtenstein later provided testimony to Congress in November 2017 about the state of the disaster response on the island. Lichtenstein reinforced to members of the U.S. House of Representatives Energy and Commerce Committee, Subcommittee on the Environment, that "the residents and visitors of Puerto Rico and the Virgin Islands deserve our focused attention, clean air, and a healthy ecosystem. The hurricanes were certainly not desired, but this is a great opportunity to build a more resilient and sustainable future, so that the islands can come back better than before" (Lichtenstein, 2017).

ESF continues to be actively engaged in pursuing research and conducting service projects in Vieques (discussed in the following section) as well as on the main island, focusing on disaster debris management, ecosystem restoration, and other environmental and sustainability issues resulting from this devastating hurricane. Moreover, a partnership of administrators, staff, and students formed the student-led Acorns2Action (A2A) response group immediately after Hurricane Maria impacted the Caribbean (ESF's mascot is the Oak Tree Acorn). The following is a student account of the moment when A2A was formed—a situation replicated at a number of SUNY campuses at the time:

> On September 21, 2017, 30 ESF students, faculty and staff gathered together. The room was solemn and still shaken by . . . recent natural disasters. . . . Some students were from [the places impacted], some had family and friends there, and others had no connection at all, but we all had the same question on our minds: "What can we do to help?" . . . Our primary goal is to connect to organization[s] local to the affected country and help them rebuild in a way that is culturally appropriate as well as sensitive to their needs. Rather than sending water and food to these countries, we provide the resources they request and the tools/knowledge required to rebuild their country in a sustainable and socially-just way. (SUNY College of Environmental Science and Forestry, n.d.)

As a testament to their understanding, care, and awareness of the seriousness of the situation on the ground, campuses across SUNY held their own fundraising drives—mainly led by students—to support the people of Puerto Rico. For example, UAlbany generated funds to help cover travel expenses for student volunteers through its Alumni Foundation, as well as individual, corporate, and other foundation gifts. UAlbany's CEHC took the lead in developing an Memorandum of Understanding (MOU) with the University of Puerto Rico—Mayagüez (UPRM), signed by the respective university presidents. CEHC also developed a conceptual joint academic research center in partnership with UPRM to study long-term recovery and societal resiliency. In addition, CEHC created courses focusing on public health issues post-Hurricane Maria on the island, which included fieldwork, as well as on disaster recovery in Puerto Rico. Other student service engagement initiatives on the island were led by other UAlbany faculty and staff, including from the Center for Leadership and Service, the Rockefeller College of Public Affairs and Policy, and the School of Public Health, among others.

VIEQUES: A COMMUNITY IMPACTED BY HURRICANE MARIA AND SUNY

It is worth highlighting that the aforementioned A2A evolved with an emphasis on the Puerto Rico island municipality of Vieques, forming

Acorns2Vieques (A2V) to focus their attention on funding support and partnerships. The ongoing "story of Vieques" continues to reinforce the importance of SUNY's efforts there and across Puerto Rico.

Vieques is a small island municipality, with approximately 9,300 inhabitants, about 7 miles off the east coast of the main island of Puerto Rico (see figure 1.1), and 20 miles long by 4.5 miles wide. The island has a resourceful resident population (Viequenses), rich culture, and an important and unique centuries-long history. Vieques is also widely known internationally as a location the United States Navy (and NATO) used as a bombing range and a military training area from the 1940s to 2003.[5] As a result, and as exacerbated by other factors, such as its isolation, even before the eastern edge of the eye of Hurricane Maria slammed into the island, the community faced many challenges, including low high school graduation rates, high unemployment rates, abject poverty, serious public health challenges, and gentrification and development pressures, among others. With Hurricane Maria, local weather watchers talk of wind gusts well over 230 miles per hour (Mark Martin, conversation with Mark Lichtenstein, November 6, 2017, Vieques, PR). This devastating hurricane added to and magnified the existing social and economic challenges in Vieques.

However, ESF encountered Viequenses determined to rise-up from the storm, even in the face of seemingly insurmountable challenges. Limited employment opportunities, extreme poverty, and lack of access to adequate healthcare, combined with the devastation caused by Hurricane Maria, as well as the slow and inefficient federal response, resulted in chronic and long-term consequences. It will take decades for the island of Vieques and its residents to recover from this disaster. Nevertheless, in the midst of this devastation, Viequenses remain cautiously optimistic. Their story is one of stress, fear, struggle but also of resolve, endurance, and resiliency.

It was largely the Viequenses themselves and a few local NGOs, such as Hope Builders and ViequesLove, who came to Vieques' rescue following Hurricane Maria. SUNY and ESF, including through A2V, played a small part in helping by providing on-the-ground staff engagement soon after the storm and throughout 2018 and 2019, and early in 2020. One simple activity A2V led was a campaign on the ESF campus to create and distribute Valentine's Day cards to ViequesLove. This heartfelt gesture had positive reverberations across the Vieques' community.

As elucidated in the passage below by Devon Camillieri, copresident of ESF's A2A, Vieques also had a profound impact on her and the other 19 ESF volunteers who traveled there:

> It's important to recognize that regardless of where you are, you can make a difference. It's easy to complain about the large organizations for the role they

> play in relief, but what is more important is that we hold them accountable. Some organizations approach disaster relief with ideas already in mind, but it is up to us to tell them what the needs of the community are. We have to insist that they build a relationship with the community first, and not after. . . . The struggles are not over for Vieques, as climate change is only causing storms to increase. . . . We spent a week asking the [Vieques] community what they needed, and getting involved. While doing so, we fell in love with the island, and continue to maintain a collaborative relationship in every way we can. (Camillieri 2019)

Vieques is increasingly being referred to as the "forgotten island" because of the dire post-hurricane needs that have gone unmet. However, SUNY did not forget Vieques and continues to play a small but important role in its recovery process.

SUNY AND INSTITUTIONS OF HIGHER EDUCATION IN PUERTO RICO: STRENGTHENING THE BONDS

With the goal of increasing bilateral cooperation between the state of New York and the Commonwealth of Puerto Rico (State University of New York, 2018), the growing SUNY/UPR partnership, and the potential for increased synergistic collaborative activities, SUNY chancellor Johnson and UPR interim president Ubaldo Cordova Figueroa signed a MOU on July 26, 2018, at UPR's headquarters. This MOU creates a framework for continued relationship building. It recognizes that these two public higher education systems "share a long history of educational, cultural and demographic ties," and it acknowledges that both systems will "dedicate themselves to long-term collaborative approaches to the issues facing New York, Puerto Rico, and the Caribbean region." It also highlights that cooperation "among students, administrators, scientists and scholars in New York and Puerto Rico will enhance the quality of the relationship between the two."

The SUNY-UPR MOU was intended to foster collaborative relationships, focusing on a number of areas that are mutually beneficial, including collaborative scientific research; disaster management, mitigation, and resilience studies; sustainable energy; visits by faculty members and researchers for conferences, seminars, lectures, and other academic and research interactions; development of dual-degree programs leading to undergraduate and graduate degrees; and enhanced experiential and service learning opportunities. This also led to the aforementioned MOU between UAlbany and UPRM, which resulted in a number of concrete academic and research collaborations between faculty and students at both institutions. SUNY continued to explore how to solidify partnerships with La Pontifícia Universidad Católica de Puerto Rico, as well as other UPR institutions.

Further, the Institute for Disaster Mental Health at SUNY New Paltz, in partnership with UNICEF USA, is leading a new initiative to help children and families cope with mental health issues resulting from Hurricane Maria. A diverse group of experts will be convened from Puerto Rico and beyond, to create actionable recommendations to expand direly needed trauma-informed mental health support across the island. Specifically, the project, supported by a grant from UNICEF USA, focuses on school-based mental health in Puerto Rico in collaboration with the island's Department of Education and the UPR at Río Piedras. As part of this process, they will meet with school principals and generate assessment data, which will be used to inform a training program to be administered to counselors in public schools throughout Puerto Rico.

SUNY also participated in the inaugural *Resilience through Innovation in Sustainable Energy (RISE)* summit held at the UPRM, hosted by the UPR faculty-led Instituto Nacional de Energía y Sostenibilidad Isleña in June 2018. RISE is a national "platform [that] seeks to re-envision how universities interact with communities, NGOs, private sector partners, and local governments and how to match the knowledge and capacities of an extended partner network with community needs. [RISE is working to] move beyond a humanitarian aid approach in the aftermath of disasters to find new ways of building collaborations that can enhance resilience and foster convergent projects among diverse disciplines and sectors" (Convergence Lab. n.d.).

Furthermore, under the leadership of the National Council for Science and the Environment, SUNY, CUNY, and the UPR, among others, a successful national and interdisciplinary conference titled *Transforming University Engagement in Pre- and Post-Disaster Environments: Lessons from Puerto Rico* was held at UAlbany in November 2019 (University at Albany, 2019). This conference provided a platform for a national conversation to explore ways through research and scholarship in which institutions of higher education can enhance community preparedness, mitigation, resiliency, and sustainability. Although Puerto Rico, in the aftermath of Hurricane Maria, was used as a case study, the conference objective focused on the well-being of communities throughout the world that are increasingly vulnerable to extreme weather due to climate change. The ultimate goal was to develop "a national platform where universities and colleges can have a greater impact in pre- and post-disaster environments." Work started on that platform at the conference.

LESSONS LEARNED: LEADERSHIP, COMMUNITY ENGAGEMENT, AND COLLECTIVE ACTION

During the two years following Hurricane Maria, the experiences of SUNY and its community members in Puerto Rico revealed many lessons. We highlight nine of these lessons here.

1. *Leadership is critical: People of positional and resource allocation power can make a substantive difference in disaster response and recovery efforts.*
   Legitimate issues and concerns about privilege, cultural relativeness, and the potential abuses and negative repercussions of volunteerism aside, the impact of altruistic actions from caring people in leadership positions is instrumental in disaster response and recovery efforts, and needs acknowledgment and validation. In this case, without the vision, leadership, and support from a variety of New York State leaders, UNICEF USA, and other partners of the New York Stands with Puerto Rico initiative, the overall impact and success of disaster response in Puerto Rico would have been diminished. Further, the active engagement and participation of faculty, staff, and students from both SUNY and CUNY in the response and recovery efforts is noteworthy. In the absence of a timely, effective, and efficient disaster response at the federal level, the response by state governments, state and national leaders, local communities, and institutions of higher education become all the more important.
2. *UNICEF USA was an essential partner.*
   Without the leadership, support, and funding from UNICEF USA, the New York Stands with Puerto Rico initiative, especially the SUNY/CUNY student service trips to the island, could have not happened. Also, it is noteworthy that, according to informal feedback from a UNICEF USA representative, Hurricane Maria marked the first time the agency funded disaster response within the United States. Moreover, UNICEF USA embedded an essential staff member in Puerto Rico preceding and throughout the student service period. This representative was actively engaged in this process, accessible, responsive, and became a critical partner and resource to all the SUNY/CUNY service participants. The model UNICEF USA employed in Puerto Rico is one worthy of replication in similar disaster situations nationally and globally.
3. *Pretrip cultural orientation is crucial.*
   SUNY and CUNY faculty, staff, and student service providers (e.g., volunteers) were required to attend a pretrip cultural orientation. This was instrumental, as was the need to reinforce that SUNY/CUNY teams were traveling to Puerto Rico to assist local leaders and activities through an

invitation from the people living and working there. Students were also informed that this trip would provide them transformational experiences in which they would learn about Puerto Rico's history and immerse themselves in Puerto Rican culture, while significantly contributing to response and recovery efforts on the island.

4. *Cultural immersion, engaging communities, and expanding worldviews.* It is critical to provide cultural immersion training, focusing on issues like cultural relativism, and emphasizing the importance of respecting local residents and their norms, and valuing their competencies and capabilities. However, it can be challenging to put these concepts into action. It entails more than being aware of one's own privileges and worldview—which is important—or understanding others' worldviews. The learning and immersion process also involves the following.
   - Being able to communicate, develop active listening skills, and effectively interact with people stricken by disaster.
   - Developing trust and credibility within the community.
   - Understanding that these learning and engagement experiences are a two-way street and that volunteers can learn from local residents and organizations and vice versa.
   - Remembering the Hippocratic Oath as it applies to relief work and resist implementing service projects that will place additional burdens on disaster-stricken communities (i.e., unskilled volunteers descending upon communities with limited capability, competing for use of already stretched resources and infrastructure, etc.).
   - Understanding that sustainable and systemic long-term change happens when people are actively engaged in solving their own problems, rather than having things done for them or external solutions imposed upon them (Cole, 2012). Cole wrote about this in a 2012 essay in *The Atlantic* ("The White Savior Industrial Complex"). Cole warned that volunteerism has the potential of being "a big emotional experience that validates privilege." He concluded that "if we are going to interfere in the lives of others, a little due diligence is a minimum requirement." In the words of one of the SUNY students in the anonymous 2018 post-service survey, "Make sure to try to speak with locals and hear their stories."
5. *Mental health preparation for responders needs more attention.* Evidence acquired through postservice trip interviews with some SUNY volunteers highlights the need to provide increased preservice preparation. This includes skill and coping mechanism development to help responders/volunteers while they are performing service. It also includes more attention to the critical stage of postservice response and potential mental health issues or concerns that may emerge.

6. *Enhance and strengthen response and recovery efforts.*
   Students and other volunteers noted the inadequacy of the government response, particularly at the federal level. Responders reported encountering devoted and capable individuals from several federal agencies, yet there was a systemic failure characterized by the absence of rapid and integrated coordination at the agency and governmental level. On the post-service survey in September 2018, one student noted, "Our government and society lack effective systems to respond to disasters. We are unprepared to mitigate crises related to climate change and need to generate innovative ideas as well as more initiatives." This further emphasizes the critical role that NGOs, such as All Hands and Hearts, the Boys and Girls Club of Puerto Rico, Heart 9/11, NECHAMA, UNICEF USA, ViequesLove, and others, can play in the disaster response and recovery process. Their rapid and effective response in many sectors of the Puerto Rican community has been instrumental and impactful.
7. *An "all-sector" partnership is vital to the success of disaster response and recovery initiatives.*
   The integration and active engagement of academic institutions; different levels of government; and local, community-based, regional, and international NGOs in disaster response results in increased inclusivity and more predictive positive outcomes. The active collaboration and coordination among and between many of these agencies had a significant and positive impact on many communities throughout the island. Also, the work and interaction between "external" and local agencies and organizations demonstrated the strong impact and effectiveness of community engagement and collaborative work in the response and recovery process. Further, the critical role and impact of institutions of higher education in the response, recovery, and reconstruction process in areas impacted by disaster events cannot be overstated. Both SUNY and CUNY have played and will continue to play a meaningful role in Puerto Rico's recovery efforts.
8. *Promoting leadership and active engagement among youth contributes to a holistic approach.*
   The aforementioned "all-sector" approach leading to successful response and recovery efforts requires the coupling of experienced disaster responders with less experienced youth and young adults. Organizations like All Hands and Hearts recognize this. Consequently, their apprenticeship and training programs are also designed to actively engage and train these groups. These groups also bring to the forefront important and much-needed skills, especially in the areas of social media and communication technology, in addition to the knowledge and skills acquired at their educational institutions. It is critically important to engage youth and young adults in the areas or communities where response/recovery

services are being provided as this also promotes a strong connection to the local community, helps establish a group of local role models, and can foster critically important informal communication and information networks. Recognizing the importance of engaging local youth, ESF's A2A group has been discussing the possibility of forming a student-led, national disaster response and recovery initiative, as a way to better tap into the traits and skills of local youth, which would also help address the gaps they witnessed in the governmental response to Puerto Rico's disaster.

9. *Community engagement and service provide hope to people and communities impacted by disasters.*
   Testimonials abound from local Puerto Ricans resulting from their interactions with or witnessing the efforts of the New York, SUNY, and CUNY responders. The pain, fear, despair, and uncertainty evident in the survivors of Hurricane Maria in many cases were replaced by hope and a renewed faith in humanity as a result of the interaction with volunteers and other responders. This is evident in the following testimonial from the executive director of ViequesLove: "The students from SUNY and ESF were very different than the volunteers from what we normally see. They did their research, they were culturally sensitive with their approach, and they gave 100 percent of themselves; not only to the recovery jobs, but they really got to know and understand the people. Most important, their strong work ethic, willingness to go the extra mile, and their caring and sensitive demeanors provided a sense of hope to local residents, particularly our youth. We now consider them family" (Kelly Thompson, in an email to Mark Lichtenstein, July 1, 2019). Gratitude and hope were also personified in the grandmother living alone in Barranquitas, whose house flooded twice during the storm, sweeping all her prized belongings away. However, an All Hands and Hearts team arrived to help rebuild her house. She went from utter misery to sheer joy in a span of minutes.

IMPACT OF DISASTER RESPONSE AND RECOVERY EFFORTS ON THE STUDENTS

The impact on student service providers was also significant, and in many instances, transformational, as manifested by these volunteers. Numerous anecdotes and stories from SUNY and CUNY students exist about how the Puerto Rico service experience was "life-changing," and how their once murky career paths suddenly came into great clarity upon their return from Puerto Rico. Some students highlighted potential changes in their career aspirations, focused on providing services to others in need. Further, being able to apply the knowledge and skills developed in the classroom to real-life situations is noteworthy; moving students from theory to praxis is a learning experience that forever impacts their personal and professional growth and development.

The significance of these experiences on SUNY students is best articulated through select sentiments shared by students in the September 2018 anonymous survey, as follows.

- "Community is the most powerful force of human nature, and it's the number one thing that pulls us out of disaster."
- "We can all make a difference, teamwork is crucial and kindness is translated in all languages/parts of the world."
- "Effective disaster relief is more than rebuilding a home, it is making personal connections with the community you are serving, and understanding their traumas."
- "The people of Puerto Rico are the most hospitable people I have ever met. They cooked lunch for us every single day. They made us jewelry charms to thank us. They treated us like family. Even strangers teared up and thanked us for our work when we said we were volunteers. It was incredible, and the kindness I received from the Puerto Ricans, I will never forget and always carry with me."

DISCUSSION AND CONCLUDING REMARKS

This disaster response and engagement by New York State, and SUNY's important role, provided the opportunity for a unique case study, one that generated and teased out the important lessons learned enumerated above. Under the leadership of the state of New York, SUNY, CUNY, NGOs, tradespeople, as well as local residents and institutional partners, establishing strong partnerships and collaborative ties between service providers and island residents, experiential learning opportunities for students, and a host of community service projects have had significant and long-lasting impacts in the recovery and rebuilding process in a number of communities in Puerto Rico.

Moreover, as this case study highlights, these projects and initiatives positively impacted the lives of hundreds of households and community members throughout the island. In addition to serving as transformational experiences for SUNY and CUNY students, they also furthered the educational mission of New York's public institutions of higher education through offering meaningful applied learning about the social and economic impacts of these devastating events. As part of this experience, students had opportunities to immerse themselves and learn about Puerto Rican history, culture, traditions, and language, and how U.S. citizens on the island were impacted, responded to, coped with, and began to recover from the catastrophic impacts of Hurricane Maria. As important, these experiences helped many of the volunteers come to know themselves better and learn about the positive impacts that individual and collective actions can have on entire communities, especially following catastrophic events, such as Hurricane Maria.

These experiences also brought to the forefront how delayed, ineffective, and inefficient disaster response, especially at the federal level, can adversely impact communities during and after calamitous events, which in the end reminds us that disasters are not "natural," but are socially constructed events that severely impact the most vulnerable of our populations. It is clear that the social, demographic, and economic outcomes of the most powerful hurricane to strike Puerto Rico in the last century, combined with preexisting and chronic socioeconomic conditions (e.g., massive debt, high levels of unemployment, unrelenting poverty, a deteriorating healthcare system, and massive migration to the U.S. mainland), will be felt for decades to come.

This case study shows that through their response efforts following Hurricane Maria in Puerto Rico, SUNY and CUNY exemplified the critical leadership role that institutions of higher education can and should play in disaster response and recovery initiatives, while also serving their communities, locally and globally. Also, the focus on developing long-term and sustainable disaster resiliency initiatives with regions impacted by disasters is critically important in the near- and long-term rebuilding process. Through these educational efforts, students move from theory to practice and are engaged in high-impact experiential learning initiatives while positively impacting communities in their recovery process.

Given the key roles that public institutions of higher education play in the education of their community members, as economic engines for the regions they serve, as important vehicles for the economic mobility of its students, and in disaster recovery and rebuilding processes, it should be emphasized that the economic future and vitality of the UPR is in peril. For example, an *Inside Higher Ed* article (July 11, 2019) highlighted the profound budget cuts the UPR System is encountering: "The appropriation for the University of Puerto Rico's operating expenses was slashed by $86 million this year, to about $501 million, following on a $44 million cut the year before that and a $203 million cut the year before that" resulting in a total budget cut of $333 million over a three-year period. These are catastrophic budget reductions for the UPR faculty, staff, students, and the communities they serve. Furthermore, these massive cuts will result in a significant impact on the economic recovery and growth of the island, which depends on a highly educated workforce.

To conclude on a more optimistic note, it is also important to highlight that the resiliency of the Puerto Rican people and the massive outpouring of support, such as that from the state of New York, SUNY, CUNY, and the Puerto Rican diaspora on the mainland, shed a light of hope and promise for the recovery and reconstruction efforts in Puerto Rico. There is certainly much more work to be done, but as demonstrated with this case study, institutions of higher education can play a critical role in significantly impacting recovery and rebuilding efforts following disasters. Moreover, Puerto Rico has no option but to continue to build resiliency into its vibrant societal web and community. Kaira Fuentes, a Puerto Rican who was a PhD candidate at ESF and a member of the SUNY Stands with Puerto Rico team, captured this succinctly: "People in Puerto Rico are resilient because they have to be resilient. They don't have an option not to be."

NOTES

1. We want to express our deepest appreciation to Governor Andrew M. Cuomo and former SUNY Chancellor Kristina M. Johnson for their strong leadership and commitment to mobilize the state of New York and SUNY, and its resources, to respond to the devastating impacts of Hurricane Maria in Puerto Rico. Thanks also goes to the SUNY Puerto Rico Task Force members, and to the SUNY faculty, staff, and students, and the volunteer organizations, that played a critical role in the aftermath of Hurricane Maria in Puerto Rico. We also want to extend our appreciation to Peter Velz and Christian Speedling for their support in the development of this chapter. Finally, "thank you" to Dr. Marie T. Mora for her excellent feedback and recommendations regarding this chapter.

2. Other members of the SUNY Task Force included Robert Balkin, director of Latin American and Caribbean Programs, SUNY; Sally Crimmins Villela, associate vice chancellor for Global Affairs, SUNY; Robert P. Griffin Jr., dean, College of Emergency Preparedness, Homeland Security and Cybersecurity, UAlbany; Mark Lichtenstein, chief of staff and chief sustainability officer, SUNY ESF; Merissa McKasty, leadership development manager, SUNY SAIL Institute; Amy Nitza, director, Institute for Disaster Mental Health, SUNY New Paltz; James Pasquill, director of International Programs, SUNY; Christian Speedling, global partnerships manager, SUNY; and Peter Velz, assistant vice chancellor for External Affairs, SUNY.

3. Another aspect of SUNY's response has been to offer in-state tuition to residents of Puerto Rico whose educational progress was interrupted by Hurricanes Maria and Irma. Despite some concerns this would further impact out-migration from the island to the U.S. mainland, the intent of this action was to contribute to the island's future economic vitality through these educational efforts. During the 2018–2019 academic year, 152 Puerto Rican students applied for this tuition benefit across SUNY institutions.

4. The SUNY institutions participating in these initiatives include Alfred State College of Technology; Binghamton University; SUNY Brockport; Broome Community College; Buffalo State; SUNY Canton; SUNY Cobleskill; Columbia-Greene Community College; SUNY Cortland; SUNY Delhi; Empire State College; SUNY Erie; College of Environmental Science and Forestry (ESF); Farmingdale State College; Fashion Institute of Technology (FIT); SUNY Fredonia; SUNY Geneseo; SUNY Maritime College; Monroe Community College; Nassau Community College; SUNY New Paltz; SUNY Old Westbury; SUNY Oneonta; SUNY Oswego; SUNY Plattsburgh; SUNY Polytechnic Institute; SUNY Potsdam; SUNY Purchase; Stony Brook University; Suffolk County Community College; SUNY Upstate Medical University; Tompkins Cortland Community College; University at Albany; University at Buffalo; and Westchester Community College.

5. Due to this activity, a significant portion of the landmass and near-shore areas (e.g., beaches, coral reefs, seagrass beds, etc.) were contaminated with unexploded ordnance and other materials related to decades of damaging military activity. These areas are now managed under the federal Superfund program, which provides resources and a management structure for the cleanup of sites contaminated with hazardous substances.

Chapter 13

A Perfect Storm and Then Maria

Alberto Dávila, Marie T. Mora,
and Havidán Rodríguez

Even before Hurricane Maria devastated Puerto Rico when it made landfall on September 20, 2017, as we discussed in chapter 1, the island was being hit by another storm "La Crisis Boricua," which started in 2006. In our 2017 book (Mora, Dávila, and Rodríguez 2017a), we pointed to a set of events that came together in 2006 that resulted in this storm, including the complete expiration of Section 936 that provided U.S. corporations tax incentives to operate in Puerto Rico; the imposition (and subsequent increase) of the island's sales tax that overwhelmingly impacted a disfranchised population at the bottom of the income distribution; the beginning of more than a decade's loss of jobs in the public and private sector, particularly in the manufacturing industry; and an escalating government debt described as "unpayable," which eventually resulted in the passage of the controversial federal PROMESA legislation. We noted that these events not only led to a deteriorating infrastructure on the island, but also to a massive net out-migration from the island that had many socioeconomic and demographic ramifications in Puerto Rico, but also in the U.S. mainland, including in Florida and other nontraditional settlement areas for Puerto Ricans.

Literally two days before we received our galley proofs for that book, Hurricane Maria brought catastrophic destruction to the island, with flooding rains and sustained winds equaling those of an EF-3 tornado (fortunately, we were able to include an addendum to initially consider the impacts of this devastating storm). As has been noted throughout this edited book, the storm left its (then) 3.3 million American citizens without electricity, a significant loss of life (2,975 lost lives according to official estimates, and higher according to unofficial estimates), a further destruction of needed capital infrastructure, and over $94 billion in damages. With its already $74 billion debt and $49 billion unfunded pension balance, Hurricane Maria added to an already bleak outlook for Puerto Rico's economic, demographic, and fiscal conditions.

This book documents socioeconomic, demographic, health, and other immediate impacts of Hurricane Maria on the island. It also offers insights on strategies that would have been useful in coping with the aftermath of this disaster and could serve the island well when other hazards—natural or otherwise—impact island residents, including the series of earthquakes in the southern area of the island that started in December 2019, as well as the COVID-19 pandemic. This book also advances other work investigating, for example, the impact that Maria and the slow recovery period had on the visual arts on the island (discussed by Carlos Rivera Santana and Bettina Pérez Martínez in chapter 10), how additional net out-migration from the island could impact voting patterns in the U.S. mainland (discussed by Mark Hugo Lopez, Antonio Flores, and Jens Manuel Krogstad in chapter 11), as well as the role that colleges and universities can play in disaster response and rebuilding (discussed by Havidán Rodríguez and colleagues in chapter 12).

On the always important topic of disasters and the economy, the set of chapters (2–4) by María E. Enchautegui, Zadia M. Feliciano, and José Caraballo-Cueto carefully sort through Hurricane Maria's multiple effects using empirical methodologies and recent data from the island and mainland to assess the impact of Hurricane Maria on key labor market variables and the Puerto Rican economy. To augment their arguments, the authors use comparisons, such as Florida (in the case of Enchautegui) and the United States (in the case of Feliciano), and in the case of Caraballo-Cueto, detailed econometric modeling. We return to some of these findings later in this chapter in the context of extant literature.

Regarding the health and psychological effects of the post-Maria period, discussed in chapters 6–9, Jose M. Fernandez (chapter 6) highlights the need for an improved economy as an essential prerequisite to help stabilize the (decaying) health industry on the island. He recommends that Medicaid be dealt in the same manner in Puerto Rico as is the case on the U.S. mainland in order to stem the out-migration of doctors and physicians, and that the federal government fund more medical residency programs to increase the number of healthcare professionals on the island.

Fernando I. Rivera and colleagues (chapter 7) discuss several post-Maria consequences, such as elevated death counts, healthcare complications resulting from the sustained lack of electricity, collective trauma experienced during and after the hurricane, as well as an increase in the number of suicides. They point to the frail state of the island's infrastructure (i.e., the power grid, roads, healthcare facilities, and communication systems) as a culprit in the storm's immediate health and psychological negative aftermath.

Amy Nitza and Shao Lin (chapter 8) also note that some of these negative consequences could have been mitigated and, just as important, *can* be mitigated in the future with regular mental health and public health screening, dissemination of information on the environmental consequences of disasters, and more effective public response mechanisms. They go on to argue that programs and initiatives to monitor the school climate and the well-being of teachers and students are equally important, as well as professional responders following the impact of disasters; these themes are further discussed by María Rolón-Martínez and colleagues (chapter 9).

LINGERING QUESTIONS

One question that is in the background as the reader sorts through these contributions is what would the impact of Hurricane Maria have been in an island with a relatively strong economy and state-of-the art infrastructure? We, of course, will never know. However, we do know that the storm's freakish strength and bullseye nature toward and across the island was rare, powerful, and destructive, regardless of the island's precarious socioeconomic conditions and its deteriorating infrastructure. One of the outcomes of La Crisis Boricua was the decade's long mass exodus from the island to the mainland, which admittedly reduced the number of potential victims of Hurricane Maria.

It also remains unknown whether a more modern infrastructure (as called for by Marla D. Pérez-Lugo, Cecilio Ortiz-García, and Didier Valdés in chapter 5) would have been destroyed by the storm (although their thesis says otherwise), resulting in structural losses, which would have been the same or greater than those actually observed. Still, it is unlikely that a more modern infrastructure would have collapsed as the existing one did, nor is it likely to have taken as long to restore basic services to millions of Americans, thousands of whom lost their lives in this catastrophic event.

Furthermore, the situation begs another question, also raised by Pérez-Lugo and colleagues, where does Puerto Rico go from here? Does it return to pre-Hurricane Maria's conditions or to a more robust socioeconomic infrastructure as the island continues to rebuild? What were the lessons learned as a consequence of this event, which will allow Puerto Rico to build better and stronger, resulting in a more resilient society?

The outlook provided by Pérez-Lugo and colleagues and the present are bleak as a consequence of the political powerbrokers in Puerto Rico. However, given what seems a better than average response on the island to COVID-19 despite a slow start (e.g., Ayala and Padilla Dalmau 2020), there is hope that Puerto Rico's resilience in the face of disaster adversity is seemingly paying off.

One of the most important themes covered in this edited book is the net out-migration of Puerto Ricans resulting from the aforementioned socioeconomic conditions and Hurricane Maria, along with the labor market and demographic consequences of this migratory phenomenon. To put labor market context into these dynamics, consider that an outflow of labor in an area reduces labor supply and should increase general wages. Other things remaining the same (one of which is the availability of the same number of jobs), the increase in wages should serve to attract labor back to the region and eventually lead toward wage parity. The higher wages should also mitigate the demand for labor in the afflicted areas, as supposedly the cost of goods produced in the area would increase, making them relatively less attractive to consumers. Also, related to the demand for labor, capital out-migration and inflows should fall, further reducing this demand. In both cases, wages would be expected to return to comparable levels prior to the decrease in labor supply.

Of course, labor market hedonics should be considered as well as cost-of-living differentials across areas. In the case of Puerto Rico, there is an obvious high concentration of Puerto Ricans on the island (likely a compensating wage differential for those who prefer residing near other Puerto Ricans and accessing the island's cultural amenities), relatively low earnings, and high poverty rates (which might reduce the hedonic effects of living in the area). In this context, it is worth noting that Enchautegui (chapter 2) reported that in almost all industries, wages grew in the aftermath of Hurricane Maria, with most industries experiencing wage growth between 2 and 5 percent, and the largest growth occurred in construction.

PRIOR LITERATURE ON LONGER-TERM IMPACTS FROM DISASTERS

Also consider that the literature provides some clues on another partial answer to the aforementioned "where do we go from here" question. Earlier work suggests that the long-run demographic impact of a natural hazard in a particular geographic area is neutral. For example, in a 1979 study of this question, Wright and colleagues, based on their statistical analysis of data on natural hazards in the United States in the 1960s, did not find significant differences in demographic and housing trajectory impacts between areas affected by natural hazards and those that were not.

Hass and colleagues (1977) referred to this type of finding as a "functional recovery," where the population and their everyday housing needs and infrastructure are replaced after the natural hazard event. The evidence provided in this book by Enchautegui and Feliciano is supportive of this possibility (as is the population data we reported in chapter 1, where for the first time in 15 years, Puerto Rico's population stopped shrinking between 2018 and 2019). Feliciano notes in chapter 3 that as the recovery started, three months after the hurricane landed in Puerto Rico, areas closer to the epicenter experienced greater employment growth than those less affected by the hurricane. She argues that this might be the result of additional resources being deployed to these areas to reconstruct roads, buildings, homes, and utilities. However, she also reports that those effects were short lived and did not offset the initial employment losses. Similarly, Enchautegui notes in chapter 2 that the longer-term effects of disasters on employment are ambiguous, raising questions whether in the mid-to-long term, employment levels will return to their prior levels.

Other studies provide a more optimistic insight into the "where do we go from here" question. Schultz and Elliot (2013), for example, discuss how natural hazards have historically evoked a "moral response" from the public as they occur without "moral reason," potentially leaving the stricken areas better off than before the event. They cite state responses to natural hazards dating back from Lisbon's 1755 earthquake to Congress' donation of public lands to those displaced by the New Madrid, Missouri earthquake in 1827. Indeed, the Disaster Relief Act of 1950 formalizes these types of assistance programs by the federal government. Others expand on this argument. For example, Pais and Elliott (2008) argue that in recent times pro-growth coalitions have promoted a disproportionately favorable reallocation of resources to areas affected by natural hazards. In their study, they combine data from the Geographic Information Systems with demographic data of the areas afflicted by the billion-dollar storms of the 1990s, and find that the afflicted areas eventually added 1.4 million residents and 600,000 housing units.

This modern phenomenon is referred to as the "recovery machine" that occurs after natural events in the United States. From the perspective of the dynamic labor market adjustment mentioned above, where theory predicts the afflicted areas would restore their stocks of labor and capital to pre-hazard levels, the recovery machine thesis is more optimistic. The added demand of disproportionate reactions to natural hazards in afflicted areas makes those areas achieve higher labor and capital stock levels than those that initially existed.

RESPONSE AND REACTION TO HURRICANE MARIA IN PUERTO RICO

Returning to Hurricane Maria, what was the public moral reaction to this storm? As the federal government's response to the Maria crisis has been controversial and subject to intense debate, we start there. Initial consideration was given to removing the Jones Act for Puerto Rico,[1] which arguably limited the aid and supplies from non-U.S.-flagged vessels from U.S. ports. However, this idea was met with resistance from the Department of Homeland Security. That federal agency disagreed that this act was a limiting factor in Puerto Rico receiving aid and support. However, in an investigative *Politico* report (March 2018), Danny Vinik documents how the federal government responded "far more aggressively" and deployed greater resources in Texas following Hurricane Harvey than in Puerto Rico following Hurricane Maria. Also, after estimates in August 28, 2018, of the nearly 3,000 deaths in Puerto Rico attributed to Hurricane Maria, President Donald Trump held steadfast that the federal government had done a "fantastic job" in its response.

The Federal Emergency Management Administration's (FEMA) official position in its response to Hurricane Maria is particularly worth noting. On its website, FEMA reported providing assistance of over $1.5 billion in aid to Puerto Rico following the aftermath of Hurricane Maria. The agency noted financial housing assistance of $780 million, direct housing assistance at $21 million, and other needs assistance (including critical needs assistance) and human services assistance at $428 and $275 million, respectively. The Defense Logistic Agency, both stateside and their liaison officer, also noted their availability to provide Puerto Rico resources to support and restore the power grid, transformers, and conductors. However, recall from Havidán Rodríguez and colleagues (chapter 12) that the *New York Times* reported that "FEMA was sorely unprepared" for a hurricane like Maria (Robles 2018). A more moderate account of the federal relief efforts by the Harvard Humanitarian Initiative highlighted that the military deployment, in March 2018, albeit with room to improve, had improved relative to that after Hurricane Katrina.

That said, concerns have arisen over whether federal resources have been properly allocated following Hurricane Maria in Puerto Rico. For example, *El Nuevo Día* (Puerto Rico's largest circulating newspaper) reported (May 25, 2019) that the U.S. attorney's office in San Juan was investigating a FEMA Deputy Regional Administrator's involvement, who was in Puerto Rico overseeing the reconstruction of the power grid, regarding the channeling of contracts to the Cobra Acquisitions Energy company. Moreover, a study by Deepak Lamba-Nieves and Raúl Santiago Bartolomei at the Center for the New Economy reported that as of August 22, 2018, nearly all (approximately 90%) of the initial federal contract spending for relief and rebuilding efforts had been awarded to firms based on the U.S. mainland ($4.3 billion in awards to mainland-based firms vs $490 million to island-based firms). They concluded that "provisions to foster local activity in the post-disaster relief and reconstruction efforts are not being adequately implemented in Puerto Rico" (Lamba-Nieves and Bartolomei 2018).

BEYOND THE FEDERAL GOVERNMENT RESPONSE

Outside federal efforts to assist Puerto Rico after the Hurricane Maria crisis, and in some cases owing to the seeming frustration with the federal government's response, other relief groups have joined the aid efforts to help in the rebuilding of the island. Oxfam, the AARP Foundation, and UNICEF were among the few entities that publicly criticized federal relief efforts and offered assistance. Also, as outlined by Rodríguez and colleagues (chapter 12), state and local government officials and agencies, including in New York and Florida, stepped up to play a role in the recovery process. They further highlighted the State University of New York Stands with Puerto Rico Initiative, which was one of the first disaster response initiatives in Puerto Rico led by a state university system.

DISCUSSION AND CONCLUDING REMARKS

Before closing, we venture some additional points in this regard. First, has Hurricane Maria triggered a new future demographic impact for Puerto Ricans, one that provides an even closer tie to the U.S. mainland? As the discussion by Mark Lopez and colleagues (chapter 11) suggests, Puerto Rican voters appeared to be part of a coalition of voters that made a difference in determining the final outcome of the 2020 presidential election, but it was too early when this book went into production to actually measure their impact. Their presence in Florida, Pennsylvania, New York, and elsewhere may have growing implications for primary and general election results into the foreseeable future, especially in swing states like Florida and Pennsylvania. However, based on recent trends, it is likely that mainland-born Puerto Ricans rather than island-born Puerto Ricans will have a larger impact compared to previous elections on the direction of the "Puerto Rican vote" and the broader statewide and national "Hispanic vote," given their size and growing voter participation in recent years. Still, the growing presence of Puerto Ricans on the mainland raises the question as to what extent will this potential Puerto Rican political clout translate into a strengthening of the island's economy.

Second, the recent work on natural hazards and their impact on areas mentioned above discusses a potential "recovery machine" phenomenon. But the Schultz and Elliott (2013) study also provides that these recoveries have been uneven, mostly favoring those at the top end of the income distribution. While it is possible, then, that on average, Puerto Rico's economy might surpass pre-Hurricane Maria levels, the question is whether this will occur at the expense of an increase in the already large income distribution gap on the island. What would this type of economic dynamic have on the socioeconomic and demographic fabric on the island?

Third, in a 2010 article, Richard W. Evans, Yingyao Hu, and Zhong Zhao found that the fertility rates of afflicted areas rise for low-advisory storms and decrease with more intense storms. We reported in chapter 1 (as well as in our aforementioned 2017 book) the issue of the shrinking and rapidly aging population, illustrated by the bulging of the age-population pyramids (recall figure 1.6) due to net out-migration of the young as well as low fertility rates on the island. While we showed an almost immediate effect of Hurricane Maria on Puerto Rico's age-population pyramid, it remains to be seen whether it will have a longer-term impact on fertility rates on the island, which are already at an all-time low. Structural changes to Puerto Rico's demographic profile will impact its future education and healthcare needs as well as its workforce and longer-term prosperity. Regardless, it remains imperative to continue rebuilding Puerto Rico and ease the effects of the prolonged crisis which has led to widespread suffering, mental and physical health issues, and fatalities that have affected millions of American citizens on the island and U.S. mainland.

NOTE

1. The 1920 Jones Act requires that goods shipped between the U.S. mainland and noncontiguous areas (including Alaska, Hawaii, Puerto Rico, the U.S. Virgin Islands, etc.) must use U.S.-owned, U.S.-crewed, and U.S.-built vessels.

Bibliography

Abel, Jaison R. and Richard Dietz. 2014. "Causes and Consequences of Puerto Rico's Declining Population." *Current Issues in Economics and Finance* 20(4): 1–8, Federal Reserve Bank of New York. https://www.newyorkfed.org/medialibrary/media/research/current_issues/ci20-4.pdf.

Acevedo-Garcia, Dolores and Lisa M. Bates. 2007. "Latino Health Paradoxes: Empirical Evidence, Explanations, Future Research, and Implications." In *Latinas/os in the United States: Changing the Face of America*, edited by H. Rodríguez, R. Sáenz, and C. Menjívar, 101–113. New York: Springer.

Acosta-Belén, Edna and Carlos E. Santiago. 2006. *Puerto Ricans in the United States: A Contemporary Portrait*. Boulder: Lynne Rienner.

Aja, Alan, Stephan Lefebvre, Williams Darity Jr., R. Ortiz-Minaya, and Darrick Hamilton. 2018. "Bold Policies for Puerto Rico: A Blueprint for Transformative, Justice-Centered Recovery." *Diálogo* 21(2): 3–14.

Alarcón, Renato D., Amrita Parekh, Milton L. Wainberg, Cristiane S. Duarte, Ricardo Araya, and María A. Oquendo. 2016 "Hispanic Immigrants in the USA: Social and Mental Health Perspectives." *The Lancet Psychiatry* 3(9): 860–870.

Aldaja, A. A., Watson, M., Bouri, N., Minton, K., Morhard, R. C., and Toner, E. S. 2014. "Absorbing Citywide Patient Surge during Hurricane Sandy: A Case Study in Accommodating Multiple Hospital Evacuations." *Annals of Emergency Medicine* 64: 66–73.

Alegría, Margarita, Norah Mulvaney-Day, Maria Torres, Antonio Polo, Zhun Cao, and Glorisa Canino. 2007. "Prevalence of Psychiatric Disorders across Latino Subgroups in the United States." *American Journal of Public Health* 97(1): 68–75.

Alm, James. 2006. "Assessing Puerto Rico's Fiscal Policies." In *The Economy of Puerto Rico: Restoring Growth*, edited by Susan M. Collins, Barry P. Bosworth and Miguel A. Soto Class. Washington, DC: Center for the New Economy, San Juan Puerto Rico and Brookings Institution.

American Psychological Association. 2008. *Children and Trauma: Update for Mental Health Professionals: Presidential Task Force on Posttraumatic Stress*

Disorder and Trauma in Children and Adolescents. Retrieved from https://www.apa.org/pi/families/resources/children-trauma-update.

American Psychological Association. 2012. *Effects of Poverty, Hunger and Homelessness on Children and Youth*. Retrieved from https://www.apa.org/pi/families/poverty.

American Society of Civil Engineers. 2019. *2019 Report Card for Puerto Rico's Infrastructure*. https://www.infrastructurereportcard.org/wp-content/uploads/2019/11/2019-Puerto-Rico-Report-Card-Final.pdf. Accessed December 22, 2019.

Aponte, J. 2018. "Hurricanes and Mental Health." *Hispanic Health Care International* 16(3): 110–111.

Aranda, Elizabeth and Fernando I. Rivera. 2016. "Puerto Rican Families in Central Florida: Prejudice, Discrimination, and Their Implications for Successful Integration." *Women, Gender, and Families of Color* 4(1): 57–85.

Aronoff, A. 2018. "Puerto Rico Governor Seizes Opportunity Created By Hurricane Maria, Plans To Privatize Electric Power." *The Intercept*, January 24, 2018. https://theintercept.com/2018/01/24/puerto-rico-prepa-opportunity-government-plans-to-privatize-electric-power/.

Arroyo, Marga Parés. 2016. "Peligrosa Fuga de Miles de Médicos." *El Nuevo Dia*. July 28, 2016. https://www.elnuevodia.com/noticias/locales/nota/peligrosafugademilesdemedicos-2225024/.

Assets for Artists. 2018. "Welcome Puerto Rican Artists!" *Blog*, April 12, 2018. https://www.assetsforartists.org/blog/2018/4/9/welcome-puerto-rican-artists. Accessed July 8, 2019.

ASSMCA. 2016. *Need Assessment Study of Mental Health and Substance Use Disorders and Service Utilization among Adult Population in Puerto Rico – Final Report*. Behavioral Sciences Research Institute, University of Puerto Rico, Medical Science Campus.

Atiles-Osoria, José M. 2013. "Environmental Colonialism, Criminalization and Resistance: Puerto Rican Mobilizations for Environmental Justice in the 21st Century." *Revista Crítica de Ciencias Sociais,* October. DOI: 10.4000/rccs.5262.

Ayala, Edmy and Camille Padilla Dalmau. 2020. *How Puerto Rican Scientists Hacked the COVID-19 Response*. New York, NY: Latino USA, June 9, 2020. https://www.latinousa.org/2020/06/09/prscientistscovid19/, podcast Accessed January 10, 2021.

Barfield Barry, Deborah. 2018. "Midterms: Puerto Ricans Displaced by Hurricane Maria may Prove Pivotal in Florida Elections." *USA Today*, October 18, 2018. https://www.usatoday.com/story/news/politics/elections/2018/10/17/midterms-displaced-puerto-ricans-courted-swing-state-florida/1518309002/.

Belasen, Ariel and Solomon Polachek. 2013. "Natural Disasters and Migration." In *International Handbook on the Economics of Migration*, edited by Amelie F. Constant and Klaus F. Zimmermann, 309–330. Edward Elgar Publishing.

Belasen, Ariel R. and Solomon W. Polachek. 2009. "How Disasters Affect Local Labor Markets: The Effects of Hurricanes in Florida." *The Journal of Human Resources* 44(1): 251–276.

Belasen, Ariel R. and Solomon W. Polachek. 2008. "How Hurricanes Affect Wages and Employment in Local Labor Markets." *American Economic Review: Papers & Proceedings*, 98(2): 49–53.

Bengtsson, Linus, Xin Lu, and Petter Holme. 2017. "Predictability of Population Displacement after the 2010 Haiti Earthquake." *PNAS* 109(29) (July): 11576–11581. https://www.pnas.org/content/pnas/109/29/11576.full.pdf.

Berkowitz, S., Bryant, R., Brymer, M., Hamblen, J., Jacobs, A., Layne, C., Macy, R., Osofsky, H., Pynoos, R., Ruzek, J., Steinberg, A., Vernberg, E., and Watson, P. 2010. *Skills for Psychological Recovery: Field Operations Guide*. Washington, DC: The National Center for PTSD & the National Child Traumatic Stress Network.

Biesenbach, Klaus, Gregory, Christopher, and Mclaughlin, Ariana. 2018. "In Puerto Rico, Artists Rebuild and Reach Out." *New York Times*, 25 January 2018, https://www.nytimes.com/2018/01/25/arts/design/puerto-rico-artists-klaus-biesenbach-hurricane-maria.html.

Blaikie, P., Cannon, T., Davis, I., and Wisner, B. 2005. *At Risk: Natural Hazards, People's Vulnerability and Disasters*. Routledge.

Blakeman, Bradley. 2017. "Puerto Rico Was a Disaster Long before Maria Ravaged the Island." *The Hill*, https://thehill.com/opinion/energy-environment/353506-puerto-rico-was-a-disaster-long-before-maria-ravaged-the-island.

Bloom, M., Palumbo, J., Sayed, N., Lauper, U., and Lin, S. 2016. "Food and Waterborne Disease in New York State Following Hurricane Sandy, 2012." *Disaster Med Public Health Preparedness* 10(3): 314–319.

Bonilla, Yarimar. 2018. "For Investors, Puerto Rico Is a Fantasy Blank Slate." *The Nation*, February 28, 2018. https://www.thenation.com/article/for-investors-puerto-rico-is-a-fantasy-blank-slate/. Accessed October 18, 2018.

Bonnano, G. A. 2004. "Loss, Trauma and Human Resilience: Have We Underestimated the Human Capacity to Thrive after Extremely Aversive Events?" *American Psychologist* 59(1): 20–28.

Bonnano, G. A., Brewin, C. R., Kaniasty, K., and La Greca, A. M. 2010. "Weighing the Costs of Disaster: Consequences, Risk, and Resilience in Individuals, Families, and Communities." *Psychological Science in the Public Interest* 11(1): 1–49.

Borrás, Susana and Jakob Edler, eds. 2014. *The Governance of Socio-Technical Systems: Explaining Change*. Edward Elgar Publishing, 2014.

Boryga, Andrew, Yvonne H. Valdez, and Mario Ariza. 2020. "How Trump Won Big with Latinos in Florida – And Then Some." *South Florida Sun Sentinel*, November 4, 2020. https://www.sun-sentinel.com/news/politics/elections/fl-ne-latinos-miami-voting-20201104-eyydu3ltkbfqrkklsg2jgtvy2i-story.html.

Bourque, L. B. 2006. "Weathering the Storm: The Impact of Hurricanes on Physical and Mental Health." *The Annals of the American Academy of Political and Social Science* 604(1): 129–151.

Bronner, Laura and Michael Tabb. 2020. "Exit Polls Came Up Short This Year. Here's Why." *FiveThirtyEight*, December 7, 2020. https://fivethirtyeight.com/videos/dont-believe-anything-the-2020-exit-polls-tell-you/.

Brown, Nick, Robin Respaut, and Jessica Resnick-Ault. 2017. "Special Report: The Bankrupt Utility behind Puerto Rico's Power Crisis." *Reuters*, October 4, 2017.

https://www.reuters.com/article/us-usa-puertorico-utility-specialreport/special-report-the-bankrupt-utility-behind-puerto-ricos-power-crisis-idUSKBN1C92B5. Accessed December 11, 2019.

Brown, Sharon P. Sandra L. Mason, and Richard B. Tiller. 2006. "The Effect of Hurricane Katrina on Employment and Unemployment." *Monthly Labor Review* 129(8): 52–69.

Brusentsev, Vera and Wayne Vroman. 2017. *Disasters in the United States. Frequency, Costs, and Compensation.* Kalamazoo: Upjohn Institute for Employment Research.

Brymer, M., Jacobs, A., Layne, C., Pynoos, R., Ruzek, J., Steinberg, A., Vernberg, E., and Watson, P. 2006. *Psychological First Aid: Field Operations Guide, 2nd Edition.* Washington, DC: National Child Traumatic Stress Network and National Center for PTSD. Retrieved from www.nctsn.org and www.ncptsd.va.gov.

Burgos, Giovani, Fernando I. Rivera, and Marc A. Garcia. 2017. "Contextualizing the Relationship between Culture and Puerto Rican Health: Towards a Place-Based Framework of Minority Health Disparities." *Centro Journal* 29(3): 36–73.

Byme, M. 2013. *New York. One Month after Sandy Weblog Entry.* Washington, DC: Federal Emergency Management Agency, US Department of Homeland Security; http://goo.gl/55IZU. Accessed April 15, 2013.

Cabán, Pedro. 2019. "Hurricane Maria's Aftermath: Redefining Puerto Rico's Colonial Status." *Latin American, Caribbean, and U.S. Latino Studies Faculty Scholarship* 34, University at Albany, State University of New York, Scholars Archive. Accessed October 14, 2019.

Caetano, Raul, Patrice A. C. Vaeth, Britain Mills, and Glorisa Canino. 2016. "Employment Status, Depression, Drinking, and Alcohol Use Disorder in Puerto Rico." *Alcoholism: Clinical and Experimental Research* 40(4): 806–815.

Cai, Weiyi and Ford Fessenden. 2020. "Immigrant Neighborhoods Shifted Red as the Country Chose Blue." *The New York Times*, December 20, 2020. https://www.nytimes.com/interactive/2020/12/20/us/politics/election-hispanics-asians-voting.html?campaign_id=29&emc=edit_up_20201221&instance_id=25263&nl=the-upshot&regi_id=15453865&segment_id=47484&te=1&user_id=087c36a117dcbd86cb675e39b2e7a1a2&fbclid=IwAR036MFSCzJUo_mOPgiRAH_32G5m6N9QIe-fqC4LsA_HRmojUDhh-fE81Fg.

Camillieri, Devon. 2019. "No Water in Sight." Storyfest Entry at Planet Forward, March 8, 2019, George Washington University, Washington, DC. Blog. https://www.planetforward.org/idea/no-water-in-sight. Accessed June 28, 2019.

Campo-Flores, Arian and Elizabeth Findell. 2020. "Latino Voters Drifted From Democrats in Florida and Texas." *The Wall Street Journal*, November 5, 2020. https://www.wsj.com/articles/latino-voters-drifted-from-democrats-in-florida-and-texas-11604582691.

Canino, Glorisa, Patrick E. Shrout, Amanda NeMoyer, Doryliz Vila, Katyana M. Santiago, Pedro García, Amarilis Quiñones, Vilmary Cruz, and Margarita Alegria. 2019. "A Comparison of the Prevalence of Psychiatric Disorders in Puerto Rico with the United States and the Puerto Rican Population of the United States." *Social Psychiatry and Psychiatric epiPemiology* 54(3): 369–378.

Caputo, Ibby. 2017. “Hurricane Maria Devastated Puerto Rico. Then It Caused a Ripple Effect in Mainland Hospitals.” *Public Radio International*, December 06, 2017. https://www.pri.org/stories/2017-12-06/hurricane-maria-devastated-puerto-rico-then-it-caused-ripple-effect-mainland.

Caraballo-Cueto, Jose and Juan Lara. 2018. “Deindustrialization and Unsustainable Debt in Middle-Income Countries: The Case of Puerto Rico.” *Journal of Globalization and Development* 8(2): 1–11.

Caragol-Barreto, Taína, 2005. “Aesthetics of Exile: The Construction of Nuyorican Identity in the Art of El Taller Boricua.” *Centro Journal*, XVII (1): 122–134.

Carey, Lois. 2006. *Expressive and Creative Arts Methods for Trauma Survivors*. Philadelphia, PA: Kingsley.

Casanova-Burgess, Alana. 2017. “Dark Humor after Maria.” Podcast audio. *WNYC Studios: On the Media*, December 15, 2017, https://www.wnycstudios.org/story/on-the-media-2017-12-15.

Castro-Sitiriche, M., Cintrón-Sotomayor, Y., and Gómez-Torres, J. 2018. “The Longest Power Blackout in History and Energy Poverty.” In *Proceedings of the 8th International Conference Appropriate Technology*, November, 36–48.

Center for Puerto Rican Studies (Centro). 2018a. *Puerto Rico after Hurricane Maria*. New York: Centro, RD2018-01, October 2018.

Center for Puerto Rican Studies (Centro). 2018b. *Post-Maria Puerto Rico*. New York: Centro. https://centropr.hunter.cuny.edu/sites/default/files/PDF/puerto_rico_post_maria-2018-final.pdf. Accessed January 11, 2021.

Centers for Disease Control and Prevention. 2017. *BRFSS Prevalence and Trends Data*, 2–3 http://wwwdev.cdc.gov/brfss/brfssprevalence/.

Centers for Disease Control and Prevention, 2018. https://www.cdc.gov/socialdeterminants/index.htm.

Chapell, Bill. 2017. “Trump Hints at a Limit on Federal Aid to Puerto Rico; San Juan Mayor Responds.” *NPR*, October 12, 2017. http://www.npr.org/sections/thetwo-way/2017/10/12/557353205/trump-hints-at-a-limit-on-federal-aid-to-puerto-rico-san-juanmayor-responds.

Cilluffo, Anthony and Richard Fry. 2019. *An Early Look at the 2020 Electorate*. Washington, DC: Pew Research Center, January 30, 2019. https://www.pewsocialtrends.org/essay/an-early-look-at-the-2020-electorate/.

CNN. 2020. “Exit Polls.” https://www.cnn.com/election/2020/exit-polls/president/national-results.

Cohen, J. A., Mannarino, A. P., and Deblinger, E. 2017. *Treating Trauma and Traumatic Grief in Children and Adolescents* (2nd ed.). New York: Guilford Press.

Cohn, D’Vera, Eileen Patten, and Mark Hugo Lopez. 2014. *Puerto Rican Population Declines on Island, Grows on U.S. Mainland*. Washington, DC: Pew Research Center Hispanic Trends Project, August 11, 2014.

Cole, Teju. 2012. “The White-Savior Industrial Savior Complex.” *The Atlantic*, March 21, 2012. https://www.theatlantic.com/international/archive/2012/03/the-white-savior-industrial-complex/254843/. Accessed June 25, 2019.

Commonwealth of Puerto Rico. 2019. "Restoring Growth and Prosperity." 2019 Fiscal Plan for Puerto Rico. https://drive.google.com/file/d/13wuVn04--JKMEPKu-u-djZJHqTK-55aV/view.

Constantino, Tracy and White, Boyd, Eds. 2010. *Essays on Aesthetic Education for the 21st Century*. Taipei: Sense Publishers.

Convergence Lab. n.d. "About Rise." https://www.umnconvergencepuertorico.org/about-rise. Accessed June 20, 2019.

COR3 Transparency Portal. n.d. "¿Cómo se distribuyen los fondos?" https://recovery.pr/home. Accessed August 19, 2019.

Corkery, Michael and Mary Williams Walsh. 2015. "Puerto Rico's Governor Says Island's Debts Are 'Not Payable'." *New York Times*, June 28, 2015.

Cruz-Cano, Raul and Erin L Mead. 2019. "Causes of Excess Deaths in Puerto Rico after Hurricane Maria: A Time-Series Estimation." *American Journal of Public Health* : e1–e3.

Cupeles, J. David. 1993. *Lorenzo Homar: Artista Ejemplar De La Grafica Contemporanea De Puerto Rico*. Mexico: S.n.

Daugherty, Alex, Caitlin Ostroff, and Martin Vassolo. 2018. "Post-Hurricane Maria Puerto Ricans Won't Swing Florida's Election." *Tampa Bay Times*, October 30, 2018. https://www.tampabay.com/florida-politics/buzz/2018/10/30/post-hurricane-maria-puerto-ricans-wont-swing-floridas-election/.

Daviglus, Martha L., Gregory A. Talavera, M. Larissa Avilés-Santa, Matthew Allison, Jianwen Cai, Michael H. Criqui, Marc Gellman Aida L. Giachello, Natalia Gouskova, Robert C. Kaplan. 2012. "Prevalence of Major Cardiovascular Risk Factors and Cardiovascular Diseases among Hispanic/Latino Individuals of Diverse Backgrounds in the United States." *JAMA* 308(17): 1775–1784.

De Jesus Salaman, Adriana. 2017. "Cambios en Juntas Públicas Bajo Rosselló Nevares." *Noticel*, July 1, 2017. https://www.noticel.com/ahora/cambios-en-juntas-pblicas-bajo-rossell-nevares/609406524.

Deloughney, Elizabeth M., and George B. Handley. 2011. *Postcolonial Ecologies: Literatures of the Environment*. New York: Oxford University Press.

Democratic Staff Report. 2018. *A FAILURE OF OVERSIGHT: How Republicans Blocked a Credible Investigation of the Trump Administration's Response to the 2017 Hurricanes*. Retrieved July 20, 2019, from Committee on Oversight and Government Reform: https://oversight.house.gov/sites/democrats.oversight.house.gov/files/documents/A%20FAILURE%20OF%20OVERSIGHT%20-%20STAFF%20REPORT.pdf.

Demos, T. J. 2016. "Introduction." *Decolonizing Nature : Contemporary Art and the Politics of Ecology*. Berlin: Sternberg Press.

Department of Health in Puerto Rico. "Estadisticos, Registros, y Publicaciones." www.salud.gov.pr/Estadisticas-Registros-y-Publicaciones/Pages/default.aspx.

Departamento de Salud, Gobierno de Puerto Rico. 2019. Estadisticas Preliminares de Casos de Suicidios, Puerto Rico, January-May 2019. Retrieved from http://www.salud.gov.pr/Estadisticas-Registros-y-Publicaciones/Estadisticas%20Suicidio/Mayo%202019.pdf.

Diario de Puerto Rico. 2019. "Trabajadores de la Construcción Inician Campaña por Sus Salarios." Diariodepuertorico.com, November 12, 2019.

Dickerson C. 2017. "After Hurricane, Signs of a Mental Health Crisis Haunt Puerto Rico." *The New York Times*. November 13, 2017. https://www.nytimes.com/2017/11/13/us/puerto-rico-hurricane-maria-mental-health.html?_r=0.

Downer, Brian, Michael Crowe, and Kyriakos Markides. 2019. "Population Aging and Health in Puerto Rico: Effects of Space, Time and Place." In *Contextualizing Health and Aging in the Americas*, 7–17. Switzerland: Springer Nature.

Eccles, J. S., Midgley, C., Wigfield, A., Buchanan, C. M., Reuman, D., Flanagan, C., and MacIver, D. 1993. "Development during Adolescence: The Impact of Stage Environment Fit on Young Adolescents' Experiences in Schools and in Families." *American Psychologist. Special Issue: Adolescence,* 48: 90–101.

Echenique, Martín and Luis Melgar. 2018. "Mapping Puerto Rico's Hurricane Migration with Mobile Phone Data." *Citylab*, May 11. https://www.citylab.com/environment/2018/05/watch-puerto-ricos-hurricanemigration-via-mobile-phone-data/559889/.

EFE. 2018. "Industriales Piden que la Camara Apruebe la Privatizacion de la AEE." *El Nuevo Dia*, November 8, 2018. https://www.elnuevodia.com/negocios/economia/nota/industrialespidenquelacamaraapruebelaprivatizaciondelaaeee-2458311/. Accessed December 11, 2019.

Enchautegui, María E. and Richard B. Friedman. 2006. "Why Don't More Puerto Rican Men Work? The Rich Uncle (Sam) Hypothesis." In *The Economy of Puerto Rico Restoring Growth,* edited by Susan M. Collins, Barry P. Bosworth and Miguel A Soto-Class, 152–182. Washington, DC: Brookings Institution Press.

Environmental Protection Agency. 2015. Hurricane Sandy Response and Recovery: Air Monitoring Results. *EPA Website*. http://archive.epa.gov/region02/sandy/web/html/. Updated November 18, 2015. Accessed November 20, 2015.

Estudios Técnicos, Inc. and University of Puerto Rico, Río Piedras. 2019. *Impact of Hurricane Maria in Puerto Rico's Children: Volume 1 Summary of Relevant Findings*. (Instituto Desarrollo Juventud report). Retrieved from http://juventudpr.org/wp-content/uploads/2019/01/20511.pdf?v=1.0.

Evans, Richard W., Yingyao Hu, and Zhong Zhao. 2010. "The Fertility Effect of Catastrophe: U.S. Hurricane Births." *Journal of Population Economics* 23: 1–36.

Ewing, Bradley T. and Jaime B. Kruse. 2005. *Hurricanes and Unemployment*. Working Paper No. 0105-002, Center for Natural Hazards Research, East Carolina University. http://citeseerx.ist.psu.edu/viewdoc/download?doi=10.1.1.694.315&rep=rep1&type=pdf.

Ewing, Bradley T., Jaime B. Kruse, and Mark A. Thompson. 2005. "Empirical Examination of the Corpus Christi Unemployment Rate and Hurricane Bret." *Natural Hazards Review* 6(4) (November):191–196. https://doi.org/10.1061/(ASCE)1527-6988(2005)6:4(191).

Farrant, Jaime. 2017. "Four Reasons Why Puerto Rico's 'Bankruptcy' Process Matters to U.S. Residents." *NBC News*, June 5, 2017. www.nbcnews.comhttps://www.nbcnews.com/news/latino/4-reasons-why-puerto-rico-s-bankruptcy-process-matters-u-n766991.

Federal Emergency Management Agency. 2018. "2017 Hurricane Season FEMA After-Action Report." https://www.fema.gov/media-library-data/1533643262195

-6d1398339449ca85942538a1249d2ae9/2017FEMAHurricaneAARv20180730.pdf?smid=nytcore-ios-share. Accessed June 13, 2019.

Feliciano, Zadia M. 2018. "IRS Section 936 and the Decline of Puerto Rico's Manufacturing." *Centro Journal* 30(3): 30–42.

Feliciano, Zadia M. and Andrew Green. 2017. "U.S. Multinationals in Puerto Rico and the Repeal of Section 936 Tax Exemption for U.S. Corporations." *NBER Working Paper Series*, Working Paper #23681, http://www.nber.org/papers/w23681.

Felix, E. D., You, S., and Canino, G. 2013. "School and Community Influences on the Long Term Postdisaster Recovery of Children and Youth Following Hurricane Georges." *Journal of Community Psychology* 41(8): 1021–1038.

Felix, E. D., You, S., Vernberg, E., and Canino, G. 2013. "Family Influences on the Long-Term Post-Disaster Recovery of Puerto Rican Youth." *Journal of Abnormal Child Psychology* 41: 111–124.

Fenelon, Andrew and Laura Blue. 2015. "Widening Life Expectancy Advantage of Hispanics in the United States: 1990–2010." *Journal of Immigrant and Minority Health / Center for Minority Public Health* 17(4): 1130–1137. https://doi.org/10.1007/s10903-014-0043-6.

Ferris, D. and Behr, P. 2017, December 8. Microgrids Could Save Puerto Rico. But First, a Fight. Retrieved October 2018, from E&E News: https://www.eenews.net/stories/1060068479/.

Figueroa-Rodríguez, Raúl. 2013. *The Elders' Colony*. San Juan, PR: Raúl Figueroa Rodríguez.

Flores, Antonio, Mark Hugo Lopez, and Jens Manuel Krogstad. 2018. "Hispanic Voter Registration Rises in Florida, but Role of Puerto Ricans Remains Unclear." Washington, DC: Pew Research Center, October 12, 2018. https://www.pewresearch.org/fact-tank/2018/10/12/hispanic-voter-registration-rises-in-florida-but-role-of-puerto-ricans-remains-unclear/.

Flores, Antonio and Jens Manuel Krogstad. 2019. "Puerto Rico's Population Declined Sharply after Hurricanes Maria and Irma." Washington, DC: Pew Research Center, July 26, 2019. https://www.pewresearch.org/fact-tank/2019/07/26/puerto-rico-population-2018/.

Food and Agriculture Organization, United Nations. 2015. *The Impact of Natural Hazards and Disasters on Agriculture and Food Security and Nutrition. A Call for Action to Build Resilient Livelihoods*. Rome: FAO, http://www.fao.org/3/a-i4434e.pdf.

Fouquet, Roger and Peter J. G. Pearson. 2012. "Past and Prospective Energy Transitions: Insights from History." *Energy Policy* 50: 1–7.

Garcia-Lopez, G. A. 2018. "The Multiple Layers of Environmental Injustice in Contexts of (un) Natural Disasters: The Case of Puerto Rico Post-Hurricane Maria." *Environmental Justice* 11(3): 101–108.

Garcia, Marc A, Catherine Garcia, Chi-Tsun Chiu, Mukaila Raji, and Kyriakos S. Markides. 2018. "A Comprehensive Analysis of Morbidity Life Expectancies Among Older Hispanic Subgroups in the United States: Variation by Nativity and Country of Origin." *Innovation in Aging* 2(2). https://doi.org/10.1093/geroni/igy014.

Garofalo, G. 2020. "Puerto Rico Experiencing 'Mental Health Pandemic.'" *The Weekly Journal,* May 15, 2020. https://www.theweeklyjournal.com/lifestyle/puerto-rico-experiencing-mental-health-pandemic/article_76625a24-9522-11ea-8f24-bf871d166d7b.html. Accessed August 31, 2020.

Gay, Hiram A., Roberto Santiago, Betty Gil, Carlos Remedios, Pedro J. Montes, Javier López-Araujo, Carlos M. Chévere, et al. 2019. "Lessons Learned from Hurricane Maria in Puerto Rico: Practical Measures to Mitigate the Impact of a Catastrophic Natural Disaster on Radiation Oncology Patients." *Practical Radiation Oncology* 9: 305–321. https://doi.org/10.1016/j.prro.2019.03.007.

Geiger, A. W. 2018. "A Look at Voters' Views Ahead of the 2018 Midterm." Washington, DC: Pew Research Center, November 1, 2018. https://www.pewresearch.org/fact-tank/2018/11/01/a-look-at-voters-views-ahead-of-the-2018-midterms/.

Glanz, James and Frances Robles. 2018, "How Storms, Missteps and an Ailing Grid Left Puerto Rico in the Dark." *New York Times,* May 6, 2018. https://www.nytimes.com/interactive/2018/05/06/us/puerto-rico-power-grid-hurricanes.html. Accessed December 22, 2019.

Glassman, Brian. 2019. "Puerto Rico Outmigration Increases, Poverty Declines." https://census.gov/library/stories/2019/09/puerto-rico-outmigration-increases-poverty-declines.html?utm_campaign=20190926msacos3ccstors&utm_medium=email&utm_source=govdelivery&fbclid=IwAR04wpvRCm06zRIBMNP8XW6kbb15EpnfVxZe33uJNgdvMFMfB5lmFZa6RYk.

Glissant, Édouard. 1997. *Poetics of Relation.* Edited by Betsy Wing. Ann Arbor: University of Michigan Press.

Goldsmith, William W. and Thomas Vietorisz. 1979. "Operation Bootstrap, Industrial Autonomy, and a Parallel Economy for Puerto Rico." *International Regional Science Review* 4(1): 1–22.

Government of Puerto Rico. 2018. "Transformation and Innovation in the Wake of Devastation: An Economic and Disaster Recovery Plan for Puerto Rico." http://www.p3.pr.gov/assets/pr-transformation-innovation-plan-congressional-submission-080818.pdf.

Government of Puerto Rico. 2018. "Construimos." https://www.construimos.pr/?gclid=EAIaIQobChMIsvrFzv7i3QIV3UwNCh2wpgEkEAAYASAAEgJw3fD_BwE. Accessed October 18, 2018.

Government of Puerto Rico. 2018. "News & Noteworthy: Press Releases, Blogs and More." *Business in Puerto Rico.* https://www.businessinpuertorico.com/noticias/for-investors-puerto-rico-is-a-fantasy-blank-slate/. Accessed October 15, 2018.

Groen, Jeffrey A., Mark J. Kutzbach, and Anne E. Polivka. 2020. "Storms and Jobs: The Effect of Hurricanes on Individuals' Employment and Earnings over the Long Term." *Journal of Labor Economics* 38(3): 653–685.

Groen, Jeffrey A., Mark J. Kutzbach, and Anne E. Polivka. 2016. "Storms and Jobs: The Effect of Hurricanes on Individuals' Employment and Earnings Over the Long Term." *U.S. Census Bureau Center for Economic Studies*, no. CES-WP-15-21R (May). http://doi.org/10.2139/ssrn.2782038.

Gros, D. F. 2012. "Relations between Loss of Services and Psychiatric Symptoms in Urban and Non-Urban Settings Following a Natural Disaster." *Journal of Psychopathology and Behavioral Assessment* 34(3): 343–350.

Guimarães, Paulo, Frank L. Hefner, and Douglas P. Woodward. 1993. "Wealth and Income Effects of Natural Disasters: An Econometric Analysis of Hurricane Hugo." *The Review of Regional Studies* 23(2): 97–114. https://pdfs.semanticscholar.org/da07/68d615db27e2bd4c2cb3489ec805157af0cf.pdf.

Guerra, N. G. and Dierkhising, C. 2011. "The Effects of Community Violence on Child Development." *Encyclopedia of Early Childhood Development*. http://www.child-encyclopedia.com/activite-physique/according-experts/effects-community-violence-child-development.

Guth, L. J., Surinon, C., Puig, A., Nitza, A., Georgiana, B., and Freytes, I. M. 2020. *The Impact of Hurricane Maria on Students and Educators in Puerto Rico: A Needs Assessment Study*. Unpublished manuscript.

Guzman, Gloria. 2019. "Household Income: 2018." *American Community Survey Briefs*. Washington, DC: U.S. Census Bureau. https://www.census.gov/content/dam/Census/library/publications/2019/acs/acsbr18-01.pdf.

Hall, Cornelia, Robin Rudowitz, and Kathleen Gifford. 2019. "Medicaid in the Territories: Program Features, Challenges, and Changes." The Henry J. Kaiser Family Foundation, January 25, 2019. https://www.kff.org/medicaid/issue-brief/medicaid-in-the-territories-program-features-challenges-and-changes/.

Hallegatte, Stéphane and Michael Ghil. 2008. "Natural Disasters Impacting a Macroeconomic Model with Endogenous Dynamics." *Ecological Economics* 68(1–2): 582–592.

Halpern J. and Vermeulen, K. 2017. *Disaster Mental Health Interventions: Core Principles and Practices*. New York, NY: Routledge.

Hass, J. E., Kates, R. W., and Bowden, M. J. 1977. *Reconstruction Following a Disaster*. Boston: MIT Press.

Head, Brian W. 2008. "Wicked Problems in Public Policy." *Public Policy* 3(2): 101.

Hernández Pérez Maribel. 2019. "Denuncian Incumplimineto al Pago de $15 la Hora a Obreros de la Construcción." *Primera Hora*, November 4, 2019.

Hernandez-Suarez, Dagmar F., Christina Rodriguez-Ruiz, Melanie Malavé-Sánchez, Javier E. Mirabal-Arroyo, Jose A. Colon-Marquez, Ivonne Z. Jimenez-Velazquez, Nicole Rassi-Stella, Arelis Febles-Negron, and Angel Lopez-Candales. 2018. "Adapt and Evolve: How Our Internal Medicine Residency Changed in Hurricane Maria." *Puerto Rico Health Sciences Journal* 37(1): 3–4.

Hinojosa, Jennifer, Nashia Román, and Edwin Meléndez. 2018. "New Estimates: 135,000+ Post-Maria Puerto Ricans Relocated to Stateside." *Centro DS2018-01*, March 2018. https://centropr.hunter.cuny.edu/sites/default/files/ data_sheets/PostMaria-NewEstimates-3-15-18.pdf.

Hinojosa, J., Melendez, E., and Pietri, K. S. 2019. *Population Decline and School Closure in Puerto Rico*. Centro Report RB2019-01). Retrieved from Center for Puerto Rican Studies, Hunter College website: https://centropr.hunter.cuny.edu/sites/default/files/PDF_Publications/centro_rb2019-01_cor.pdf.

Hobfoll, S. E., Watson, P. J., Bell, C.C., Bryant, R. A., Brymer, M. J., Friedman, M. J., et al. 2007. "Five Essential Elements of Immediate and Mid-Term Mass Trauma Intervention: Empirical Evidence." *Psychiatry: Interpersonal and Biological Processes* 70(4): 283–315.

Hohmann, James. 2018. "The Daily 202: Puerto Ricans Who Fled to Florida after Hurricane Maria Are Not Registering to Vote." *The Washington Post*, July 27, 2018. https://www.washingtonpost.com/news/powerpost/paloma/daily-202/2018/07/27/daily-202-puerto-ricans-who-fled-to-florida-after-hurricane-maria-are-not-registering-to-vote/5b5a82a61b326b0207955dcb/.

Houston, J. Brian. 2015. "Bouncing Forward: Assessing Advances in Community Resilience Assessment, Intervention, and Theory to Guide Future Work." *American Behavioral Scientist* 59(2): 175–180.

Huss, Ephrat, Roni Kaufman, Amos Avgar, and Eitan Shuker. 2015. "Arts as a Vehicle for Community Building and Post-Disaster Development." *Disasters* 40(2): 284–303. https://doi.org/10.1111/disa.12143.

Inside Higher Ed. 2019. "Deep Cuts in Puerto Rico." Printed July 11, 2019. https://www.insidehighered.com/news/2019/07/11/university-puerto-rico-faces-deep-cuts-appropriations?utm_source=Inside+Higher+Ed&utm_campaign=83997d87a2-DNU_2019_COPY_01&utm_medium=email&utm_term=0_1fcbc04421-83997d87a2-234736905&mc_cid=83997d87a2&mc_eid=379d544af2. Accessed July 13, 2019.

Institute for Energy Economics and Financial Analysis. 2018. "Op-Ed: Rampant Political Hiring at PREPA Only Makes Matters Worse." *News Is My Business*, September 17, 2018. https://newsismybusiness.com/rampant-political-matters/. Accessed December 11, 2019.

Instituto Nacional de Energia y Sostenibilidad Islena. 2016. "Informe de Estado Energetico 2015." Universidad de Puerto Rico, San Juan, PR.

Isidore, Chris, Tal Kopan, and Julia Horowitz. 2017. "Closed Puerto Rico Factories Are the Sole Source of Some Critical Drugs." *CNN Money,* September 29, 2017. https://money.cnn.com/2017/09/29/news/companies/puerto-rico-drug-makers/index.html.

Jacobs, Karen and Charles Davidson. 2017. "Hurricane Andrew, 25 Years Later." *Economy Matters*, August 24, 2017. Federal Reserve Bank of Atlanta. https://www.frbatlanta.org/economy-matters/regional-economics/2017/08/24/hurricane-andrew-25-years-later.

Jervis, Rick. 2018. "'I Sit and Cry All Day': Suicide Hotline Calles Double in Puerto Rico 6 Months after Hurricane Maria." *USA Today*, March 23, 2018. https://www.usatoday.com/story/news/2018/03/23/mental-health-crisis-puerto-rico-hurricane-maria/447144002.

Kaiser Family Foundation. 2016. "Behavioral Risk Factor Surveillance." https://www.kff.org/disparities-policy/fact-sheet/puerto-rico-fast-facts/#footnote-238005-7.

Karoly, Lynn A. and Julie Zissimopoulos. 2010. "The Workforce and Economic Recovery Effects of Hurricane Katrina." *Research Briefs*. RAND Corporation. https://www.rand.org/pubs/research_briefs/RB9531.html.

Klein, N. 2007. *The Shock Doctrine: The Rise of Disaster Capitalism*. Macmillan.

Klein, N. 2015. *This Changes Everything: Capitalism Vs. the Climate.* Simon and Schuster.

Kirchberger, Martina. 2017. “Natural Disasters and Labour Markets.” *Journal of Development Economics* 125: 40–58. http://doi.org/10.1016/j.jdeveco.2016.11.002

Kishore, Nishant, Domingo Marqués, Ayesha Mahmud, Mathew V Kiang, Irmary Rodriguez, Arlan Fuller, Peggy Ebner, Cecilia Sorensen, Fabio Racy, and Jay Lemery. 2018. “Mortality in Puerto Rico after Hurricane Maria.” *New England Journal of Medicine* 379(2): 162–170.

Klinger, Chaamala and Virginia Murray Owen Landeg. 2014. “Power Outages, Extreme Events and Health: A Systematic Review of the Literature from 2011–2012.” *PLoS Currents* 6.

Krogstad, Jens Manuel. 2015. “In a Shift Away from New York, More Puerto Ricans Head to Florida.” *Pew Research Center*, October 30, 2015. https://www.pewresearch.org/fact-tank/2015/10/30/in-a-shift-away-from-new-york-more-puerto-ricans-head-to-florida/.

Krogstad, Jens Manuel. 2018. “Key Takeaways about Latino Voters in the 2018 Midterm Elections.” *Pew Research Center*, November 9, 2018. https://www.pewresearch.org/fact-tank/2018/11/09/how-latinos-voted-in-2018-midterms/.

Krogstad, Jens Manuel, Mark Hugo Lopez, Gustavo López, Jeffrey S. Passel and Eileen Patten. 2016. “Millennials Make Up Almost Half of Latino Eligible Voters in 2016.” *Pew Research Center*, January 19, 2016. https://www.pewresearch.org/hispanic/2016/01/19/millennials-make-up-almost-half-of-latino-eligible-voters-in-2016/.

Krogstad, Jens Manuel, Luis Noe-Bustamante, and Antonio Flores. 2019. “Historic Highs in 2018 Voter Turnout Extend across Racial and Ethnic Groups.” *Pew Research Center*, May 1, 2019. https://www.pewresearch.org/fact-tank/2019/05/01/historic-highs-in-2018-voter-turnout-extended-across-racial-and-ethnic-groups/.

Kronenberg, M. E., Cross Hansel, T., Brennan, A. M., Osofsky, H. J., Osofsky, J. D., and Lawrason, B. 2010. “Children of Katrina: Lessons Learned about Postdisaster Symptoms and Recovery Patterns.” *Child Development* 81: 1241–1259. https://doi.org/10.1111/j.1467-8624.2010.01465.

Krueger, Anne O., Ranjit Teja, and Andrew Wolf. 2015. *Puerto Rico – A Way Forward.* Report for the Commonwealth of Puerto Rico and the Government Development Bank of Puerto Rico, June 29, 2015.

Kwasinski, A., Andrade, F., Castro-Sitiriche, M., and O’Neill-Carrillo, E. 2019, March. “Hurricane Maria Effects on Puerto Rico Electric Power Infrastructure.” *IEEE Power and Energy Technology Systems Journal* 6(1): 85–94.

Lamba-Nieves, Deepak and Raúl Santiago Bartolomei. 2018. *Transforming the Recovery into Locally-led Growth: Federal Contracting in the Post-Disaster Period*, Washington, DC: Center for a New Economy, https://grupocne.org/wp-content/uploads/2018/09/Federal_Contracts_FINAL_withcover-1.pdf.

Lassman, David, Andrea M. Sisko, Aaron Catlin, Mary Carol Barron, Joseph Benson, Gigi A. Cuckler, Micah Hartman, Anne B. Martin, and Lekha Whittle. 2017. “Health Spending by State 1991–2014: Measuring per Capita Spending by Payers and Programs.” *Health Affairs* 36(7): 1318–1327.

Lawrence, W. R., Lin, Z., Lipton, E., Birkhead, G., Primeau, M., Dong, G. H., and Lin, S. 2019. "After the Storm: Short- and Long-term Health Effects Following Superstorm Sandy among the Elderly." *Disaster Medicine and Public Health Preparedness* 13(1): 28–32.

Lauper, U., Chen, J., and Lin, S. 2017. "Window of Opportunity for New Disease Surveillance: Developing Keyword Lists for Monitoring Mental Health and Injury through Syndromic Surveillance." *Disaster Med Public Health Preparedness* 11(2): 173–178. DOI:101017/dmp.2016.99.

Lester, W. 2018. *Transforming Disaster Response: Federalism and Leadership*. Routledge.

Levantesi, Stella. 2018. "Rising Crime and a Shrinking Police Force Stunt Puerto Rico's Recovery." *Centro de Periodismo Investigativo*, April 30, 2018.

Lichtenstein, Mark. "Verbal Testimony" (transcript). US House of Representatives Energy and Commerce Committee, Subcommittee on Environment. Public Hearing: Response and Recovery to Environmental Concerns from the 2017 Hurricane Season. November 14, 2017. Washington, DC.

Lin, S., Fletcher, B., Luo, M., Chinery, R., and Hwang, S. A. 2011. "Health Impact in New York City during the Northeastern (US) Blackout of 2003." *Public Health Report* 126(3): 384–393.

Lin, S., Lu, Y., Justino, J., Dong, G., and Lauper, U. 2016. "What Happened To Our Environment and Mental Health as a Result of Hurricane Sandy?" *Disaster Med Public Health Preparedness* 10: 314–319.

Lin, S., Luo, M., Walker, J. R., Liu, X., Hwang, S. A., and Chinery, R. 2009. "Extreme High Temperature and Hospital Admissions for Respiratory and Cardiovascular Diseases." *Epidemiology* 20(5): 738–746.

Loorbach, D. 2015, October 6. "Derk Loorbach on Transition Management and Ideas that Have and Impact." Transformation 2015 Conference. (S. R. Center, Interviewer) Stockholm Resilience Center TV. You Tube.

Lopez-Araujo, Javier and O. Lee Burnett. 2017. "Letter from Puerto Rico: The State of Radiation Oncology After Maria's Landfall." *International Journal of Radiation Oncology, Biology Physics* 99(5): 1071–1072. https://doi.org/10.1016/j.ijrobp.2017.10.012.

Lucas, Robert E. and Leonard A. Rapping. 1969. "Price Expectations and the Phillips Curve." *The American Economic Review* 59(3): 342–350.

Lui, Kevin, "Puerto Rico Could Be Left Without Electricity for Months. Here's What to Know." Time, http://time.com/4951048/puerto-rico-power-blackout-hurricane-maria-electricity-prepa/.

Mach, Annie L., Patricia A. Davis, Sarah A. Donovan, Jim Hahn, Suzanne M. Kirchhoff, Alison Mitchell, Paulette C. Morgan, C. Stephen Redhead, and Scott R. Talaga. 2016. "Puerto Rico and Health Care Finance: Frequently Asked Questions." Washington, DC: Congressional Research Service, 1–34.

Malo, Sebastien and Adriana Brasileiro. 2018. "Puerto Rico Hurricane Migrants May Be Wild Card in U.S. Elections." *Reuters*, March 28, 2018. https://www.reuters.com/article/us-migration-usa-puertorico/puerto-rico-hurricane-migrants-may-be-wild-card-in-u-s-elections-idUSKBN1H500P.

Manuel, J. 2013. "The Long Road to Recovery: Environmental Health Impact of Hurricane Sandy." *Environmental Health Perspectives* 121(5): A152–A159.

Manyena, Bernard, Geoff O'Brien, Phil O'Keefe, and Joanne Rose. 2011. "Disaster Resilience: A Bounce Back or Bounce Forward Ability?" *Local Environment: The International Journal of Justice and Sustainability* 16(5): 417–424.

Marmot, Michael. 2004. "The Status Syndrome: How Your Social Standing Affects Your Health and Life Expectancy." *Journal of Knowledge, Culture and Communication.* Bloomsbury, London 21(1–2): 231–233. https://doi.org/10.1007/s00146-006-0037-6.

Mass MoCA. n.d. "Focus on Puerto Rico Residency." https://www.manacontemporary.com/residencies/focus-on-puerto-rico/. Accessed July 8, 2019.

Masses, Rodrigo. 2018. "Congressional Hearing on Puerto Rico's Electric Grid." C-Span. (May 8, 2018).

Mattei, Josiemer, Martha Tamez, Carlos F. Ríos-Bedoya, Rui S. Xiao, Katherine L. Tucker, and José F. Rodríguez-Orengo. 2018. "Health Condition and Lifestyle Risk Factors of Adults Living in Puerto Rico: A Cross-Sectional Study." *BMC Public Health* 18(1): 491. https://doi.org/10.1186/s12889-018-5359-z.

Mbaye, Lingere Mously and Klaus F. Zimmermann. 2016. "Natural Disasters and Human Mobility." *Working Papers Series.* UNU- MERIT. https://www.merit.unu.edu/publications/working-papers/abstract/?id=6082.

Mbaye, Lingere Mously. 2017. "Climate Change, Natural Disasters, and Migration." *IZA World of Labor*, 346. https://wol.iza.org/uploads/articles/346/pdfs/climate-change-natural-disasters-and-migration.pdf).

McIntosh, Molly F. 2008. "Measuring the Labor Market Impacts of Hurricane Katrina Migration: Evidence from Houston, Texas." *The American Economic Review* 98(2): 54–57.

Medical Schedule Inc. 2018. "Aftermath Of Hurricane Maria and the Emigration of Healthcare Professionals to Mainland US." Npidashboard.Com. July 1, 2018. https://www.npidashboard.com/puerto-rico-doctors-emigration-to-us-mainland-updated#change/2018.

Meléndez, Edwin and Charles Venator-Santiago. 2018. "Introduction to Puerto Rico Post-Maria: Origins and Consequences of a Crisis." *CENTRO Journal* 30(3): 5–29.

Meléndez, Edwin. 2018a. "The Politics of PROMESA." *Centro Journal* 30(3): 43–71.

Meléndez, Edwin. 2018b. "The Economics of PROMESA." *Centro Journal* 30(3): 72–103.

Melin, Kyle, Wanda T. Maldonado, and Angel López-Candales. 2018. "Lessons Learned from Hurricane Maria: Pharmacists' Perspective." *Annals of Pharmacotherapy* 52(5): 493–494. https://doi.org/10.1177/1060028017751691.

Michaud, Josh and Jen Kates. 2017a. "KFF: Filling the Need for Trusted Information on National Health Issues." *The Henry J. Kaiser Family Foundation*, November 17, 2017. https://www.kff.org/other/issue-brief/public-health-in-puerto-rico-after-hurricane-maria/.

Michaud, Josh and Jen Kates. 2017b. "Public Health in Puerto Rico after Hurricane Maria." *Henry J. Kaiser Foundation*, November 8, 2017.

Misra, Jordan. 2019. "Behind the 2018 U.S. Midterm Election Turnout: Voter Turnout Rates Among All Voting Age and Major Racial and Ethnic Groups Were Higher Than in 2014." *U.S. Census Bureau*, April 23, 2019. https://www.census.gov/library/stories/2019/04/behind-2018-united-states-midterm-election-turnout.html.

Mora, Marie T., Alberto Dávila, and Havidán Rodríguez. 2019. "Puerto Rican Migration and Mainland Settlement Patterns before and after Hurricane Maria." *The Minority Report*, 1, 4–7.

Mora, Marie T., Alberto Dávila, and Havidán Rodríguez. 2018. "Migration, Geographic Destinations, and Socioeconomic Outcomes of Recent Puerto Rican Migrants during La Crisis Boricua: Implications for Island and Stateside Communities Post-Maria." *Centro Journal* 30(3): 208–229.

Mora, Marie T., Alberto Dávila, and Havidán Rodríguez. 2017a. *Population, Migration, and Socioeconomic Outcomes among Island and Mainland Puerto Ricans: La Crisis Boricua*. Lanham, MD: Lexington Books.

Mora, Marie T., Alberto Dávila, and Havidán Rodríguez. 2017b. "Education, Migration, and Earnings of Puerto Ricans on the Island and U.S. Mainland: Impact, Outcomes, and Consequences of an Economic Crisis." *Migration Studies* 5(2): 168–189.

Morris, Zachary, Hayward, R., and Otero, Yamirelis. 2018. "The Political Determinants of Disaster Risk: Assessing the Unfolding Aftermath of Hurricane Maria for People with Disabilities in Puerto Rico." *Environmental Justice* 11. 10.1089/env.2017.0043.

Murphy, Sheila. *Puerto Rico Hurricanes Map*. Digital Image, 1435 × 1125. Available from: USGS, https://www.usgs.gov/media/images/puerto-rico-hurricanes-map. Accessed August 17, 2019.

National Hurricane Center. 2018. *Costliest U.S. Tropical Cyclones Tables Updated*, National Oceanic and Atmospheric Administration, January 26, 2018, https://www.nhc.noaa.gov/news/UpdatedCostliest.pdf.

Negrón-Muntaner, Frances. "Blackout: What Darkness Illuminated in Puerto Rico." *Politics / Letters*, March 2, 2018, http://quarterly.politicsslashletters.org/blackout-darkness-illuminated-puerto-rico/.

New York State. 2019. *The Empire State Relief and Recovery Effort for Puerto Rico*. Albany, NY. https://www.ny.gov/empire-state-relief-and-recovery-effort-puerto-rico-and-us-virgin-islands/empire-state-relief-and#_blank. Accessed June 23, 2019.

New York Times. July 12, 2018. "*FEMA Was Sorely Unprepared for Puerto Rico Hurricane, Report Says.*" https://www.nytimes.com/2018/07/12/us/fema-puerto-rico-maria.html. Accessed June 20, 2019.

Nieves, Javier, Jan Cordero, Cecilio Ortiz-Garcia, y Marla Perez-Lugo. 2019. "From Sikorsky to Tesla: Exploring the Limits of Puerto Rico's Energy Transitions." NCSE Conference 2019. Washington, DC: National Council for Science and the Environment.

Nitza, A. 2019. "International Disasters: Introduction." In *Disaster Mental Health Case Studies: Lessons Learned from Counseling in Chaos*, edited by J. Halpern, A. Nitza, and K. Vermeulen, 130–138. New York, NY: Routledge.

Nitza, A., and Surinon, C. 2019. *The Perceived Needs of Teachers in Supporting Students' Long-Term Recovery Following Hurricane Maria in Puerto Rico. International Society of Traumatic Stress Studies Conference, Boston, MA.*

Noe-Bustamante, Luis. 2020. "Latinos Make Up Record 17% of Florida Registered Voters in 2020." *Pew Research Center*, October 19, 2020. https://www.pewresearch.org/fact-tank/2020/10/19/latinos-make-up-record-17-of-florida-registered-voters-in-2020/.

Norris, F. H., Friedman, M. J., and Watson, P. J. 2002. 60,000 Disaster Victims Speak, Part II: Summary and Implications of the Disaster Mental Health Research. *Psychiatry* 65(3): 240–260.

O'Keefe, Phil, Geoff O'Brien, Zaina Gadema, and Tahia Devisscher. 2008. "From Vulnerability to Resilience: The Adaptation Continuum." In *Multi-stakeholders Partnership for Disaster Risk Reduction From National to Local,* 3rd Asian Ministerial Conference on Disaster Risk Reduction, pp. 1–10.

Okun, Arthur M. 1963. *Potential GNP: Its Measurement and Significance.* New Haven: Yale University, Cowles Foundation for Research in Economics.

O'Neill-Carrillo, Efrain. 2010. "Una Nueva AEE: Energía Eléctrica para la Sociedad Puertorriqueña del Siglo XXI." Instituto Tropical de Energia, Ambiente y Sociedad, Universidad de Puerto Rico-Mayaguez. Último acceso: 11 de December de 2019. http://iteas.uprm.edu/docs/Resumen_Una_Nueva_AEE_8_dic_fci.pdf.

O'Neill-Carrillo, Efraín, and Miguel A. Rivera-Quinones. 2018. "Energy Policies in Puerto Rico and Their Impact on the Likelihood of a Resilient and Sustainable Electric Power Infrastructure." *Centro Journal* 30(3): 147–171.

Orange County Florida Supervisor of Elections. 2020. "2020 General Election." November 3, 2020. https://www.ocfelections.com/election-record/2020-general-election-2020-11-03.

Padró Ocasio, Bianca and Adelaide Chen. 2018. "Despite National Push, Puerto Rican Voter Turnout in Florida Lagged Other Groups, Early Data Suggests." *Orlando Sentinel*, November 21, 2018. https://www.orlandosentinel.com/politics/os-ne-hispanic-puerto-rican-voter-turnout-20181121-story.html.

Orengo-Aguayo, Rosaura, Regan W. Stewart, Michael A. de Arellano, Joy Lynn Suárez-Kindy, and John Young. 2019. "Disaster Exposure and Mental Health among Puerto Rican Youths after Hurricane Maria." *JAMA*, Published online April 26, 2019, 2(4): e192619.

Orengo-Aguayo, R., Stewart, R., de Arellano, M., Pastrana, F. A., Villalobos, B. T., Martínez-González, K. G., Suarez-Kindy, J. L., and Brymer, M. 2019. "Implementation of a Multi-Phase, Trauma-Focused Intervention Model Post-Hurricane Maria in Puerto Rico: Lessons Learned from the Field Using a Community Based Participatory Approach." *Journal of Family Strengths* 19(1), Article 7. https://digitalcommons.library.tmc.edu/jfs/vol19/iss1/7.

Orengo-Aguayo, Rosaura, Regan W. Stewart, Karen G. Martínez González, Joy Lynn Suárez-Kindy, María C. Christian Herrero, and Inés Rivera Colón. 2019. "Building Collaborative Partnerships across Professions to Implement Trauma-Focused

Cognitive Behavioral Interventions After Hurricane Maria in Puerto Rico." *The Behavior Therapist* 42(4): 727–54.

Ortiz-Garcia, C. 2018, May. Rebuilding in Puerto Rico: Universities as Leaders in Community Resilience. (N. C. Environment, Producer) Retrieved August 2019, from Webinars: https://www.ncseglobal.org/webinars.

Pacheco, Istra. 2018. "Puerto Rico's Police Stage Sickout over Unpaid Overtime." *NBC News,* January 8, 2018; https://www.nbcnews.com/storyline/puerto-rico-crisis/puerto-rico-s-police-stage-sickout-over-unpaid-overtime-n835111. Accessed December 12, 2019.

Pacific Disaster Center Global. 2017. "Hurricane María- Exposure Based on Observed Wind Impacts Puerto Rico." Accessed August 19, 2019. https://reliefweb.int/map/puerto-rico-united-states-america/hurricane-maria-exposure-based-observed-wind-impacts-puerto.

Pais, J. F. and J. R. Elliott. 2008. "Places as Recovery Machines: Vulnerability and Neighborhood Change after Major Hurricanes." *Social Forces* 86(4): 1415.

Pan American Organization of Health. Health in the Americas, Puerto Rico. 2–3. https://www.paho.org/salud-en-las-americas-2017/?p=4295&lang=en.

Pasch, Richard J., Andrew B. Penny, and Robbie Berg. 2019. "Hurricane Maria (AL152017): 16-30 September 2017." *National Hurricane Center Tropical Cyclone Report*, February 14, 2019. U.S. National Hurricane Center, Washington, DC. Accessed December 30, 2020. https://www.nhc.noaa.gov/data/tcr/AL152017_Maria.pdf.

Pérez, Jackie. 2018. "El Arte de Bregar." *Defying Darkness* exhibition catalogue. Albuquerque, NM: 516 Arts.

Pérez Pedrogo, C. Sánchez Cesáreo, M. Martínez Taboas, A., Colón Jordán, H. & Morales-Boscio, A. 2016. Violencia comunitaria: Programas basados en la evidencia como alternativa para su mitigación. *Revista Puertorriqueña de Psicología* 27(1): 26–42.

Pérez, José Javier. 2018. "A Puerto Rican Look on Florida Elections." *El Nuevo Día*, November 4, 2018. https://www.elnuevodia.com/english/english/nota/apuertoricanlookonfloridaelections-2457326/.

Perez-Lugo, Marla, y Cecilio Ortiz-Garcia. 2018. "'No Blank Slates': Socio-technical Systems Theory as a Guiding Principle for Disaster Response and Recovery." Seismological Society of the Americas, Session on Emergency Management, Resilience and Preparedness. Miami, FL.

Perreira, Krista, Rebecca Peters, Nicole Lallemand, and Stephen Zuckerman. 2017. "Puerto Rico Health Care Infrastructure Assessment." Washington, DC: Urban Institute.

Perrow, Charles. 1984. *Normal Accidents: Living With High-Risk Technologies.* New York: Basic Books, 1984.

Pew Research Center. 2020. "Sharp Divisions on Vote Counts, as Biden Gets High Marks for His Post-Election Conduct; Large Majority of Americans Say Additional COVID-19 Aid is Needed – And Want Congress To Pass It As Soon As Possible." November 20, 2020. https://www.pewresearch.org/politics/2020/11/20/sharp-divisions-on-vote-counts-as-biden-gets-high-marks-for-his-post-election-conduct/.

Pietri, K. S., Figueroa, D. I., Hinojosa J., Roman, N., Meléndez, E., Yong-Garcia, C., and Vargas-Ramos C. 2018. *Puerto Rico: One Year after Hurricane Maria.*

(Centro Report RD2018-01). Retrieved from Center for Puerto Rican Studies, Hunter College website: https://centropr.hunter.cuny.edu/sites/default/files/data_briefs/Hurricane_maria_1YR.pdf.

Pinel, John P. J. and Steven J. Barnes. 2018. *Biopsychology*. Harlow: Pearson.

Plyer, Allison. 2013. "Facts for Features: Katrina Impact." *The Data Center*. Accessed June 29, 2019. https://www.datacenterresearch.org/data-resources/katrina/facts-for-impact/.

Portela, Maria and Benjamin D Sommers. 2015. "On the Outskirts of National Health Reform: A Comparative Assessment of Health Insurance and Access to Care in Puerto Rico and the United States." *The Milbank Quarterly* 93(3): 584–608.

Puerto Rico Planning Board. 2017. "Economic Report to the Governor—Statistical Appendix—2016." March 2017. http://www.aafaf.pr.gov/spanish/assets/apendiceestadistico2016.pdf.

Ramírez, Yasmín. 2005. "Nuyorican Visionary: Jorge Soto and the Evolution of an Afro-Taíno aesthetic at Taller Boricua." *Centro Journal* XVII(1): 150–178.

Ramos, Ricardo. 2017. Congressional Hearings: Hurricane Recovery Efforts in Puerto Rico and Virgin Islands, Power Utility Officials. (November 14, 2017).

Richman, Eli. 2018. "Medicare Advantage Enrollment Soared in Puerto Rico. Now It's Starving the Island's Healthcare System." *FierceHealthcare*. August 8, 2018. https://www.fiercehealthcare.com/payer/puerto-rico-s-medicare-advantage-participation-through-roof-but-program-s-low-reimbursement.

Pullen, Lara C. "Puerto Rico after Hurricane Maria. 2018." *American Journal of Transplantation* 18(2): 283–284. DOI:10.1111/ajt.14647.

Rivera-Santana, Carlos. 2019. "Aesthetics of Disaster as Decolonial Aesthetics: Making Sense of the Effects of Hurricane Maria through Puerto Rican Contemporary Art." *Cultural Studies* 3: 341–362, DOI: 10.1080/09502386.2019.1607519.

Rivera, Fernando I., Peter J. Guarnaccia, Norah Mulvaney-Day, Julia Y. Lin, Maria Torres, and Margarita Alegria. 2008. "Family Cohesion and its Relationship to Psychological Distress Among Latino Groups." *Hispanic Journal of Behavioral Sciences* 30(3): 357–378. https://doi.org/10.1177/0739986308318713.

Rivera, Fernando, Irene López, Peter Guarnaccia, Rafael Ramirez, Glorisa Canino, and Hector Bird. 2011. "Perceived Discrimination and Antisocial Behaviors in Puerto Rican Children." *Journal of Immigrant and Minority Health* 13(3): 453–461. https://doi.org/10.1007/s10903-010-9421-x.

Rivera, Fernando I., and Giovani Burgos. 2010. "The Health Status of Puerto Ricans in Florida." *Centro Journal* 22(1): 199–219.

Rivera, Fernando I., Molina M., Kristine, and Ethel Nicado. 2019. "Psychological Distress Differentials as a Function of Subjective Social Status Among Latino Subgroups in the United States." In Jennie Jacobs Kronenfeld (Ed.), *Underserved and Socially Disadvantaged Groups and Linkages with Health and Health Care Differentials (Research in the Sociology of Health Care)*, 37: 53–67. https://doi.org/10.1108/S0275-495920190000037007.

Rivera, Jose and Fernando I. Rivera. 2019. "A Content Analysis on the Phases of Emergency Management for Hurricane Maria in Puerto Rico." *The Pegasus*

Review: University of Central Florida Undergraduate Research Journal 11(1): 8–17.

Rivera-Batiz, Francisco L., and Carlos E. Santiago. 1996. *Island Paradox: Puerto Rico in the 1990s*. New York: Russell Sage Foundation.

Rivera Sánchez, Maricarmen. 2018. "Ojo de Turismo a hoteles que siguen cerrados." *El Vocero de Puerto Rico*, June 13, 2018. https://www.elvocero.com/gobierno/ojo-de-turismo-a-hoteles-que-siguen-cerrados/article_f276f910-6ea2-11e8-b55d-ab7f33d1d146.html.

Robles, Frances. 2018. "FEMA Was Sorely Unprepared for Puerto Rico Hurricane, Report Says." *New York Times,* July 12, 2018. https://www.nytimes.com/2018/07/12/us/fema-puerto-rico-maria.html?smid=nytcore-ios-share. Accessed June 28, 2019.

Robles, Frances. 2017. "23% of Puerto Ricans Vote in Referendum, 97% of Them for Statehood." *New York Times*, June 11, 2017, https://www.nytimes.com/2017/06/11/us/puerto-ricans-vote-on-the-question-of-statehood.html.

Rodríguez, Havidán and Marie T. Mora. 2020. "Hurricane Maria: Disaster Response in Puerto Rico." *Oxford Research Encyclopedia of Crisis Analysis,* September 2020, https://doi.org/10.1093/acrefore/9780190228637.013.1609.

Rolon-Martínez, M. and Moreno-Torres, M. A. 2018. Psicología de la salud con poblaciones escolares: una perspectiva integrativa. *Revista Puertorriqueña de Psicología* 29(1): 146–162.

Roman, Jesse. 2015. "The Puerto Rico Healthcare Crisis." *Annals of the American Thoracic Society* 12(12): 1760–1763. https://doi.org/10.1513/AnnalsATS.201508-531PS.

Román Miguel O., Eleanor C. Stokes, Ranjay Shrestha, Zhuosen Wang, Lori Schultz, Edil A. Sepulveda, Qingsong Sun, et al. 2019. "Satellite-Based Assessment of Electricity Restoration Efforts in Puerto Rico after Hurricane Maria." *PLoS One* 14(6): e0218883. https://doi.org/10.1371/journal.pone.0218883.

Roulet, Laura. 2017. "Aglutinación: The Collective Spirit of Puerto Rican Art." In *Relational Undercurrents: Contemporary Art of the Caribbean Archipelago,* edited by Tatina Flores and Michelle Ann Stephens. Long Beach, CA: Museum of Latin American Art.

Ruggles, Steven, Sarah Flood, Ronald Goeken, Josiah Grover, Erin Meyer, Jose Pacas, and Matthew Sobek. 2019. IPUMS USA: Version 8.0 [dataset]. Minneapolis, MN: IPUMS. https://doi.org/10.18128/D010.V8.0.

Sanchez, Ray "How Puerto Rico's Death Toll Climbed from 64 to 2,975 in Hurricane Maria." *CNN*, August 29, 2018. https://edition.cnn.com/2018/08/29/us/puerto-rico-growing-death-toll/index.html.

Santos-Burgoa, Carlos, Ann Goldman, Elizabeth Andrade, Nicole Barrett, Uriyoan Colon-Ramos, Mark Edberg, Alejandra García-Meza, et al. 2018. "Ascertainment of the Estimated Excess Mortality from Hurricane Maria in Puerto Rico." Milken Institute School of Public Health. https://hsrc.himmelfarb.gwu.edu/sphhs_global_facpubs/288.

Santos-Burgoa, Carlos, John Sandberg, Erick Suárez, Ann Goldman-Hawes, Scott Zeger, Alejandra Garcia-Meza, Cynthia M. Pérez, et al. 2018. "Differential and Persistent Risk of Excess Mortality from Hurricane Maria in Puerto Rico: A Time-Series Analysis." *The Lancet Planetary Health* 2(11): e478–e488.

Santos-Lozada, Alexis R., and Jeffrey T. Howard. 2017. "Estimates of Excess Deaths in Puerto Rico Following Hurricane Maria." November 2017. https://doi.org/10.31235/osf.io/s7dmu.

Santos-Lozada, Alexis R, and Jeffrey T. Howard. 2018. "Use of Death Counts from Vital Statistics to Calculate Excess Deaths in Puerto Rico Following Hurricane Maria." *JAMA* 320(14): 1491–1493.

Scaramutti, Carolina, Christopher P. Salas-Wright, Saskia R. Vos, and Seth J. Schwartz. 2019. "The Mental Health Impact of Hurricane Maria on Puerto Ricans in Puerto Rico and Florida." *Disaster Medicine and Public Health Preparedness* 13(1): 24–27. DOI: 10.1017/dmp.2018.151.

Schaul, Kevin, Kate Rabinowitz, and Ted Mellnik. 2020. "2020 Turnout Is the Highest in Over a Century." *The Washington Post*, November 5, 2020. https://www.washingtonpost.com/graphics/2020/elections/voter-turnout/.

Schoen, John W. 2017. "Here's How an Obscure Tax Change Sank Puerto Rico's Economy." September 26, 2017. https://www.cnbc.com/2017/09/26/heres-how-an-obscure-tax-change-sank-puerto-ricos-economy.html.

Schnall, A., Law, R., Neinzerling, A., Sircar, K., Damon, S., Yip, R., Schier, J., Bayleyegn, T., and Wolkin, A. 2017. Characterization of Carbon Monoxide Exposure during Hurricane Sandy and Subsequent Nor'easter. *Disaster Medicine Public Health Preparedness* 11(5): 562–567. https://doi.org/10.1017/dmp.2016.203.

Schultz, J. and J. R. Elliot. 2013. "Natural Disasters and Local Demographic Change in the United States." *Population and the Environment* 34: 293–312.

Scurria, Andrew and Heather Gillers. 2017. "Puerto Rico to Square Off with Creditors." *Wall Street Journal*, May 4, 2017.

Serra-Taylor, José and Carol Irizarry-Robles. 2015. "Factores protectores de la depresión en una muestra de adultos mayores en Puerto Rico: autoeficacia, escolaridad y otras variables socio- demográficas." *Acta Colombiana de Psicología* 18(1): 125–134. DOI: 10.14718/ACP.2015.18.1.12.

SESA. s.f. Solar and Energy Storage Association of Puerto Rico. https://www.sesapr.org/.

Sesin, Carmen. 2020. "Trump Cultivated the Latino Vote in Florida, and It Paid Off." *NBC News Latino*, November 4, 2020. https://www.nbcnews.com/news/latino/trump-cultivated-latino-vote-florida-it-paid-n1246226.

Shabnam, Nourin. 2014. "Natural Disasters and Economic Growth: A Review." *International Journal of Disaster Risk Science* 5(2): 157–163. https://link.springer.com/article/10.1007/s13753-014-0022-5.

Sharac, Jessica, Sara Rosenbaum, Jennifer Tolbert, Anne Markus, Peter Shin, Maria Diaz Published: Sep 19, and 2018. 2018. "The Recovery of Community Health Centers in Puerto Rico and the US Virgin Islands One Year after Hurricanes Maria and Irma - Issue Brief." *The Henry J. Kaiser Family Foundation* (blog). September 19, 2018. https://www.kff.org/report-section/the-recovery-of-community-health-centers-in-puerto-rico-and-the-us-virgin-islands-one-year-after-hurricanes-maria-and-irma-issue-brief/.

Sharp, M., Ledneva, T., Sun, M., Pantea, C., Lauper, U., and Lin, S. 2016. Effect of Hurricane Sandy on Health Care Services Utilization under New York State Medicaid. *Disaster Med Public Health Preparedness* 10(3): 472–484.

Shin, Peter, Jessica Sharac, Rachel Gunsalus, Brad Leifer, and Sara Rosenbaum. 2017. "Puerto Rico's Community Health Centers: Struggling to Recover in the Wake of Hurricane Maria." *Geiger Gibson/RCHN Community Health Foundation Research Collaborative*, Policy Issue Brief #50.

Smith-Nonini, Sandy. 2019. *Dis.em.POWER.ed: Puerto Rico's Perfect Storm.* Video. Dirigido por Roque Nonini.

Solomon, Judith. 2019. "Medicaid Funding Cliff Approaching for U.S. Territories." *Center on Budget and Policy Priorities*. June 18, 2019. https://www.cbpp.org/blog/medicaid-funding-cliff-approaching-for-us-territories.

Sommerfeldt, Chris. 2020. "Trump Administration Refuses to Release All Available Aid to Puerto Rico Despite Earthquakes, Citing 'Corruption' Concerns." *New York Daily News,* January 9, 2020. https://www.nydailynews.com/news/politics/ny-trump-refuses-aid-puerto-rico-earthquakes-20200109-leu5ushanzcnlehtnqucr6btze-story.html. Accessed January 9, 2020.

State University of New York. n.d. "SUNY Stands with Puerto Rico." https://www.suny.edu/puerto-rico/. Accessed April 3, 2019.

State University of New York / University of Puerto Rico. 2018. *Memorandum of Understanding for Academic Collaboration between the State University of New York and the University of Puerto Rico.* San Juan, Puerto Rico: July 26, 2018:1.

State University of New York, 2019. *Commonwealth Caribbean.* Albany, NY: The State University of New York. https://system.suny.edu/global/caribbean/. Accessed April 3, 2019.

Strobl, Eric. 2011. "The Economic Growth Impacts of Hurricanes: Evidence from U.S. Coastal Counties." *The Review of Economics and Statistics* 93(2): 575–589. https://EconPapers.repec.org/RePEc:tpr:restat:v:93:y:2011:i:2:p:575-589.

Subramanian, R., Aja Ellis, Elvis Torres-Delgado, Rebecca Tanzer, Carl Malings, Felipe Rivera, Maité Morales, Darrel Baumgardner, Albert Presto, and Olga L. Mayol-Bracero. 2018. "Air Quality in Puerto Rico in the Aftermath of Hurricane Maria: A Case Study on the Use of Lower Cost Air Quality Monitors." *ACS Earth and Space Chemistry* 2(11): 1179–1186. https://doi.org/10.1021/acsearthspacechem.8b00079.

Sudmeier-Rieux, Karen I. 2014. "Resilience–An Emerging Paradigm of Danger or of Hope?" *Disaster Prevention and Management* 23(1): 67–80.

Sullivan, L. and Swartz, E. 2018, July 13. *FEMA Report Acknowledges Failures In Puerto Rico Disaster Response*. Retrieved August 2019, from NPR: https://www.npr.org/2018/07/13/628861808/fema-report-acknowledges-failures-in-puerto-rico-disaster-response.

Sutter, John D. and Sergio Hernandez. 2018. "'Exodus' from Puerto Rico: A Visual Guide." *CNN*, February 21, 2018. https://www.cnn.com/2018/02/21/us/puerto-rico migration-data-invs/index.html.

Szentpetery, Sylvia E., Erick Forno, Glorisa Canino, and Juan C. Celedón. 2016. "Asthma in Puerto Ricans: Lessons from a High-Risk Population." *The Journal of Allergy and Clinical Immunology* 138(6): 1556–1558. https://doi.org/10.1016/j.jaci.2016.08.047.

Taylor, Wendell C., Dena Shugart, and Raheem J. Paxton. 2018. "Healthy Lifestyle Behaviors and Disparities between the United States Mainland Compared to Puerto Rico, Guam, and United States Virgin Islands (ie, United States territories)." *Journal of Health Disparities Research and Practice* 12(1): 3.

Torres, McNelly. 2019. "Puerto Rico's Post-Maria Medicaid Crisis." *DCReport.Org* (blog), June 11, 2019. https://www.dcreport.org/2019/06/11/puerto-ricos-post-maria-medicaid-crisis/.

United States Election Project. 2020. "2020 November General Election Turnout Rates." December 7, 2020 update. http://www.electproject.org/2020g.

University at Albany. 2019. *RISE 2019: Transforming University Engagement in Pre- and Post-Disaster Environments: Lessons from Puerto Rico.* Albany, NY: University at Albany, SUNY. https://www.albany.edu/rise2019/home.html. Accessed December 30, 2020.

U.S. Bureau of Labor Statistics. 2006. "The Labor Market Impact of Hurricane Katrina: An Overview." *Monthly Labor Review* (August): 3–10. https://www.bls.gov/opub/mlr/2006/08/art1full.pdf.

U.S. Census Bureau. 2019. "Annual Estimates of the Resident Population for the United States, Regions, States, and Puerto Rico: April 1, 2010 to July 1, 2019 (NST-EST2019-01)." Washington, DC: U.S. Census Bureau, Population Division, December 2019. Accessed January 12, 2020.

U.S. Department of Commerce. National Center for Environmental Information. 2019. "Billion Dollar Weather and Climate Disasters: Table of Events." Accessed June 13, 2019. https://www.ncdc.noaa.gov/billions/events.

U.S. Department of Health and Human Services. 2019. "Designated Health Professional Shortage Areas Statistics." *HRSA Data Warehouse. Last Modified January* 1(June): 16.

U.S. Department of Health and Human Services. 2017. "Evidence Indicates a Range of Challenges for Puerto Rico Health Care System." ASPE Issue Brief. https://aspe.hhs.gov/system/files/pdf/255466/PuertoRico_Assessment.pdf.

U.S. Department of Homeland Security. 2018. "Infrastructure Interdependency Assessment Puerto Rico." May 2018 http://www.camarapr.org/Camara-en-Accion-18-19/17-nov-8/gob/PR-Infrastructure-Interdependency-Assessment-Report-Sept-2018.pdf.

U.S. Department of Labor, Bureau of Labor and Statistics. 2018. *Hurricane Florence and September 2018 Payroll Data.* October 5, 2018. https://www.bls.gov/ces/notices/2018/hurricane-florence-payroll-data.htm.

U.S. Department of Labor, Bureau of Labor and Statistics. 2017. *Hurricanes Irma and Maria and September, October, November and December 2017 Payroll Data for Puerto Rico and the U.S. Virgin Islands.* January 24, 2017. https://www.bls.gov/sae/notices/2017/hurricanes-irma-maria-september-october-november-december-2017-payroll-data-for-puerto-rico-and-the-us-virgin-islands.htm.

U.S. Government Accountability Office. 2020. Puerto Rico Disaster Recovery: FEMA Actions Needed to Strengthen Project Cost Estimation and Awareness of

Program Guidance. Washington, DC: U.S. Government Accountability Office. https://www.gao.gov/assets/710/704282.pdf. Accessed January 9, 2021.

U.S. Federal Emergency Management Agency. 2018. "Puerto Rico One Year after Hurricanes Irma and María." Release number 269. Last modified September 7, 2018. https://www.fema.gov/news-release/2018/09/06/puerto-rico-one-year-after-hurricanes-irma-and-maria.

U.S. Federal Reserve Bank of Dallas. 2017. "Texas Loses 4,400 Jobs in September Due to Hurricane's Impact; State Employment Forecast Remains at 2.6 Percent for 2017." *News Releases*. https://www.dallasfed.org/news/releases/2017/nr171020.aspx.

Valle, Ariana J. 2018. "¡Puerto Rico Se Levanta!: Hurricane María and Narratives of Struggle, Resilience, and Migration." QR 279. Quick Response Reports, Natural Hazards Center, University of Colorado-Boulder.

Velez-Velez, R. and Villarubia-Mendoza, J. 2018. *Cambio desde abajo y desde adentro*: Notes on *Centros de Apoyo Mutuo* in post-Maria Puerto Rico. *Latino Studies* 16: 542–547.

Venator-Santiago, Charles. 2018. "Territorial Incorporation: A Note on the History of Territorial Incorporation Bills for Puerto Rico, 1898–2017." *Centro Journal* 30(3): 313–331.

Venator-Santiago, Charles R. 2017. "Are Puerto Ricans American Citizens?" *U.S. News and World Report*, March 3, 2017. https://www.usnews.com/news/national-news/articles/2017-03-03/are-puerto-ricans-american-citizens.

Venegas, Haydée. 1985. *Oller Maestro*. Puerto Rico: Universidad Católica De Puerto Rico.

Venegas, Haydeé, and Marimar Benítez. 1986. *25 Años De Pintura Puertorriqueña*. Ponce: Museo De Arte De Ponce.

Vigdor, Jacob. 2008. "The Economic Aftermath of Hurricane Katrina." *Journal of Economic Perspectives* 22(4): 135–154.

Villafane, Veronica. 2017. "Puerto Rico's GFR Media Sends Perez as Correspondent to Orlando." *Media Moves,* December 15, 2017. https://www.mediamoves.com/2017/12/puerto-ricos-gfr-media-sends-perez-as-correspondent-to-orlando.html.

Vinik, Danny. 2018. "How Trump Favored Texas over Puerto Rico." *Politico*, March 27, 2018, https://www.politico.com/story/2018/03/27/donald-trump-fema-hurricane-maria-response-480557.

Vygotsky, Lev. 1972. "The Psychology of Art." *The Journal of Aesthetics and Art Criticism* 30(4): 564. https://doi.org/10.2307/429477.

Walker, B., Holling, C. S., Carpenter, S., and Kinzig, A. 2004. "Resilience, Adaptability and Transformability in Social–Ecological Systems." *Ecology and Society*, 9(2): 5.

Willison, C., Singer, P., and Creary, M. 2019. "Quantifying Inequities in US Federal Response to Hurricane Disaster in Texas and Florida Compared with Puerto Rico." *BMJ Global Health* 4: e001191.

World Energy Council. 2014. "Global Energy Transitions A Comparative Analysis of Key Countries and Implications for the International Energy Debate." Weltenergierat – Deutschland.

World Bank. 2019. "Life Expectancy at Birth, Total for Puerto Rico." FRED, Federal Reserve Bank of St. Louis. March 12, 2019. https://fred.stlouisfed.org/series/SPDYNLE00INPRI.

Wright, J. D., Rossi P. H., Wright, S. R., and Weber-Burdin, E. 1979. *After the Cleanup: Long Range Effects of Natural Disasters,* Beverly Hills, CA: Sage.

Xiao, J., Huang, M., Zhang, W., Rosenblum, A., Meng X., Ma, W., and Lin S. 2019. "The Immediate and Lasting Impact of Hurricane Sandy on Pregnancy Complications in Eight Affected Counties of New York State." *Science of the Total Environment* 678: 755–760.

Xu, Jiaquan, Sherry L. Murphy, Kenneth D. Kochanek, Brigham Bastian, and Elizabeth Arias. 2018. "Deaths: Final Data for 2016." *National Vital Statistics Report* 67(5): 1–76.

Youth Development Institute of Puerto Rico. 2017. Índice de bienestar de Puerto Rico. Retrieved from http://juventudpr.org/datos/estadisticas/.

Youth Development Institute of Puerto Rico. 2017, December. The Impact of Hurricane Maria on Puerto Rico's Children: Analysis and Initial Recommendations. Retrieved from http://juventudpr.org/wp-content/uploads/2017/12/86104.pdf.

Youth Development Institute of Puerto Rico. 2018, December. Impact of Hurricane Maria in Puerto Rico's Children. Retrieved from: http://juventudpr.org/sobre-nosotros/biblioteca/?libroId=20511.

Youth Development Institute of Puerto Rico. 2019, June. Continúa el crecimiento población infantil en Estados Unidos; mientras que en Puerto Rico, se reduce drásticamente. Retrieved from http://juventudpr.org/continua-el-crecimiento-poblacion-infantil-en-estados-unidos-mientras-que-en-puerto-rico-se-reduce-drasticamente/.

Zissimopoulos, Julie and Lynn A. Karoly. 2010. "Employment and Self-Employment in the Wake of Hurricane Katrina." *Demography* 47(2): 345–367.

Index

Note: *Italic* page number refer to figures and tables; Page numbers followed by "n" denote endnotes.

About the Contributors

Marie T. Mora is provost and executive vice chancellor for Academic Affairs and professor of Economics at the University of Missouri—St. Louis. She has been invited to share her research expertise on Hispanic/Latino socioeconomic outcomes with institutions and agencies across the country, including the White House, Board of Governors of the Federal Reserve System, and the Puerto Rico Institute of Statistics. Mora has published numerous journal articles and book chapters, two coauthored books (including *Population, Migration, and Socioeconomic Outcomes among Island and Mainland Puerto Ricans: La Crisis Boricua*, Lexington Books 2017, with Dávila and Rodríguez), and three coedited volumes. Among her honors are the 2020 *Presidential Award for Excellence in Science, Mathematics, and Engineering Mentoring* from the White House Office of Science and Technology Policy; 2019 *Outstanding Service Award* from the American Society of Hispanic Economists (ASHE); 2016 *Outstanding Support of Hispanic Issues in Higher Education Award* (American Association for Hispanics in Higher Education, 2016); and the 2015 *Cesar Estrada Chavez Award.* Mora is a distinguished alumnus of the Department of Economics at the University of New Mexico where she earned her BA and MA degrees; she earned her PhD in Economics from Texas A&M University.

Havidán Rodríguez is president and professor in the College of Emergency Preparedness, Homeland Security and Cybersecurity, and professor of Sociology at the University at Albany, State University of New York (SUNY). He is also co-chair of the SUNY Stands with Puerto Rico Task Force. Rodríguez's research focuses on the social science aspects of disasters and the socioeconomic outcomes of Hispanics. In addition to numerous journal articles and book chapters, his publications include

Population, Migration, and Socioeconomic Outcomes among Island and Mainland Puerto Ricans: La Crisis Boricua (Lexington Books 2017, with Mora and Dávila), and the *Handbook of Disaster Research, 2nd Edition* (Springer 2018, coedited with Donner and Trainor). Rodríguez has led and participated in a number of field research projects, including to Honduras following Hurricane Mitch, India and Sri Lanka following the Indian Ocean Tsunami, and the Gulf Coast following Hurricane Katrina. His recognitions include *Man of the Year* (New York League of Puerto Rican Women, 2018); *Cesar Estrada Chavez Award* (American Association for Access, Equity and Diversity, 2016); *Alfredo G. de los Santos, Jr. Distinguished Leadership Award* (American Association of Hispanics in Higher Education, 2015); *National Disaster Medical System Outstanding Achievement Award* (FEMA, 2004); among others. He earned his PhD in Sociology from the University of Wisconsin-Madison.

Alberto Dávila is dean of the Harrison College of Business and Computing and professor of Economics at Southeast Missouri State University. His research interests include the economics of the U.S.-Mexico border, Hispanic labor markets, and the economics of immigration. Along with numerous journal articles and book chapters, his publications include *Population, Migration, and Socioeconomic Outcomes among Island and Mainland Puerto Ricans: La Crisis Boricua* (Lexington Books, 2017, with Mora and Rodríguez); the award-winning *Hispanic Entrepreneurs in the 2000s* (Stanford University Press, 2013, with Mora); and two coedited volumes. Moreover, Dávila has received such professional honors as the 2021 *Outstanding Service Award* from the ASHE, *Small Business Administration District Research Advocate Award for the Lower Rio Grande Valley* (2003), the *Distinguished Alumnus award* from the College of Business Administration at U.T.-Pan American's 75th Anniversary (Fall 2002), and the 2014 *Academic Achievement Award* from the ASHE. He earned his PhD and MS degrees in Economics from Iowa State University and a BA degree in Economics from Pan American University.

Michael A. Alfultis was named president of the SUNY Maritime College in June 2014. He previously served 28 years as an officer in the U.S. Coast Guard, including service as a Coast Guard Academy faculty member and academic department chair. Upon his retirement, he served as director and chief operating officer of the University of Connecticut's Avery Point campus. Alfultis graduated from the Coast Guard Academy in 1982 with a degree in Marine Science. He has an MS degree from the University of Washington and a doctorate from the University of Rhode Island, both in Oceanography.

Veronica Arroyo Rodríguez is a student at the University of Central Florida pursuing an undergraduate major in Biomedical Sciences with a minor in

Business Administration. Born in San Juan, Puerto Rico, Arroyo Rodríguez has always had an interest in the socioeconomic and health factors of the island, even after moving to the U.S. mainland. The Puerto Rico Research Hub at UCF gave her the opportunity to further her investigative interests in regards to the well-being of Puerto Rico and its people. In addition, Arroyo Rodríguez dedicates her free time by volunteering at local free clinics and Nemours Children's Hospital.

José Caraballo-Cueto is associate professor at the University of Puerto Rico, Cayey, where he is also a researcher in the Institute for Interdisciplinary Research and director of the Census Information Center of Puerto Rico. He is past president of the Puerto Rico Association of Economists and was the general coordinator of the first Human Development Report of Puerto Rico. His research, which includes studies on the Puerto Rican economy, has been published in international outlets. Caraballo-Cueto recently received a fellowship from Princeton University and from the Global Foundation for Democracy and Development. He earned his PhD in Economics at The New School for Social Research.

Sally Crimmins Villela is an international educator at the SUNY System with specific interests in language acquisition and sociolinguistic aspects of literacy development. In her role as associate vice chancellor for Global Affairs for SUNY, her areas of responsibility include collaborative international academic programs and research, education abroad, exchange, international student and scholar services, and curricular internationalization. Crimmins Villela is responsible for overseas offices in Mexico, Russia, and Turkey, as well as the SUNY Confucius Institute for Business and the SUNY COIL Center. She has studied, worked, and resided in Brazil, Mexico, Spain, and Portugal and speaks fluent Spanish and Portuguese.

María E. Enchautegui is research director of the Youth Development Institute in Puerto Rico. Prior to this position, she was the acting director of the Department of Economics at the University of Puerto Rico—Río Piedras. Enchautegui was also a senior fellow at the Urban Institute and senior economic advisor at the Office of the Assistant Secretary for Policy at the U.S. Department of Labor under the Obama administration. She has provided consulting services to a variety of Puerto Rico's government agencies based on her research areas of expertise, which include labor markets, migration, and family economic security. Enchautegui's PhD is in Economics from Florida State University.

Zadia M. Feliciano is professor of Economics at Queens College, City University of New York; a faculty member at The Graduate Center,

CUNY; and a Research Economist in the Program of International Trade and Investment at the National Bureau of Economic Research. Feliciano's research is in international trade, foreign direct investment, and labor economics. Her latest research is on the impact of the repeal of Internal Revenue Code Section 936 tax exemption for U.S. corporations in Puerto Rico in 2006 on the island's manufacturing industry. She earned her PhD in Economics at Harvard University.

Jose M. Fernandez is associate professor of Economics and Department chair at the University of Louisville. His research focuses on the areas of health economics, labor economics, and industrial organization. His research has appeared in leading economics journals, including the *American Economic Review Papers and Proceedings*, *International Economic Review*, and *Journal of Business Venturing* as well as media outlets such as the *Wall Street Journal Blog*, *Washington Post Wonkblog*, and *The Economist* magazine. He is also serving as the President of the American Society of Hispanic Economists. Fernandez earned his PhD in Economics from the University of Virginia.

Antonio Flores is a former research assistant at the Pew Research Center. He performs research and data analysis on global migration, U.S. Hispanic demographic trends, and public opinion of Latinos. He has coauthored Pew Research publications on the Hispanic population and electorate in the United States, Hispanic identity, and Puerto Ricans and Florida's electorate. Flores has also done research on European unemployment and assisted in a variety of Pew Research publications concerning global attitudes and African immigrants around the world.

Jens Manuel Krogstad is a senior writer and editor at Pew Research Center. He studies global migration, U.S. Hispanic demographic trends, and public opinion of Latinos. He has coauthored reports on the concerns Latinos have about their place in America, Puerto Rico out-migration to the U.S. mainland, and the Hispanic electorate in Florida. Krogstad has also contributed to research on asylum seekers in Europe, and a variety of reports about the U.S. immigration system and its foreign-born population.

Mark Lichtenstein is chief of staff, chief sustainability officer, and adjunct faculty at the SUNY College of Environmental Science and Forestry (ESF), and a faculty associate in Syracuse University's Program for the Advancement of Research on Conflict and Collaboration. He has focused on post-disaster response in New Orleans, New York, Puerto Rico, and the Virgin Islands and is a SUNY Puerto Rico Task Force member. Lichtenstein has an MA in Public Administration and a Graduate Certificate of Advanced

Studies in Conflict Resolution from Syracuse, and a BS in Environmental Studies from ESF.

Shao Lin is professor and associate director for Global Health Research at the University at Albany, SUNY. She has over 25 years of experience in directing various environmental health studies, especially assessing the impacts of extreme weather/hurricanes on human health. Lin has been a principal investigator for over $17 million in grants, served on multiple national climate-health committees, and was an invited Presidential Expert Panelist for the National Climate Health Report. She is frequently invited to speak internationally, and her studies regarding power outage-mental health have been featured in multiple media, such as the *New York Times Magazine*.

Mark Hugo Lopez is the director of race and ethnicity research at Pew Research Center, where he leads planning of the Center's research agenda focused on chronicling the diverse, ever-changing racial and ethnic landscape of the United States. He is an expert on issues of racial and ethnic identity, Latino politics and culture, the U.S. Hispanic and Asian American populations, global and domestic immigration, and the U.S. demographic landscape. Lopez was previously the Center's director of Global Migration and Demography, and of Hispanic research. He earned his PhD in Economics from Princeton University.

Amy Nitza is the director of the Institute for Disaster Mental Health at SUNY New Paltz. She specializes in trauma and disaster mental health, with a particular interest in the role of cultural factors in this work. She served as a Fulbright scholar at the University of Botswana and has over 15 years of experience in training mental health professionals internationally. Among numerous other publications, Nitza is the coeditor of the forthcoming book *Disaster Mental Health Case Studies: Lessons Learned from Counseling in Chaos*. She earned her PhD in Counseling Psychology from Indiana University.

Rosaura Orengo-Aguayo is assistant professor and bilingual clinical psychologist at the Medical University of South Carolina where she also codirects the World Changers Lab. Her research focuses on addressing mental health disparities among Hispanic and other underserved populations through innovative implementation and dissemination methods, including telehealth. Orengo-Aguayo directs the Puerto Rico Outreach Model in Schools-Esperanza, a SAMHSA-funded program aimed at bolstering resiliency and promoting psychological recovery among Puerto Rican youth after Hurricane Maria. She also codirected a USAID-funded program aimed at creating trauma-informed systems and services for children in El Salvador.

Cecilio Ortiz-García is professor of Political Science and Public Policy in the Department of Social Sciences, University of Puerto Rico—Mayagüez. He is also a founding member and part of the Steering Committee for the National Institute for Energy and Island Sustainability of the UPR, ascribed to the President's Office. His areas of interests are environmental policy, energy transitions, and governance. Ortiz-García's work after the impact of Hurricane Maria in Puerto Rico has also revolved around community resilience through innovations in sustainable energy and the role of universities' disaster response and recovery.

Marla D. Pérez-Lugo is an environmental sociologist and professor at the Department of Social Sciences, University of Puerto Rico—Mayagüez. She is also a founding member and part of the Steering Committee for the National Institute for Energy and Island Sustainability of the UPR, ascribed to the President's Office. Her areas of interests are disaster vulnerability, disaster communication, and most recently energy governance and transitions in the face of climate change. After the impact of Hurricane Maria on Puerto Rico, Pérez-Lugo has also focused on university-community relations in disaster and postdisaster environments.

Bettina Pérez Martínez is a curator, researcher, and MA candidate at the University of Concordia in Montréal, Canada. Pérez Martínez's current research focuses on navigating Caribbean identity, decolonial studies, geopolitics, and ecology through the work of contemporary visual artists in the region. Her thesis work addresses Puerto Rico's colonial relationship with the United States as the pivotal agent for the country's growing economic and social crisis and how this relationship pertains to the representation and exploitation of nature. Pérez Martínez holds a BA and BFA in art history and printmaking from SUNY Purchase in New York.

Valeria Quiñones Rodríguez is a recent graduate with a BS in Biomedical Sciences from the University of Central Florida and a past researcher for the Puerto Rico Research Hub. Part of her research involved, belonging to the medical sociology field, was about how the mental health of both mainland and island Puerto Ricans was effected by natural disaster. Quiñones Rodríguez plans on pursuing a medical degree from a medical school in Puerto Rico and becoming a gynecologist with a specialty in infertility in the near future.

Carlos Rivera Santana is assistant professor of Hispanic Studies at the College of William & Mary, specializing in visual culture and contemporary art, Puerto Rican and Indigenous studies, and decolonial theories. Rivera Santana was based in Australia for over seven years where he completed his PhD and was a lecturer at the University of Queensland. He was also a research associate at the Center for Puerto Rican Studies at Hunter College. Rivera Santana's work has been published in peer-reviewed journals, including *Cultural Studies*, *Qualitative Inquiry*, and *Third Text*, and in 2019 his first book was released, *Archaeology of Colonisation: From Aesthetics to Biopolitics* (Rowman & Littlefield International).

Fernando I. Rivera is professor of Sociology and director of the Puerto Rico Research Hub at the University of Central Florida. His research interests and activities are in the sociology of health/medical sociology, disasters, and race and ethnicity. Rivera's published work has investigated how different mechanisms are related to certain health and mental health outcomes with a particular emphasis on Latino populations. His disaster research has explored the investigation of factors associated with disaster resilience and restoration and resilience in coupled human-natural systems. Rivera has also studied the Puerto Rican diaspora in Florida. He earned his PhD in Sociology from the University of Nebraska-Lincoln.

María Rolón-Martínez earned her PhD in School Psychology, BA in Early Childhood Education, and BA in Psychology from the Interamerican University of Puerto Rico. She also completed a Post Graduate Certificate in Integrated Health Services and in Preschool Psychological Assessment. Rolón-Martínez has worked in private practice as a psychologist with children and youth with behavioral, academic, and social-emotional difficulties. She is an adjunct faculty member at Ana G. Méndez University and Sacred Heart University. Her numerous service roles include being president of the Puerto Rico School Psychology Association and the National Association of School Psychologists Delegate for Puerto Rico.

Rebecca Sanchez Santiago is an assistant undergraduate researcher at the Puerto Rico Research Hub at the University of Central Florida. Her research interests and activities are in the sociology of mental health and risk factors that could lead to mental illnesses in Puerto Ricans. Sanchez Santiago graduated with her BS degree in Biomedical Sciences from the University of Central Florida.

Adriana Solla is an undergraduate student at the University of Central Florida pursuing a degree in Biomedical Sciences. Solla's research interests surround healthcare with a focus on underdeveloped populations and their effect after severe natural disasters. Solla has provided medical assistance as a volunteer in undeserved countries like Honduras. Her plan is to continue in the medical field and become a physician focused on women's health.

Joy Lynn Suárez-Kindy was a clinical psychologist and assistant professor at the University Carlos Albizu, San Juan Campus in Puerto Rico before her tragic passing in January 2020. She also served as a consultant to the Secretary of the Puerto Rico Department of Education on student socioemotional needs. Suárez-Kindy's expertise was in bullying prevention and intervention, including for cyber-bullying, with youth within schools. In 2016, Suárez-Kindy was named Psychologist of the Year (Psicóloga del Año) by the Association of Psychologists of Puerto Rico (Asociación de Psicología de Puerto Rico).

Didier Valdés is professor of Civil Engineering at University of Puerto Rico—Mayagüez and a member of the National Institute for Energy and Island Sustainability of the UPR, ascribed to the President's Office. His work focuses on the design of transportation systems, resilience of critical transportation infrastructure in disaster situations, and engineering education in civil engineering.

Ruth Enid Zambrana is professor in the Department of Women's Studies; director of the Consortium on Race, Gender and Ethnicity; and adjunct professor of Family Medicine at the University of Maryland, Baltimore, School of Medicine. Zambrana's scholarship applies a critical intersectional lens to structural inequality and racial, Hispanic ethnicity, and gender disparities in population health and higher education trajectories. She has published extensively and serves on many social science and public health journal editorial boards. Awards include the 2019–20 *Distinguished University Professor* at the University of Maryland; 2013 *Founding Member Award for Vision and Leadership* from the American Public Health Association Latino Caucus; 2013 *University of Maryland Outstanding Woman of Color Award*; and the 2011 *Julian Samora Distinguished Career Award* by the American Sociological Association, Sociology of Latinos/as Section.

www.ingramcontent.com/pod-product-compliance
Ingram Content Group UK Ltd.
Pitfield, Milton Keynes, MK11 3LW, UK
UKHW041842031026
15587UKWH00002B/947